"Who Are You, Lord?"

Footpaths beyond a Street Called Straight

Mark A. Luther

WESTBOW
PRESS®
A DIVISION OF THOMAS NELSON
& ZONDERVAN

WestBow Press books may be ordered through booksellers or by contacting:

WestBow Press
A Division of Thomas Nelson & Zondervan
1663 Liberty Drive
Bloomington, IN 47403
www.westbowpress.com
1 (866) 928-1240

ISBN: 978-1-5127-2091-4 (sc)
ISBN: 978-1-5127-2092-1 (hc)
ISBN: 978-1-5127-2093-8 (e)

Library of Congress Control Number: 2015919169

Print information available on the last page.

WestBow Press rev. date: 2/10/2016

Contents

Preface

It happened on an otherwise ordinary winter night in the late nineteen seventies. I was still very young, and my father had recently lost a long battle with kidney cancer. My mom was just leaving to take the babysitter home and I was high from having taken Magic (hallucinogenic) Mushrooms an hour or so earlier. I remember sitting on my living room couch, not feeling so hot, feeling scared, and listening to the radio. That popular song by Joe Jackson, "Is she really going out with him?" came on. As I was listening, the end of the chorus caught my attention, not at all by accident, and that was likely my first encounter with the Living God. The lyric I heard hit me in the heart on such a deep level that I can still remember that moment all these years later. I thought to myself, *"Someone is trying to tell me something"* as Joe's familiar refrain rang out in my head:

"And if my eyes don't deceive me there's somethin' goin' wrong around here."—Is she really going out with him? by Joe Jackson

The next significant encounter I had with God happened when I was around fifteen, and it changed the course of my life forever. I was at a Christian YMCA camp called "Camp Fox" on Catalina Island for the summer. I had been attending this camp for the previous three years. I was not a Christian, so it did little more than annoy me that any of the other campers were. I was always there for three reasons: to be away from my parents, score babes, and crank tunes. That particular year I met up with one guy; I don't even remember his name. He had a bunch of those fake, mail order caffeine pills that were made to look like the drug "Speed." He gave me a handful of what we called fake "cross tops," and I took four or five, I think. About an hour later it was bedtime. I was shaking and sweating, and I felt like my heart might just stop beating at any time. It was not good. At that moment, all I wanted was to be home with my mom, in my room, in my own bed. I think I prayed some desperate prayer to whatever I thought God was at the time. It was something like, *"Lord if you get me through this and let me live, I will never _____ (you fill in the blank) again."* Sound familiar?

Fast forward to the following evening at campfire. Everyone who has ever been to a Christian camp, knows that after all the skits and singing, it's usually "alter call" time. But for some reason, that night it caught me completely by surprise. I want you to understand I had absolutely no conception of what it meant to, "Ask Jesus to be my Lord and Savior." As you may image then, I was thoroughly shocked to find that my hand did shoot straight up in the air the moment that man up front asked if anybody wanted Jesus come and live in their heart. I don't know what it was, or why God chose that particular moment to lay hold of me, but he did. I may not have properly understood the confession I was making, but I can tell you it was a sincere confession of what I now understand to be "Faith." Though I pushed, kicked, and struggled mightily against it for many years after, I had been changed on the inside, and nothing was ever the same for me.

The final encounter with God happened during a very dark period of my adult life at the age of thirty. I was a full-blown alcoholic, married, with two children that I hadn't the foggiest idea how to care for. On that particular day, I was coming off a bad weekend bender. My wife at the time, who is now my ex-wife, was visiting her sister for the weekend, and I had hit the bar no less than one hour after seeing her off. From that time on Friday night, I had not stopped drinking until I woke up on Sunday morning with the worst hangover I'd ever known. I was feeling the kind of emptiness that is so powerful it consumes every part of you. I was literally feeling soul-sick. So as I was busy wallowing in self-pity and despair, I heard a knock at the front door. My first thought was, *"Who on earth would be knocking on my door so early on a Sunday morning?"* My first inclination was annoyance. But after debating for a moment whether to ignore the knock entirely, I got up and answered it. There before me stood this little Christian woman named Cheri. I knew her primarily as a friend to my wife; to me, she was an acquaintance at most. But there she was all the same, standing on my doorstep with a Bible in her hand. She looked at me lovingly and said, "*I was just walking by your house and God told me to come knock on your door and tell you to read Psalm 139.*" I remember responding dubiously, but agreed to do what she asked—if for no other reason than to get her off my porch. She waited for some semblance of acknowledgement in my eyes, and even offered to let me use her Bible. Then, being convinced she had gotten my attention as God had instructed her, she very sweetly bid me farewell and went on her way. I had absolutely no intention of reading that verse right then or ever. All I wanted was to get back to my sulking and be left to my toxic thoughts, thank you very much! But at the same time, in spite of myself, I could not shake the feeling that I really needed to go get my Bible and read Psalm 139. It was like a compulsion that I could not ignore for another second, so now I was curious. I went and grabbed the *NIV Study Bible* on my night table and quickly thumbed through the Psalms until I hit 139. What happened next I can only describe as the hand of God reaching down and touching the deepest, darkest part of me—saying gently, "*I am real, I am here, and I have you Mark, it's going to be okay.*" I only got to the second verse before I started weeping uncontrollably, so much so that I could barely see to continue reading. Through deep sobs, and many tears, I managed to finish the whole chapter. I fell to my knees and kept on crying for what seemed like nearly an hour. It was the kind of crying that is more than a surface level emotional response. It was as if something or someone was finding every piece of my pain all at once and scooping it out of me by force until it was gone. When I finally recovered, my entire attitude and countenance had changed. I felt complete peace. I felt inexplicably loved, like I had never known love before. From that moment on, for some reason I could not quite wrap my head around, I knew that the God of the Bible was both present and deeply interested in me. He had again changed something inside me, and I was now aware. Though I still struggled with addiction and did not truly surrender my heart to him for another five years or so, my life was never the same after that day.

I have included Psalm 139, verses 1-18 to give you some idea of what God used to evoke such a profound reaction.

You have searched me, LORD,
and you know me.
² You know when I sit and when I rise;
you perceive my thoughts from afar.
³ You discern my going out and my lying down;
you are familiar with all my ways.
⁴ Before a word is on my tongue
you, LORD, know it completely.
⁵ You hem me in behind and before,
and you lay your hand upon me.
⁶ Such knowledge is too wonderful for me,
too lofty for me to attain.
⁷ Where can I go from your Spirit?
Where can I flee from your presence?
⁸ If I go up to the heavens, you are there;
if I make my bed in the depths, you are there.
⁹ If I rise on the wings of the dawn,
if I settle on the far side of the sea,
¹⁰ even there your hand will guide me,
your right hand will hold me fast.
¹¹ If I say, "Surely the darkness will hide me
and the light become night around me,"
¹² even the darkness will not be dark to you;
the night will shine like the day,
for darkness is as light to you.
¹³ For you created my inmost being;
you knit me together in my mother's womb.
¹⁴ I praise you because I am fearfully and wonderfully made;
your works are wonderful,
I know that full well.
¹⁵ My frame was not hidden from you
when I was made in the secret place,
when I was woven together in the depths of the earth.

¹⁶ Your eyes saw my unformed body;
all the days ordained for me were written in your book
before one of them came to be.
¹⁷ How precious to me are your thoughts, God!
How vast is the sum of them!
¹⁸ Were I to count them,
they would outnumber the grains of sand—
when I awake, I am still with you.

Psalm 139:1-18 (NIV)

By way of introduction, I am now, at age forty-five, a man who loves God above all else, because I am above all else loved by him. There isn't a single part of me that does not have roots in a daily, active relationship with my Abba Father, his Son Jesus Christ, and the Holy Spirit promised in his Word. They are at once the substance and evidence of everything I hope for in life. So everything that I was, am, or ever will be is by him, for him, from him, through him, and to him.

Here are a few things I am not:

- a pastor, ordained or endorsed by any church or any denomination
- a biblical scholar or theologian of any kind
- anything even remotely resembling perfect in my walk with God
- I am not an Island (I am, however, a large fjord)
- I am not normal in any sense of the word
- I am not purposely pretentious, irresponsible, or a member of any major food group (unless "Mexican" counts as a food group)
- I am not a grown up, an adult, or what most people call mature, unless I absolutely must be—with only two exceptions: my commitment to friendships and personal relationships, and my faith in Jesus Christ.

Oh, and to remove any lingering doubt you may have, I am not Kilroy, nor am I John Gault.

Everything God gives me to write begins with his doing business with me and dealing with my heart. All of my struggles, victories, failures, and faith in him are the only fuel and content for every pure, good, or true thing that comes out of me. I am being obedient, in that what he gave me to do is this: when he moves me, I write what his heart speaks to mine.

When I surrender to his will and, as my good friend James says, "*Let you all in on the conversation,*" God fills me up and comforts me with the knowledge that he is in control and my worth, every bit of it, comes from him. The closest I can come to explaining my process is contained in the doctrine of *Sola Scriptura*. Sola Scriptura, "*by Scripture alone,*" is a formal principle of Protestantism. It was a foundational doctrinal principle of the Protestant Reformation held by the Reformers who taught that authentication of Scripture is governed by "*the discernible excellence of the text* as well as *the personal witness of the Holy Spirit to the heart of each one who hears or reads it.*"

Having said that, my deepest intimacy with God comes when you see the least of me and the most of him. When I am totally submitted to what he desires, and everyone else's attention is focused on him and his Word, all of his Love and attention are focused on me. There is nothing I would rather have, and there is no place that I would rather be than in his warm embrace, at the center of his will for me. Intimacy with Jesus Christ, and the way it comes through bringing him glory in the use of every good gift he gave, is everything to me. Until the day he chooses to take me home, I understand that I am in this world only as a sojourner, a traveler who had lost his way and has now been irrevocably and finally found in Hope. The things that are as yet unseen—his *eternal* things—are more real and beautiful than the wind in my lungs or the fragile earth I now stand upon. These heavenly things, given by an always good, always loving Father to all humankind are what I have done my best to describe to you. Through what you are about to read, my prayer is that you receive from God in the same manner, with the same passionate, gentle, and quite heart, all of that which he has imparted to me. It took me over thirty-five years of life to hear and understand even a small part of his character. In sharing my prayers, stories, and revelations, I want to give you truths that I wish I had known then, so that you might encounter in them the Love of the Living God in a practical way as you read. I write to you with the hope that God's Spirit would bring Hope in your darkest moments, and with it his peace that passes all understanding, even on your brightest days. My faith in believing is that when you are finished reading, Jesus Christ will have touched you with a Joy that can come only from him. This is a Joy that brings balance and gives you, the seeker and my fellow traveler, the tools to see and hear from him on a daily basis.

If you are anything like me, there will be many times when it's really hard to be a Christian. You can expect some really lonely, ugly times when you strain to remember why you don't just say, *"Why should I even care or try anymore? This is all too hard, I'm outa' here!"* I call those "David days." If you have read any of the psalms in the Bible, then you will understand why. If you have not, then do so as soon as possible. David had really hard days too. Like each one of us, he felt hopelessness, fear, desperation, insecurity, anxiety and just about every other nasty thing you can imagine. Many of his songs and poems to God began with him in deep pain and confusion. Then as he wrote, I imagine they became more like prayers. Further still, as he began to pray with his pen, God would bring to David's remembrance his promises, his faithfulness, and his deep Love for David. As God filled him in this way, David was reminded of his Faith. He was reminded why he believed God, even though his circumstances often told him the exact opposite. Those psalms are the ones that always end with David singing God's praises, shouting his victory, praising him as he slips slowly from the arms of the enemy's lies and accusations back into the gentle embrace of truth, comfort, and love.

Honestly, I was, and still am, scared to death of what you might make of me by the time you've reached the last page of this book. It matters very little to me if my writing is approved of publicly, as long as even one person who needed to read it gets same the opportunity I did, to know Jesus. God's heart is and always has been turned toward the one sheep who needs to hear the voice of the Good Shepherd in order to find their way home. So the strong, reassuring voice of my Savior urging me letter by letter, word by word, page after page, trumped even the most vehement apprehensions I could muster. My only reasonable response to such a furious, amazing Love is to agree, and to do all I can to imitate him, no matter the consequences. I am compelled daily to say, as Isaiah the prophet said when he was confronted with the immutable presence and grace of God, **"Here am I Lord, send me" (Isaiah 6:6-8 NASB).**

Introduction

Beyond the obvious, the more subtle meaning behind the title of the book, "**Who Are You, Lord?,**" is a question all of us have or will have asked in the moments following our having come face to face with the God of all creation, Yahweh—*YHVH* **(Exodus 3:14-15 NLT)**. I am equally certain that each of us did or will respond in accordance with the unique way he made us. The Jewish Pharisee in the Bible, called Saul of Tarsus, was no exception.

It was Saul's experience on the road to Damascus that inspired me. When I was praying through how God wanted this to all come together and asking him what he wanted to say, he showed me three distinct events that compelled Saul to give a definitive response to God. Three decisions would turn the course of Saul's entire life. Three opportunities that God gave him to move forward or stay where he was all occurred in the book of Acts in Chapter 9, between verses 1 and 20.

The first was this:

"**Meanwhile, Saul was still breathing out murderous threats against the Lord's disciples. He went to the high priest and asked him for letters to the synagogues in Damascus, so that if he found any there who belonged to the Way, whether men or women, he might take them as prisoners to Jerusalem. As he neared Damascus on his journey, suddenly a light from heaven flashed around him. He fell to the ground and heard a voice say to him, 'Saul, Saul, why do you persecute me?'**

'Who are you, Lord?' Saul asked.

'I am Jesus, whom you are persecuting,' he replied. 'Now get up and go into the city, and you will be told what you must do'" **(Acts 9:1-6 NIV).**

He was literally stopped in his tracks. Then Saul asked, and Jesus answered. He also gave Saul a command: *"Get up and go."* Saul's response was, "Yes," in that he immediately got up and let his companions lead him into the city.

*"**Saul got up from the ground, but when he opened his eyes he could see nothing. So they led him by the hand into Damascus. For three days he was blind, and did not eat or drink anything.** In Damascus there was a disciple named Ananias. The Lord called to him in a vision, 'Ananias!'*

'Yes, Lord,' he answered.

The Lord told him, 'Go to the house of Judas on Straight Street and ask for a man from Tarsus named Saul, for he is praying. In a vision he has seen a man named Ananias come and place his hands on him to restore his sight.'

'Lord,' Ananias answered, 'I have heard many reports about this man and all the harm he has done to your holy people in Jerusalem. And he has come here with authority from the chief priests to arrest all who call on your name.'

But the Lord said to Ananias, 'Go! This man is my chosen instrument to proclaim my name to the Gentiles and their kings and to the people of Israel. I will show him how much he must suffer for my name'" (Acts 9:8-16 NIV).

Next God made Saul wait; blind and helpless in the house of a complete stranger, he was left three days to contemplate what had just happened to him. Saul could have been impatient, he could have dismissed all of it as a hallucination, and he could have even tried to leave. But instead his response was again, "Yes," in humility, prayer, and fasting. He knew God had spoken to him on the road, so he was obedient.

"Then Ananias went to the house and entered it. Placing his hands on Saul, he said, 'Brother Saul, the Lord—Jesus, who appeared to you on the road as you were coming here—has sent me so that you may see again and be filled with the Holy Spirit.' Immediately,

something like scales fell from Saul's eyes, and he could see again. *He got up and was baptized, and after taking some food, he regained his strength. Saul spent several days with the disciples in Damascus. At once he began to preach in the synagogues that Jesus is the Son of God"* (Acts 9:17-20 NIV).

Finally, God showed Saul in a vision what would happen next. Immediately after regaining his sight and his strength, and being filled with the Holy Spirit, he began to preach. He believed God and was filled. He waited on God and was clothed with power. He surrendered and was restored. What happened next to Saul, who soon became known to all as Paul, the Apostle to the Gentiles, fills two-thirds of what we know today as the New Testament.

Those three opportunities which afforded Saul the grace to become the person God created him to be are not so different from the way he deals with each of us. If we are ready to be honest with ourselves, we must come to grips with these things as they occur over the course of our lives. We must also be prepared and willing to respond when Heaven knocks.

- God compels us to face him, to see him and ourselves through open eyes.
- God asks us to hear and obey him to the exclusion of all other voices, including our own.
- God asks us to leave what is familiar and comfortable behind, to trust him, learn from him, and follow him.

Our heavenly Father is a gentleman, and though all God does is for our good, he does not force his will upon anyone. But when we ask the question, *"Who Are You, Lord?"* we had better expect, and be prepared to hear, an honest answer.

This book is a direct result of my wanting to share the answers he gave me. I want to give you a glimpse of what God has done in my life and where he has taken me. About three years ago, I had come to a point in my life and my Christian faith where I was asking God to give me more of him and take me deeper. I guess I had been praying along those lines for around a month when he spoke this to my heart: going deeper or knowing more would be impossible as long as the obstacle of substance abuse and addiction was still in the way. God is jealous for us in the way he loves, and his furious Love will always demand first place in our hearts if we desire to be in real, intimate relationship with him.

I eluded to it earlier in the Preface, but to be clear, I was a substance abuser for the better part of my life. At this point in my journey, God had delivered me from many things already, sometimes through a lot of surrender and prayer, sometimes by just allowing my self-will to run me to ground. But I had been addicted to nicotine consistently since the age of nine or ten, first in the form of cigarettes and chewing tobacco, then later, nicotine gum. It was so much a part of my identity by the time God confronted me that I was terrified to give it up. I was afraid I would lose all that was familiar to me, and about me, if I put it down. That, however, was a well-crafted lie born of old wounds, fear, and selfishness. The truth was that nicotine had held me in bondage and was slowly destroying what remained of my life—step by step, day by day. What was worse is that I knew it, and I continued to let it go on for far too long.

This brings me back again to God's answers when I prayed. Confronted with the truth, I now had a choice to make. I could take a leap off the cliff, trusting that he would catch me, or I could remain stagnant in this thing that had been making me a slave for so many years. I had to ask, *"Who are you really, Lord? Who are you to me? Are you really who your Word says you are? Is your Word really true? Or is it just a nice story I told my kids?"* Things get serious very quickly when you have to start answering those questions in the context of your own self-sacrifice. In the end I decided to take the leap and for the first time in my life I can now say that I am free. I am completely free from any kind of addiction, any kind of substance abuse. I am free because God cared enough to save me. What has happened since has been a flood—a Niagara Falls-sized flood of God's Holy Spirit poured out into my life. My quiet time with him almost immediately went from around fifteen minutes of mostly stale, dry prayer, to an hour or more. Sometimes I did not even realize the amount of time that had passed.

My relationship with God has turned from uninspired and lifeless to intimate and intense. Now, whether I am reading, praying, or just spending time writing, it is always a new adventure.

My submission to God's voice, to step out and walk in faith beyond the "Street called Straight" continues to be an exciting, difficult, and exhilarating journey. It is a journey I honestly never imagined I would take. If someone had told me I might be called into some sort of ministry, I would have laughed in their face. If anybody had ever told me I'd end up here, actually writing a book, I would have said they were crazy. Everything that lies ahead for you in the pages of this book is personal to me. They are my personal stories, my personal experiences, my prayers, failures, victories, revelations, and hopefully even a good helping of heavenly wisdom. But the real "surprise in the pack" is this: I am confident God will use each and every one of those things to bless you as well. So grab your favorite drink, maybe a comfy blanket, and take some time to find out what God might have to speak into your life. One thing is for sure, with him, you never know what you may encounter once the door shuts behind you and your feet start moving on down the road. Enjoy!

Acknowledgement

Immeasurable appreciation and deepest gratitude for all of their help and support are extended to the following persons who, in one way or another, made this book possible.

Maria Luther, Editor. My wife, my partner in Christ for life, my lover, and my constant companion. You are God's wisdom imparted to me and His Love poured out to me every day. Your patience and perseverance in helping me to sort through God's many revelations, your help in editing all of them two full times through, and your steadfast friendship (Even during those times when I did not deserve it), were invaluable to put it mildly. From beginning to end your encouragement and support moved me through each step along this sometimes arduous process. I couldn't have done it without you. I love you more and more every day, and I can't wait to experience every moment of what God has in store for us next!

Pastor Scott Tannehill, BTh. You have been, and will continue to be, my mentor, my teacher and my good friend. You are also one of the few people in this world I would share my deepest joys and fears with. Your love for, and knowledge of God's word are unequalled in any other person I know. Being able to process through my thoughts with you, and everything that God was showing me during the time this was all coming together was vital. Your friendship and support from the first time I met you have always been an encouragement to me. The life of Christ in you inspires me to be a better man, and to properly handle God's truth. I love you brother!

Pastor Rob McKenna. You have been a continual example to me of what it looks like to walk authentically before God as a man, a servant, a Husband, and a lover of people. Your obedience to God's voice in the way you Pastor is one of the things that stirred my spirit and the spirit of God in me to begin this adventure. Every time I see you stand up on a Sunday morning, I know I am going to get fed solid food from God because I know the One who feeds you. Thank you for your transparency and your willingness to share your life for the glory of God. You helped me to see that a title is not the measure of a man, but instead his courage and character in humility and submission to the headship of Christ.

Bruce Garrison, Pastor/Editor. When one of my brothers in Christ, who had written his own book recently, recommended you as an Editor I knew it would be a perfect fit. I had been praying all along for God to send the right man for the job, and He certainly did. Little did I know that in addition to your editing prowess, you were also a Pastor. Your wisdom and insight in both vocations helped me to critically examine not only the particulars like punctuation and sentence structure, but also the spiritual content. Your positive feedback made me want to take a second look. You showed me my writing from a readers standpoint and it blessed me and helped me to put on all of the right finishing touches.

Dr. David Frisbee, Family counselor and author. When I sat down to speak with you about my work at the San Diego Christian Writers Conference, I was flying low and lacking confidence. The way you put on the life of Christ became immediately apparent in the way you greeted me, the way you spoke to me, and the encouragement you gave. Ever since we met you have been a constant resource to me in the way your experiences have shaped you, and the way God is using you. You always made yourself available despite a full schedule, and you always urged me forward to finish well!

CHAPTER 1

LOVE

So what is Love?

I have asked that question many times in my heart and in prayer. When I felt God answer, it was like looking in a mirror and not being able to turn away, looking intently even when the reflection made me uncomfortable. Ironically but perfectly, as I consider God's attention to every last detail of the man I see staring back at me, the only vehicle by which I can arrive and remain in front of that mirror is his Love. The only way I am able to see myself clearly in all of my imperfection as I consider Love and what it means, is by receiving the acceptance, redemption, and forgiveness that are evidence of God's Love. I am truly a new creature **(2 Corinthians 5:16-17 NASB)**. This revelation staggered me and left me shaking my head in awe and wonder.

What I see in the mirror when I ask *"What is Love?"* allows me to know both Love and its antithesis. Laid over the echo of my **"natural face,"** the **"kind of person I was,"** is the image of all that I am now through God's perfect law that brings life. There is a good reason however for the often repeated adage, *"The mirror always lies."* Mirrors are designed to show reality in reverse. Consequently, apart from Him, what I am able to see is a **"forgetful hearer"** of the promises in his Word and never a proper reflection. It is only when I use the eyes of my heavenly Father, who views me through the lens of his precious Son Jesus, that perfect intimacy stares back at me. This perfect intimacy, my face now unveiled and being transformed to reveal his glory, is pure Love **(2 Corinthians 3:16-18 NASB), (James 1:23-25 NASB).**

"In this is love, not that we loved God, but that he loved us and sent his Son to be the propitiation for our sins" (1 John 4:10 NASB).

- God is Love and Love is real. **"The one who does not love does not know God, for God is love" (1 John 4:8 NASB).**
- God Loves us! He is the reason we understand Love at all. **"We love, because he first loved us" (1 John 4:19 NASB).**

- Love is not all about *me*. "**A new command I give you: Love one another. As I have loved you, so you must love one another**" (John 13:34 NIV).
- Real Love never seeks its own ends, for its own purpose. "**Love does not act unbecomingly; it does not seek its own**" (1 Corinthians 13:5 NASB).
- Love is also a verb. "**Dear children, let us not love with words or speech but with actions and in truth**" (1 John 3:18 NIV).
- Love would rather serve than be served. "**Greater love has no one than this, that one lay down his life for his friends**" (John 15:13 NASB).
- Real Love is never false and always puts others first. "**Love must be sincere ... Be devoted to one another in love. Honor one another above yourselves**" (Romans 12:9-10 NIV).
- Real Love does not keep lists, it always forgives. "**Above all, love each other deeply, because love covers over a multitude of sins**" (1 Peter 4:8 NIV).
- Love is the greatest virtue to which we aspire. "**And now these three remain: faith, hope and love. But the greatest of these is love**" (1 Corinthians 13:13 NIV).
- Real Love never fails us, will never leave us, and never forsake us. "**Love never fails**" (1 Corinthians 13:8 NIV). " **...God has said, 'Never will I leave you; never will I forsake you'**" (Hebrews 13:5 NIV).

I know the things I know about Love through Jesus Christ. If God is Love, then "Love" is as vast and immeasurable as he is. What completely blows my mind, and makes me want to drop down to my knees and never get up again is this: I know that I only see a very small piece, so how much more of him and his Love must still be obtainable?

As all of that sinks in, accompanied by every emotion that follows, I imagine the funniest picture of this exchange between a proud and loving heavenly Father and his grateful child, seeking always to emulate him, and in deference, to exalt him. For those of you who have seen the movie, "Analyze This," picture yourself in the role of

Robert De Niro as Paul Vitti, and God in the role of Billy Crystal as Dr. Ben Sobel ... totally paraphrased of course.

Me: You know, God, I don't think I ever thanked you properly for healing me.

God: We don't say "healed." We say you had a "corrective spiritual experience."

Me: You, you, you're very good.

God: (pointing) No. you, you.

I started laughing out loud when he showed it to me that way. Anyone who does not believe God has a sense of humor is sorely mistaken.

Oh, how he Loves!

Did you know that all of the things you have done in secret, the things that other people don't see, God does see? He smiles down on you even when it seems that nobody else cares. Those good deeds in giving, intercession through prayer, the thankfulness and faith in your deepest heart that you give only to him and do just for him, make a difference to him. Even if they don't matter to anyone else, they matter to God. In those secret places, he sees you and Loves you more than you could ever conceive.

"Then your Father, who sees <u>what is done in secret</u>, will reward you" (Matthew 6:4, 6, 18 NIV).

On an ordinary night in August, 2012 I was recounting the most foolish and careless things I had done as a child and as a young adult. Afterward, I felt soiled, just dirty on the inside. Then God—everything good, right, pure, praiseworthy, or admirable in my life begins with those two words: *"Then God"*—reminded me to look at those things through the enormity of his Love and grace. He also reminded me of the price (his Son's life) that was paid for me. I had heard part of a sermon that morning and the pastor said, *"The harder we seek after humility the less humble we are. The best we can do is to be like Jesus Christ in this world, and somehow inexplicably humility accompanies that."* I'd imagine the same is true with Love, or humility that accompanies Love. Jesus' first inclination everywhere he went and with everyone he met was to find their pain and Love them. So I should **"go and do likewise" (Luke 10:37 NIV).**

"Dear children, let us not love with words or tongue but with actions and in truth. This then is how we know that we belong to the truth, and how we set our hearts at rest in his presence whenever our hearts condemn us. For God is greater than our hearts, and he knows everything" (1 John 3:18-20 NIV).

"You did not choose me, but I chose you and appointed you to go and bear fruit—fruit that will last. Then the Father will give you whatever you ask in my name. This is my command: Love each other" (John 15:16-17 NIV).

As I continued to meditate on this, God showed me another way he Loves you and me. Most of us can remember coming to our mom or dad with something we had made that we thought was the most wonderful thing in the entire world. Desiring their approval, we approached them with total abandon because we knew they would love it, and how much they loved us. I had a parent that loved me as much as one here on earth could, and every day she made sure I knew it.

I am reminded of a time when I wanted to make my own peanut butter. Being about six years old, I grabbed some walnuts and cracked them open, then grabbed the butter from the fridge (back when butter was a solid bar). I then proceeded to strategically place each walnut into the butter until there were "just enough." I thought I had done it, Eureka! So I brought it to my mom, and I remember the look of love, amusement, pride, and finally resignation on her face when she knew she had to try some. She knew my heart, and she knew she'd have to clean up my mess, but she just loved me anyway and treated me like it was the most special thing she had seen all day.

God showed me that this is the way he sees us, in everything, every day. When we come to him, even having made a total hash of things, he knows the motives of our hearts. He Loves us and what we offer him—no conditions, no strings attached, no judgments, just his warm embrace.

I especially want to say this to those of you who did not feel that kind of Love or anything resembling that from an earthly parent: there is one God, and he is your heavenly Father, full of authentic Love. He will never laugh at you, reject you, push you away, or abuse you. He will always encourage you, always look at your attempt at "peanut butter" with a proud parent's eyes, and reward you with a hug that says it's the best thing he has seen all day. He knows your most tender parts, and sees that you made it just for him. If you are hurting right now, let that truth about him become real to you, and allow your heart to cry out "Abba" (which means Daddy). He desires constant intimacy with you, and he will never let you fall or be put to shame for offering him your best.

"Every good and perfect gift is from above, coming down from the Father of the heavenly lights, who does not change like shifting shadows. He chose to give us birth through the word of truth, that we might be a kind of firstfruits of all he created" (James 1:17-18 NIV).

How we Love

"Do not waste time bothering whether you 'love' your neighbor; act as if you did. As soon as we do this we find one of the great secrets. When you are behaving as if you loved someone, you will presently come to love him."—C.S. Lewis, **Mere Christianity**

"Be kind and compassionate to one another, forgiving each other, just as in Christ God forgave you" (Ephesians 4:32 NIV).

Recently I had the honor of being used by God to speak into the life of a man whose marriage was in danger of failing. I went, or I should say that God had me go, to his business for what I thought would be pretty routine service. The funny thing is, he ended up warning me against the service that I went to him for. Instead he gave me much better advice. Then he asked me the big question: *"So, you are divorced, how's that going for you?"* From that point on God pretty much took over. I had nothing out of myself to tell him, since I had more or less ruined my marriage with selfishness and alcoholism (for those of you who don't know). God's Love spoke through me to this hurting man who desperately wanted to save his marriage. I think it ministered to me as much or more than it did to him.

The first thing I shared with him was the look on my son's face and his reaction when I told him that mom and dad weren't going to be together anymore. I have been divorced twelve years now, and that is a moment and a memory that I would do anything to reverse. It still breaks me when I think of it, but it also reminds me of God's grace and mercy to comfort and heal us as we come to him with repentance and a contrite heart.

Next he told me about his own situation. He also related all of the things that people around his wife were telling her. I asked him if there was any desire on her part to reconcile. His response was all too familiar to me, because I was once in the same place she was. It reminded me of the counterfeit truths that our enemy, Satan, brings against families. Things like, "The grass is greener," "You just need to be free and do your own thing," or "You need to make you happy." Not surprisingly, none of those involve "Turn your heart back to your partner." By human standards, he is a good man who was not abusive to his wife, who was faithful to her even then, and who dearly loves his children.

The rest of our conversation was about the crux of any relationship—that real sacrificial Love is not just good feelings and warm fuzzies, rather it is a daily choice we make to say "Yes I will" or

"No I won't," despite every flaw, despite all the things that irritate us beyond rational thought, and the humdrum of an everyday existence. It is the preciousness of exclusivity, the "Yes" of daily choosing to love that says, "I remember, I will notice the little things that endear and endure, I will unzip my guts for another day and risk bearing my whole heart to only you."

In any relationship there is no empowerment in bitterness, anger, malice, indifference, or selfishness. There is only a mask for your own desperation and wounds. Indifference, rejection, and giving up don't make us stronger. By their nature they only have the ability to tear down and destroy. This story is only one example, and I know that sometimes there are very valid reasons for two people to separate. But through the experience I was again reminded that, all things being equal, if two people can get over themselves and remember why they first chose to make the journey together, the Love of God is able to heal and restore 100 percent of the time.

I ended our talk by asking if I could pray for his family and his marriage, and he allowed me. I do not know what happens next for them, but God does. I only know that I was there at just that time, for just that reason because God loves that family. I felt it; he used me and I was blessed.

Why we love

"We love because he first loved us" (1 John 4:19 NIV).

Lately I am learning lots from God, with a special emphasis on the reason why we love. He is really answering when I pray the prayer, **"Here am I Lord. Send me!" (Isaiah 6:8 NASB)**. I'm learning, as a friend of mine with a beautiful heart observed one morning, that sometimes "real life" just happens. Terrible things happen; there is no magic pill to make pain and desperation go away. God is showing me instead that his heart is so grieved by all of it, because his Love is so immense and indescribable. It was not by accident that Jesus gave us one primary command, a command that superseded every other that came before, and that still does.

"A new command I give you: Love one another. As I have loved you, so you must love one another. By this everyone will know that you are my disciples, if you love one another" (John 13:34-35 NIV).

Jesus left only that one answer. Some even call it the eleventh commandment, and it's not always an easy one to obey. It is however in his own words, the sum total of all teaching of the Law and the prophets in Old Testament scripture. So to anyone who gets hung up on silly arguments like what The Bible says about eating shellfish, the kind of clothes you can wear, the length of your hair, tattoos, or any other such thing, I would say think on this verse today. Get out in the world and go love somebody; be the hands and feet of Jesus.

"One of them, a lawyer, asked him a question, testing him, 'Teacher, which is the great commandment in the Law?' And he said to him, 'YOU SHALL LOVE THE LORD YOUR GOD WITH ALL YOUR HEART, AND WITH ALL YOUR SOUL, AND WITH ALL YOUR MIND. This is the great and foremost commandment. The second is like it, YOU SHALL LOVE YOUR NEIGHBOR AS YOURSELF. On these two commandments depend the whole Law and the Prophets'" (Matthew 22:35-40 NASB).

"This is my command: Love each other" (John 15:17 NIV).

It was not an accident or a coincidence. This is the reason why, each Easter, we celebrate Jesus Christ's rising from the dead. Having our hearts renewed, our past wrongs totally forgiven, and our lives returned to us as a gift are all reasons why we love. As I said before, there is no magic pill that makes difficulties go away or that takes away all of the pain and makes everything better. But this I do know; giving back the Love and grace of God that is poured out to us is our first and only response to him. It is above anything in this life, singular in its ability as an avenue for us to even begin to make sense of all we see, hear, touch, taste, and feel. The more we endeavor to become like him, the better we understand him.

"You, LORD, hear the desire of the afflicted; you encourage them, and you listen to their cry" (Psalm 10:17 NASB).

I am thankful that the love of Jesus is strong enough to hold me fast and able to correct my course and compel me. There is a song called "Beyond The Blue" by Josh Garrels, and he puts the response to such a furious Love into perfect context:

"Yellow and gold as the new day dawns
Like a virgin unveiled who waited so long
To dance and rejoice and sing her song
And rest in the arms of a love so strong
No one comes unless they're drawn
By the voice of desire that leads 'em along
To the redemption of what went wrong
By the blood that covers the innocent one" ... —Josh Garrels

That our life is no longer our own is never more lovely, never more fulfilling, than when we come to our Savior Jesus, heavy laden and weary from the battle. He takes it all—every anxiety—off our shoulders, returning to us only the yoke of his love and the burden to learn from him and come after him. As a result, his weight for us to carry is both light and easy. Every fragment, every jot and tittle of our divinely imprinted humanity now begins to respond to what he desires with joy and rejoicing. Whenever his Spirit is quickened within us and we are led to move or to go, we do it just because he would.

"For the love of Christ controls us, having concluded this, that one died for all, therefore all died; and he died for all, so that they who live might no longer live for themselves, but for him who died and rose again on their behalf" (2 Corinthians 5:14-15 NIV).

The King James Version of the Bible says his love *"constrains"* us, so I looked up that word to see what it means to be constrained by love.

Constrain: Verb

- *Severely restrict the scope, extent, or activity of.*
- *Compel or force (someone) toward a particular course of action.*

I had occasion one time to meet and fellowship with two guys from South Africa who were straight off the mission field. Their total abandon, hunger for God, and desire to share the Love of Jesus Christ was palpable. It radiated off of them and poured onto every word they spoke. One of them said something that I initially took issue with. But while praying about it later, the Holy Spirit actually gave me an answer to a rhetorical question that I had asked myself earlier in the week. The missionary said (paraphrasing), "It's more important for me to Love you than to be right." It brought me back again to Jesus' primary command, "**Love one another, just as I have loved you, so you should love one another.**" The Holy Spirit rose up in me and reminded me of a picture my friend Dana posted on the social networking website called Facebook that had also given me pause. Two of the things it said seemed to be in opposition: "Live without pretending," and "Speak without offending." I asked myself and God, how anyone could possibly do both? The following morning in my prayer time I again recalled what the missionary had said, and both statements became crystal clear as The Holy Spirit answered me: "It's more important for me to Love people than to be right." Beginning there, and only there, our walk with God in Christ begins to be authentic.

"Be wise in the way you act toward outsiders; make the most of every opportunity. Let your conversation be always full of grace, seasoned with salt, so that you may know how to answer everyone" (Colossians 4:5-6 NIV).

11

"See what great love the Father has lavished on us, that we should be called children of God! And that is what we are!" (1 John 3:1 NIV).

God's Word says that when we grope for him and seek him, we find him because he is near to us **(Acts 17:27 NASB)**. His loving response is present in us before the fading of our afflicted cry even leaves the air. It is his face in a random act of kindness by a total stranger that alters the entire course of our day and scatters the darkness around us. It is his power released in the concern of every praying saint, when we are lifted up inexplicably out of our circumstances to suddenly know his peace which transcends all understanding **(Philippians 4:7 NIV)**. All of our hope is in him, and we all get the opportunity to be his child. Those and so many other reasons are why we love.

- Love is not afraid to get dirty. Real Love is no respecter of position or authority **(Luke 10:26-37 NASB)**.
- Love does not call down into the pit and point to a ladder. Real Love becomes the ladder **(James 2:14-18 NASB), (1 John 3:18 NASB)**.
- Love is no respecter of appearances, it sees through to the heart of the matter, holds on, and always stays **(Matthew 15:22-28 NASB), (John 14:18-19 NASB)**.
- Love can be uncomfortable. It is rarely convenient and will certainly cost us something **(Luke 9:23-24 NASB)**.
- Love gets down in the muck. It washes us clean in giving and receiving; ultimately, real Love begets Love **(Philippians 2:5-11 NIV)**.

Love in itself

"Knowledge makes arrogant, but love edifies. If anyone supposes that he knows anything, he has not yet known as he ought to

know; but if anyone loves God, he is known by him" (1 Corinthians 8:1-3 NASB).

The reality is that anything apart from God by comparison is empty, since he is the origin of all things **(John 1:1-5 NASB), (Colossians 1:15-17 NASB)**. But this is especially the case when we are talking about love.

Agápe—means love in a "spiritual" sense. It often refers to a general affection or deeper sense of "true unconditional love." When The Bible talks about God as "Love," *Agape* is the word behind it. Whether the love given is returned or not, *Agape* continues to love (even without any self-benefit). It is also used by Christians to express the unconditional love of God for us **(John 3:16 NASB).**

Éros—is "physical," passionate love, with sensual desire and longing. Romantic, pure emotion without the balance of logic. "Love at first sight." *Erotas* means "intimate love"; however, *eros* does not have to be sexual in nature. It can also be applied to dating relationships and marriage. A great example from scripture would be the Old Testament book, The Song of Solomon.

Philia—is "mental" love. It means affectionate regard or friendship. This type of love has a sense of give and take. It is a dispassionate, virtuous love. It includes loyalty to friends, family, and community, and requires virtue, equality and familiarity. In ancient texts, *philos* denoted a general type of love, used for love between family, and between friends. *Philia* refers to brotherly love and is most often exhibited in a close friendship. The scriptural account of David and Jonathan is an excellent illustration of *phileo* love **(1 Samuel 18:1-3 NASB).**

Storge—means "affection." It is natural affection, like that felt by parents for offspring. It is also known to express mere acceptance or putting up with situations. In the New Testament, the negative form of *storge* is used twice. First in describing sinful humanity as having "no understanding, no fidelity, no love, no mercy." The

other instance is translated "without love." **(Romans 1:31 NASB),
(2 Timothy 3:3 NASB)** We also find an interesting compound: *philostorgos* is translated as "be devoted." The word combines *philos* and *storge* means "to cherish one's kindred." As part of God's family, we should show loving affection toward each other and be prone to love **(Romans 12:10 NASB).**

Ref: http://www.gotquestions.org

It matters very little which of the four most popular meanings we attach to the word. All of our attempts to make anything substantial of love without Jesus Christ as the foundation end up falling desperately short of the mark. Why? Because while acting out of our own humanity, the results of our attempts at love are never what they ought to be. We are helpless to reproduce any form of authentic Love apart from the source of all Love, which is God alone. Independent of Him, our most excellent efforts are still only counterfeit currency.

However, sometimes perception is reality. Even the defining of love in itself is affected. In the same way that the taste of a filet mignon cooked to perfection or the beauty that resounds in a masterful symphony are unknown to those who have never partaken, so the idea of all love having God as both its origin and its end must seem like total foolishness to one who has never known it. Understandable? Absolutely. Without consequences? Not so much.

"For since the creation of the world his invisible attributes, his eternal power and divine nature, have been clearly seen, being understood through what has been made, so that they are without excuse. For even though they knew God, they did not honor him as God or give thanks, but they became futile in their speculations, and their foolish heart was darkened" (Romans 1:20-21 NASB).

If we could only see ourselves the way God sees us, past all of the clutter and garbage as if it were invisible, so that we could realize the heart of who he intended us to be. Knowledge absent the presence of wisdom that is from Heaven produces arrogance. This same arrogance is that which would look full in the face, the One who crossed all time and space for us and say, *"I think I know something that You don't."*

We are well aware of what we have done, and of all the vacant things to which we were once beholden, but it is Jesus' Love combined with knowledge that assures us we are fully known by God. It releases his power in building us up, so we are able to build one another up in love through him. Bearing that in mind, what if our friends and loved ones could see themselves as we see them through the lens of Jesus Christ? If only we'd all let his light shine through us, and we would put Jesus' Love on the same way we put on clothes every morning. If he was all they saw when they looked at us, wouldn't they understand who he is? Wouldn't they run to him with abandon and never let go? Maybe, maybe not. But I do know one thing for certain: with God's authentic Love, all things are possible!

"Arise, shine, for your light has come, and the glory of the LORD rises upon you. See, darkness covers the earth and thick darkness is over the peoples, but the LORD rises upon you and his glory appears over you. Nations will come to your light, and kings to the brightness of your dawn" (Isaiah 60:1-3 NASB).

In this is love

"Instruct them to do good, to be rich in good works, to be generous and ready to share, storing up for themselves the treasure of a good foundation for the future, so that they may take hold of that which is life indeed" (1 Timothy 6:18-19 NASB).

"Life indeed," however, isn't always so easy to give. Time, love, or even a warm smile are a rare commodity to the badly wounded. "Life indeed," however, isn't always so simple to receive. A heart pierced through by the world and sin is above all a senseless thing, a cornered animal, alone and ignorant of all but preservation.

"Life indeed," though there is only One who is willing and able to give it. There is only One who sees and hears every afflicted cry. In his eyes are comfort, surrender, and release. In his eyes are every answer, every assurance of a good foundation for the future. There is only One in whom the quiet refrain of "*I Love You*" becomes the longing of every human heart. Jesus Christ is "He," and he alone is Life indeed.

"I descended to the roots of the mountains. The earth with its bars was around me forever, but you have brought up my life from the pit, O Lord my God" (Jonah 2:6 NASB).

So where did he find you? That question always evokes an immediate sensory response. No matter what it looked like relatively speaking, the only right answer is "*The pit.*" God showed compassion, that he neither earned nor deserved, to the prophet Jonah because God is Love. Jesus died for all humanity because God is Love.

"We have come to know and have believed the love which God has for us. God is love, and the one who abides in love abides in God, and God abides in him" (1 John 4:16 NASB).

Coming to know God as Love requires that we see our fallen condition, cry out, and then receive his mercy. However, having done all of these things, when we truly understand that "God is Love," what follows is an involuntary and irrevocable transformation. He imparts to us an equity of redemption in the way we view everyone and everything from that point forward.

"We love, because he first loved us ... And this commandment we have from him, that the one who loves God should love his brother also" (1 John 4:19, 21 NASB).

Jonah knew God's love, but he did not understand that "God is Love." He knew the pain of the pit, but he had no long term grasp of where God had found him. The evidence is in his own reply after God had shown mercy to deliver him. He was a man ultimately concerned with his own comfort; when things got uncomfortable for him, God's Love and the desire of God's heart for others took a back seat.

"But I will sacrifice to you with the voice of thanksgiving. *That which I have vowed I will pay.* Salvation is from the Lord" (Jonah 2:9 NASB).

Paul the apostle was a man who did properly understand that "God is Love." Comparing Jonah and Paul, as well as their responses, is a study in contradictions.

"But whatever things were gain to me, those things I have counted as loss for the sake of Christ. More than that, I count all things to be loss in view of the surpassing value of knowing Christ Jesus my Lord, for whom I have suffered the loss of all things, and count them but rubbish so that I may gain Christ, and may be found in him" (Philippians 3:7-9 NASB).

Paul's long-term grasp of where God found him was the fruit borne in everything he said and evidenced in everything he did. Paul's understanding that "God is Love" became his identity. In the same way, God has called us in Jesus to let it become ours.

"This is love: not that we loved God, but that he loved us and sent his Son as an atoning sacrifice for our sins" (1 John 4:10 NIV).

Prayer: *Lord you weave all things together in quiet, subtle beauty. The elegance and poetry of your Love in motion sets my heart at rest and quickens my spirit to Joy. "Such knowledge is to wonderful for me" and leaves me speechless but for the intimate fellowship of your heart reaching into mine and perfectly, gently, drawing out of me the deep praise and adoration for you that is too lofty for words. This Love that stands by my side and holds my hand in the face of every charge and deception is the same Love that never lets go of me while insults and accusations are piled so high that I can scarcely see through them. When all is quiet, without wavering, though many of the accusations are true, you stay by my side.*

Darkness can find no respite, my enemy's hate stands unrequited; even fear must bow its knee. In the face of your Love's declaration, all creation is silenced and in that moment, whether I am coming to you for the seventh or the seventy-seventh time, I know you will never let me fall. I know when my heart is so anxious that my vision is blurred, and my feet are mired so deeply that I become stuck, you will always be there. With an outstretched hand you will always say, "This is my son or my daughter, I Love them so much, and I am so very proud of them." Your words to me will always be, "It's okay, I'm here, and even if you can't see the next step, I can. If you walk with me, I won't ever lead you where you can't go. I will never allow you to be put to shame." Abba, the gentle embrace of your unfailing Love is more precious to me than life. Every morning I remember all that your Love is, and in turn my soul sings. What other love could ever compare? There just isn't any.

Scripture: **"If I speak in the tongues of men or of angels, but do not have love, I am only a resounding gong or a clanging cymbal. If I have the gift of prophecy and can fathom all mysteries and all knowledge, and if I have a faith that can move mountains, but do not have love, I am nothing. If I give all I possess to the poor and give over my body to hardship that I may boast, but do not have love, I gain nothing. Love is patient, love is kind. It does not envy, it does not boast, it is not proud. It does not dishonor others, it is not self-seeking, it is not easily angered, it keeps no record of wrongs. Love does not delight in evil but rejoices with the truth. It always protects, always trusts, always hopes, always perseveres. Love never fails" (1 Corinthians 13:1-8 NIV)**

CHAPTER 2

JESUS

Who is this Jesus?

To be honest, I'm not really sure where to begin. So many writers of so many great books have made this same attempt with mixed results. I only know that my little contribution to the subject is supposed to be added. The "how" part I don't know, but God does and I trust him. So to start I will defer to John the Baptist who was born for the express purpose of announcing Jesus to the world. As the Bible says, John came to "**Prepare the way for The Lord" (Isaiah 40:3 NASB), (John 1:23 NASB), (Mark 1:3 NASB), (Matthew 3:3 NASB), (Luke 3:4 NASB).**

"Behold, the Lamb of God who takes away the sin of the world!" (John 1:29 NASB).

Jesus accepts all who come, receives all who ask, and loves all he accepts as though they are his most precious. He is intimacy that defies anything in all creation to match it. He is the sudden awareness of our present condition—the grave and beautiful reality of a flashing neon, spiritual "VACANCY" sign inherent in every human soul. He is to each of us the full assurance of Life that takes back every inch of stolen ground, the One who retrieves all about us that had been lost or forsaken when we were at our very worst and weakest. He's the big brother who beats down every bully, the friend who stands by our side no matter how ugly things get. He is the One who offered to give his life for us because he was the only One who could.

But that alone isn't the Jesus I mean to convey to you. The Jesus I mean to convey is perfect and personal. He is the solution to every difficult equation my heart has tried to solve from birth. He is the answer to the deepest intimate questions I have cried out to the air in desperation when I thought nobody could hear. He is the lone embrace that enfolds a murderer's repentant heart and accepts the contrition and brokenness of a liar and a thief. He is the strong arm that holds every disease-ravaged body, every grieving, soul-sick lover, and every weary and burdened mind. He is the strength in the legs of the widow and widower, the glimmer of hope to the barely open eyes of an addict, the still small voice speaking gently in the ear of the one who has begun to believe they can no longer bear the pain of life. He is lovingkindness so complete, so all encompassing, and so real, that the finest words ever imagined to describe who He is fall pathetically short. He is my Abba Father, my daddy **(John 10:29-30), (John 14:8-9)**. He is the One I can run to anytime, anywhere, for any reason. He is the shoulder I cry on and the hand I hold when I feel most alone. He is the first thought I have every morning, the One I think of when I want to express my joy, the substance in my every emotion. He is the color and beauty in every sunset and the excellence in each of my most treasured moments. He is the delicate intricacy of a baby in the womb, the thrill of love in a new mother at the sound of her infant's first plaintiff cry. He is the only One who will ever truly understand me, the only One who will ever truly know me, the only One who will never judge me, the only One who always completely sees me. He is the only One who daily takes what is broken in me and makes it whole again. HE IS WHO HE IS, and he is the only One who will ever be enough. He is my unfailing, immovable, unshakeable, unchanging, wonderful Savior.

He is Jesus who is called Christ—not a coping mechanism, and not a crutch. He is not a nice idea or just a good man. He is more than a prophet, a wise teacher, or someone's opinion. He is neither a philosophy nor a religion. He is relationship. He is not some corner store "drive by" daily affirmation to build our self-esteem. He is the only Son of the One True God. Jesus is Love for Love's sake, looking straight through what we are not. He sees the intentionality of what formed us because he was there when it happened. He speaks and reality is born. He has the blueprints folks! He is the foundation, the cornerstone, and the capstone! **(Psalms 118:21-22 NASB), (1 Corinthians 3:11 NASB), (Ephesians 2:20-22 NASB), (1 Peter 2:6 NASB), (Acts 4:11 NASB).**

"In the beginning was the Word, and the Word was with God, and the Word was God. He was in the beginning with God. All things came into being through him, and apart from him nothing came

into being that has come into being. In him was life, and the life was the light of men ... And the Word became flesh, and dwelt among us, and we saw his glory, glory as of the only begotten from the Father, full of grace and truth" (John 1:1-4,14 NASB).

That is such an awesome revelation. He is the foundation upon which everything we are or ever will become is built. He is the integral piece that holds us up, and together, He is the final exquisite element that seals up our lives.

"Who do you say I am?"

"Now when Jesus came into the district of Caesarea Philippi, he was asking his disciples, 'Who do people say that the Son of Man is?' And they said, 'Some say John the Baptist; and others, Elijah; but still others, Jeremiah, or one of the prophets.' He said to them, 'But who do you say that I am?' Simon Peter answered, *'You are the Christ, the Son of the living God.'* And Jesus said to him, 'Blessed are you, Simon Barjona, because flesh and blood did not reveal this to you, but my Father who is in heaven. I also say to you that you are Peter, and upon this rock I will build my church; and the gates of Hades will not overpower it" (Matthew 16:13-18 NASB).

I am unashamed to declare your glory, Lord. How can I be silent? What a sweet reminder to me this verse is—that he is my portion. He is my Rock in all things, and the strength of my heart.

So, are we to understand that "**this rock**" is Peter? Weak, human, fallible, Peter? Or is "**this rock**" the proclamation and the reality that Jesus is "**the Christ, the Son of the living God**"? I believe it is certainly the latter. Though you could be asking yourself right now, *"What happens then if I reject him, or refuse to believe? What if I ask, even knowing who he is, what it takes to get to heaven, then decide I don't like the answer?"*

"As Jesus started on his way, a man ran up to him and fell on his knees before him. 'Good teacher,' he asked, 'what must I do to inherit eternal life?'

'Why do you call me good?' Jesus answered. 'No one is good—except God alone. You know the commandments: You shall not murder, you shall not commit adultery, you shall not steal, you shall not give false testimony, you shall not defraud, honor your father and mother.'

'Teacher,' he declared, 'all these I have kept since I was a boy.'

Jesus looked at him and loved him. 'One thing you lack,' he said. "Go, sell everything you have and give to the poor, and you will have treasure in heaven. Then come, follow me.'

At this the man's face fell. He went away sad, because he had great wealth" (Mark 10:17-22 NASB).

Jesus looked at him and loved him. He knew what was in the man's heart as surely as he knows what is in ours. He knows precisely what we need to hear and when, and he even knows if "today" will not be the day for us. But does Jesus hate us? Does he condemn us or put us down? Does he try to change our minds or make snarky, foolish comments about our character? No, Jesus looks at us and loves us, even if we turn our backs to him. Another piece of Jesus' character is well-defined here. He is release, compassion, and sympathy. He will always be jealous for us, but he is also patient with us.

"But do not forget this one thing, dear friends: With the Lord a day is like a thousand years, and a thousand years are like a day. The Lord is not slow in keeping his promise, as some understand slowness. Instead he is patient with you, not wanting anyone to perish, but everyone to come to repentance" (2 Peter 3:8-9 NIV).

"Because God has made us for himself, our hearts are restless until they rest in him."—Augustine of Hippo

"He has made everything beautiful in its time. He has also set eternity in the human heart; yet no one can fathom what God has done from beginning to end" (Ecclesiastes 3:11 NIV).

Sometimes it's hard for me to see how he makes everything beautiful in its proper season. But to get the correct context, my goal every day is to try to understand him better. That he has set eternity in my heart is my vehicle to faith, both at the times and in the manner that his splendor is being revealed. Though King Solomon qualifies his statements with a contrary declaration, much like the whole of the book of Ecclesiastes, all three in the above verse still point me to Jesus whenever I read it. In Jesus I have seen, I have been told, and I can know what God has done from beginning to end. Moreover, I am a partaker in his uniqueness each time I pray or read his Word simply because of who he is.

So I say to you all, hold onto your faith today however large or small it may be. He stands at the door of your heart and knocks. He is patient and waits for you because he understands you, He pursues you because he cares for you more than you could ever comprehend.

"I am HE"

"From now on I am telling you before it comes to pass, so that when it does occur, you may believe that I am He" (John 13:19 NASB).

Because he is Wholeness, I am whole.

Because he is Love, I am lovely.

Because he is Salvation, I am saved.

Because he is everything, who I am is enough.

"The seventy returned with joy, saying, 'Lord, even the demons are subject to us in your name.' And he said to them, 'I was watching Satan fall from heaven like lightning. Behold, I have given you authority to tread on serpents and scorpions, and over all the power of the enemy, and nothing will injure you. Nevertheless do not rejoice in this, that the spirits are subject to you, but *rejoice that your names are recorded in heaven'"* (Luke 10:17-20 NASB).

We pray all of the time for all sorts of things— physical healing, deliverance from bondage, sicknesses, or freedom from sin. We pray for more love, peace, wholeness, and clarity. We pray for all of these and any other thing we can imagine based on the promises in God's Word. Rightly so! All of his promises are "Yes and Amen" in Jesus, when we pray in agreement with His revealed will **(2 Corinthians 1:20 NIV), (1 John 5:14-15 NASB)**. But our focus is too often on the gift rather than the gift giver. My pastor is fond of saying, "*Sometimes we are so focused on wanting to see the miraculous that we miss the supernatural.*"

In Luke, chapter 10, Jesus' followers struggle with that very same issue. He waits patiently for them to finish talking, then without missing a step reminds them where the real power lies. What he said to them he is still saying to us today—that the miracle isn't in power over the demons, in a healing, or a spiritual gift of any other kind, the true power, the real miracle is Life. The miracle is Jesus himself. God reminded me, as I thought about it, that even the most amazing things done in his name, or anything that we would call extraordinary, are only temporal. They are done for a specific purpose and only for a time. Are they good? Absolutely! But are they really anything at all when we look full into the face of the precious Savior and truly see him? No, since there is only One true gift giver, and he is full of grace to remind us where our focus should be: "**Rejoice that your names are recorded in heaven.**"

"The kingdom of God does not come with observation; nor will they say, 'See here!' or 'See there!' For indeed, the kingdom of God is within you" (Luke 17:20-21 NKJV).

That is a fine thing indeed! God's kingdom is within us. So what is "**the kingdom of God**"? Jesus used parables to describe it. He compared it to a mustard seed that gets planted and grows into a tree **(Luke 13:19 NIV)**. He compared it to seeds being scattered on good and bad soil **(Matthew 13:1-8 NASB)**. He compared it to good seeds sown in a field **(Matthew 13:24 NASB)**. He compared it to yeast mixed with flour that is worked all through the dough **(Luke 13:21 NIV)**. Still another time he compared it to seed that is scattered, but that grows independent of any effort on the part of the sower **(Mark 4:26-29 NIV)**.

In every passage of scripture, the seeds and the yeast are the Word of God, the soil and the flour are the human heart. The crop, the wheat, the tree, and the dough are all the effect of the Word of God on the human heart. So following that logic, the "**kingdom of God**" is the Word of God, and secondarily it is the Word of God bestowed. Now consider this; we already know the Word is not just an "it," but the Word is also a "who."

"**In the beginning was the Word, and the Word was with God, and the Word was God. *He was with God in the beginning***" **(John 1:1-2 NASB).**

Jesus Christ is the kingdom and the Word of God! He is both all at once, and so very much more. This really confused me at first, but now, after doing a bit more reading, it is so simple and perfectly clear to me.

Name above all Names

"**For a child will be born to us, a son will be given to us; And the government will rest on his shoulders; And his name will be called Wonderful Counselor, Mighty God, Eternal Father, Prince of Peace**" **(Isaiah 9:6 NASB).**

He was assinged, and allowed himself to be called by, many different names. He was called son of Joseph, son of David, Son of Man, and Son of God. Just as he is perfect, no name chosen for him could be anything less than perfect. The prophet Isaiah gave a few of them in the verse above. But here are a few more you may not have known, along with their meanings:

- Emmanuel—"God with us"
- Shiloh—"Peace bringer"
- Messiah—"Anointed One"
- Adonai—"Master or Great Teacher"
- Daystar—"Light bringing"
- Alpha and Omega—"The beginning and the end of all things"
- The Amen—"The Faithful, the True"
- I AM—"The name of God"

"He is the image of the invisible God, the firstborn of all creation" (Colossians 1:15 NASB).

Most of those names are proud, some even majestic, but there are other names you rarely ever hear spoken out loud. They are not as comely, but they still describe important aspects of Christ. Although they do not whisk our minds away to happy or peaceful places, they are most precious and worthy of our attention. They proclaim the essential character traits of both a man and a Savior. He became sin who knew no sin. He was the servant of all and for all.

"Jesus then came out, wearing the crown of thorns and the purple robe. Pilate said to them, 'Behold, the Man!'" (John 19:5 NASB).

Behold! Jesus the Despised and Stricken! Behold! Jesus the Forsaken! They are, much like the thorny crown and gaudy purple robe on a beaten, bloodied prisoner, extremely unimpressive. No matter how hard we try to dress them up, they are just never going to sound triumphant. That isn't at all how most people see him, and that was not what anyone, including those on earth who knew him best, expected their king to be. Lowly and humble, in meekness he came.

"For he grew up before him like a tender shoot, and like a root out of parched ground; he has no stately form or majesty that we should look upon him, nor appearance that we should be attracted to him. He was despised and rejected by mankind, a man of suffering, and familiar with pain. Like one from whom people hide their faces he was despised, and we held him in low esteem. Surely he took up our pain and bore our suffering, yet we considered him punished by God, stricken by him, and afflicted" (Isaiah 53:2-4 NASB).

Many still were attracted, not to Jesus the man, but to "**the image of the invisible God**" in this particular man. You can feel it come through pages in the Bible when a person really saw him, the revealed Word of God who became a human being and lived a real human life **(John 1:14 NASB)**. They saw the Truth in Jesus that was for them, and is still for us—the reality of restored intimacy with Heaven.

"**God created man in his own image, in the image of God he created him; male and female he created them. God blessed them …**" **(Genesis 1:27-28 NASB).**

Jesus Christ is his (God's) image, the firstborn over all creation; we are his creation, in his image from the beginning. Once lost, now again found, once blind, now again seeing, once with a heart of stone, now having a heart of flesh, all because of who he is.

God woke me up one morning saying to me repeatedly, "Christ who is your life" **(Colossians 3:4)**. It was like some awesome song that you just can't get out of your head. When I started to meditate on it and consider it, God showed me another something special about who he is. Jesus, who is our life, *is our life every day*. Jesus, the Name above all Names!

"**God exalted him to the highest place and gave him *the name that is above every name*, that at the name of Jesus every knee should bow, in heaven and on earth and under the earth, and every tongue acknowledge that *Jesus Christ is Lord*" (Philippians 2:9-11 NIV).**

The word about "The Word"

Let me try to sum this all up in a way that will make sense to you. This chapter has been a daunting and rewarding exercise for me, to say the least. I mean, really, how could anyone accurately describe "the King of Kings"? It's like trying to explain and to describe Creation or the Universe; how do you express the attributes of that which is absolutely everything, everywhere, all the time? So to close out my very humble attempt, I thought it would be appropriate to let the words about "The Word" do the talking.

Jesus Christ is the exact representation of God:

"He who has seen me has seen the Father" (John 14:9 NASB).

Jesus Christ is directly representative of the Holy Spirit:

"Now the Lord is the Spirit" (2 Corinthians 3:17 NASB).

The three are really one (*another full chapter on its own*), though they are all mentioned separately at times as well. Confused? I know I would be. So rather than trying to explain how that all fits, let me show you.

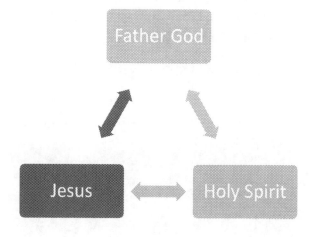

Finally, *all that Jesus was and still is, are in the things he did.* Many of those are in the Bible, even more of them are not. As for everything we can know, I hope to have at least sparked your curiosity, and I encourage you to seek even more of him in the pages of his Book. Beyond that, I think I'll let John, **"the apostle who Jesus loved"** finish up the talking.

"And there are also many other things which Jesus did, which if they were written in detail, I suppose that even the world itself would not contain the books that would be written" (John 21:25 NASB)

Prayer: *I worship you God, and I am in awe of the truth that my Savior Jesus calls me brother, that he calls me a friend. He is never ashamed of me, no matter how many times I fail or how far I might fall. He calls me his child and he is my Freedom. I am so thankful that I live today in Jesus Christ, and that I am all of those things by his grace, just because he lives. Praise God!! Lord Jesus you are my life. I turn my heart and my eyes toward heaven and sing your praise! Amen!*

Scripture: **"When my heart was grieved and my spirit embittered, I was senseless and ignorant; I was a brute beast before you. Yet I am always with you; you hold me by my right hand. You guide me with your counsel, and afterward you will take me into glory. Whom have I in heaven but you? And earth has nothing I desire besides you. My flesh and my heart may fail, but God is the strength of my heart and my portion forever" (Psalms 73:21-26 NIV).**

CHAPTER 3

GRACE

Grace upon Grace

Grace is most accurately defined as unmerited, undeserved favor—God's favor. I am not sure why, but sometimes I have trouble receiving it, and all that God has for me. It could be because I've had a good hard look at what I was before he poured out his grace and made me whole again. If you are in a similar place today and remember only one thing you read in this chapter, let it be that when God looks at you he doesn't see what you or anyone else sees. He sees only beauty.

"For of his (Jesus') fullness we have all received, and grace upon grace" (John 1:16 NASB).

God gave me an awesome picture of his **"grace upon grace"** a year or so ago, and I want to start by sharing that with you. I heard this passage of scripture in a sermon one day and he just sort of hit me over the head with it.

"And some men were carrying on a bed a man who was paralyzed; and they were trying to bring him in and to set him down in front of him. But not finding any way to bring him in because of the crowd, they went up on the roof and let him down through the tiles with his stretcher, into the middle of the crowd, in front of Jesus. Seeing their faith, he said, 'Friend, your sins are forgiven you'" (Luke 5:18-20 NASB).

I've read it a hundred times if I have read it once, but this time God wanted me to see it from an entirely different angle.

Though we are not all physically paralytic, we are all apart from Jesus, and in our sin, spiritual paralytics. Each and every one of us can become mired down and unable to move in our own power. We all have need to be brought to him, and lowered down or carried into his presence by the Holy Spirit. We are all powerless to come unless we're drawn. And if that were not enough, Jesus, knowing every part of us and seeing that we bring nothing of any worth, still calls us *"Friend"* and forgives our sin. Rather than healing us in spite of our weakness, he sees in our humility the recognition of how vulnerable we truly are, and in healing us actually esteems it. That is grace.

"No one can come to me unless the Father who sent me draws him; and I will raise him up on the last day" (John 6:44 NASB).

There was a period of my life, sometime in my late 20's to very early 30's, when I met and got to know a man named Bill. I was a father, a husband, and a confessed Christian. The more relevant part of the story is that I was also a raging alcoholic. Functional to be sure, but an alcoholic if ever there was one. So what does any of that have to do with Grace? Back to Bill—also a father, a husband, and a confessed Christian. Bill was a recovering alcoholic and far more mature in his relationship with Jesus than I was. Bill is an African-American man who came up hard as a kid. This is only significant because, to this day, I still don't know what he saw in some entitled, drunk white guy from the suburbs who had a really bad attitude.

Anyway, Bill started to come alongside me and tried to show me things in the Bible. I usually responded either poorly or dubiously, and I always wondered why this guy would never stop coming around. He just never stopped being interested in me or my faith, no matter how foolish my questions were—and they were foolish. No matter how obstinate I was, whether or not I made any attempt at all to keep in touch with him, he always kept coming around, finding me. This went on for the better part of a year until I finally realized, *"This guy doesn't care about all my junk, and he just genuinely cares about me."*

Why say all of that? Well, simply to say this: Jesus Christ used that man's life to change mine. I can honestly say I would not be alive, nor would I be the man I am today, if it had not been for him and God's grace. There are many things I could share about Bill, many amazing experiences, but one stands above the rest and illustrates the perfect way that the embodiment of Grace was imparted to me through him.

There was a day, like many others I had been having at that time, when I just decided it was all too much. My marriage was in shambles. I was selfishly fed up with raising kids, and all I saw around me in church at the time was a bunch of hypocrisy. All of that sort of converged at once and I certainly did not have any desire to be at work. I'd had it with just about everyone and everything. So I decided I was going to bail from work and go have a beer. I went to a bar around lunch time and had one, then I decided it would be even better to get a 40 oz. or two and go park at the beach.

As you might imagine, the absolutely last thing I wanted was to see or talk to anyone, most especially not, sober, loving, Spirit-filled Bill. I even thought about what time of the day it was, specifically because I knew that Bill took walks on the beach to pray and read, usually really early in the morning. Anyway, after doing some quick math, I decided I was safe and it was way past the time when he would be there anyway, right?

Wrong. God had other plans. I got my beer, pulled into the beach parking lot, and had my windows rolled up listening to some toxic, hateful band that was saying exactly what I wanted to hear: "*Shine the world, people are false, religion is false, live for yourself,*" and "*Die young.*" You get the idea. I'm drinking my beer and feeling sorry for myself, and out of the corner of my eye, in the distance, I start to see a figure of this bald, black guy walking down the bike path in my direction. He kind of looked familiar but was still far enough away that I couldn't see his face, so I remembered my earlier self-assurances about Bill and the time he usually came to the beach and convinced myself there was no way it could be him. Well, as the man got closer and closer, I was able to recognize that, to my complete shock, it was in fact Bill walking straight toward my car. At this point I got really religious again! I was praying, "*Please don't let him see me. Please don't let him see me.*" But in retrospect, he and God probably saw me before I even woke up that morning—kind of like Jesus with Nathaniel **(John 1:47-50 NASB)**. So as he got closer, I could tell he saw me, and I could tell he was coming to my window and looking a bit confused.

To set the stage for you, I was not supposed to be drinking at all, nor was I supposed to be playing hooky from work. I was already frantically trying to figure out how I would explain myself, or what lie I would tell him just to get him to move along and let me get back to my self-pity party. He calmly walked up to my window and I rolled it down, expecting just about anything. What I got, with his big welcoming smile, was, *"Hey Mark! How are you doing?"* He knew how and what I was doing both by sight and smell, I'm sure (with one giant beer already opened, and another in the passenger seat), but he did not act like it.

At that moment the strangest thing happened. Nothing I had rehearsed, none of the lies I wanted to tell him, would come out of my mouth. I could only manage the words, *"Not so hot Bill."* This was said with tears in my eyes, which I definitely had not intended. Then I looked up at him, and all I could see in him was the face of Jesus, looking straight back at me. All he had to say was, *"Tell me about it brother, what's wrong?"* Then, it was like I couldn't shut my mouth or turn it off. I kept going on and on about everything negative and cruddy that I had pent up inside of me, until I finally looked up and saw that he now also had tears in his eyes.

I will never forget the look of compassion and pain in his eyes. He looked at me, said something like *"I get it"* or *"I understand,"* reached into my truck window, and gave me the biggest hug you can imagine. Then he said, *"Hey why don't you come back to my house and let's get you cleaned up so you can go home to your family tonight."* I didn't want to go, but I could not have refused if I had tried. Something, or someone, was drawing me forward, whether I liked it or not. It was the most bizarre couple of hours. We talked a lot, and he just cared for me. His wife, Denise, even made me dinner. He called my wife and explained where I was and why I was there. He smoothed things over with her, and I went home.

That was a pivotal moment for me, because for the first time in my life I understood Grace. God had known that I needed Bill right there, right then, and he sent him straight up to my window. He sent his best to me in one of the worst moments of my life. Rather than disgust, anger, disappointment, or condemnation, what I got was kindness, sympathy, and mercy, because all God saw when he looked at me was "beautiful."

"For we also once were foolish ourselves, disobedient, deceived, enslaved to various lusts and pleasures, spending our life in

malice and envy, hateful, hating one another. But when the kindness of God our Savior and his love for mankind appeared, he saved us, not on the basis of deeds which we have done in righteousness, but according to his mercy, by the washing of regeneration and renewing by the Holy Spirit, whom he poured out upon us richly through Jesus Christ our Savior, so that being justified by his grace we would be made heirs according to the hope of eternal life" (Titus 3:3-7 NASB).

No one can boast

Grace upon Grace! God opens our eyes and hearts to see Jesus. By his Spirit the declaration, *"You are the Christ, the Son of the Living God,"* erupts from within us **(Matthew 16:15 NASB)**. His majesty is uncontested. His glory is uncontainable, and as we declare this reality, grace follows.

"But he gives us more grace. That is why Scripture says: "God opposes the proud but shows favor to the humble.""" (James 4:6 NIV)

We all fall, and foolishly so. Pride, which sent Satan hurtling to earth, is the very same perversion that exists in our flesh. It is, on our lips, the accelerant darkness that feeds an adolescent sin on to maturity, then **"sets the whole course of one's life on fire" (James 3:6 NIV)**. Thankfully our enemy's own pride blinds him. The same grace that defeated Satan at the Cross, repeatedly overcomes him to this day. So much so that, in what appears to me a residual of his curse, pride irresistibly hastens him to err in exactly the same manner over and over for all time. For the instant the enemy has tasted any sort of success, in our utter weakness and fallen nature, humility takes over. Through this affliction, we are then afforded from the pit a perfect view of God's immutable grace and lifted up. When combined with the revelation that we are in no way able to save ourselves, one might say as Paul the apostle did, "**where sin increased, grace increased all the more" (Romans 5:20 NIV)**. In fact, because of God's grace that runs to embrace us when we turn back to him, we can gratefully say to the darkness and to our enemy, "**when I am weak, then I am strong" (2 Corinthians 12:10 NIV)**. Amen!

"So he got up and came to his father. But while he was still a long way off, his father saw him and felt compassion for him, and ran and embraced him and kissed him" (Luke 15:20 NASB).

However, we still have to live in the world, every day all day. Dependence on, and a type of familiarity with, things that "seem" the most real is a given. However, a friendship-type of love (*philos*) toward them is not; it's a choice. By his Spirit, when our hearts are turned inwardly on ourselves or away from him, God always brings awareness. He will not compete for our affection nor will the intimacy we desire with him abide anything other than total surrender. Since the fruit of rebellion is always division, and the declaration, *"Who will set me free?"* **(Romans 7:24 NASB)** spills from somewhere deep within us, Grace always runs to meet us.

"No temptation has overtaken you but such as is common to man; and God is faithful, who will not allow you to be tempted beyond what you are able, but with the temptation will provide the way of escape also, so that you will be able to endure it." (1 Corinthians 10:13 NASB)

Our actions are as much a confession as our words, probably more. Our countenance will never hide the abundance of what our hearts intend or feel **(Matthew 6:21-23 NASB)**. Body language, the lamp of our eyes, most of who we are from moment to moment, speaks out of those things with which we fill our hearts. We fool ourselves by saying, *"They can't possibly know what I'm thinking or feeling."* True enough, though we all have loud spiritual and emotional "tells" that thankfully betray the silence. More often it is the hidden things that give us away more than what we say. God knows all of them already.

He is concerned with our actions and our confessions only as they relate not as much to the present condition of our heart but to that which ultimately measures its full burden. His grace is most apparent when we rip off the Band-Aids and let his love go to work, in full view of all that we lack apart from him. He is most candidly everything our hearts will ever need.

"Thanks be to God, who delivers me through Jesus Christ our Lord!" (Romans 7:25 NIV)

As I was still thinking about Satan's downfall because of pride, God in his beautiful, perfect way showed me the possibility of our own intermittent downfall through false humility. The grace of God is so complete and final that often it is far too easy, if we aren't careful, to begin to believe we have anything at all to bring to the party apart from obedience, reverence, and deference to him. In the same way, an airplane pilot is keenly aware that, despite his skill, the engines on either side of him are the only thing keeping the hulk of dead metal around him from plummeting to the ground. We need always be aware, despite our gifts and no matter their measure, that God's grace is the only thing between us and our own sudden encounter with "high speed dirt." Thankfully, God understands our weaknesses intimately and we daily receive from him a mercy we could never earn that covers a debt we could never repay.

C.S. Lewis, as the infamous demon "Screwtape," quips at our folly most candidly and comically: *"Catch him (the human) at the moment when he is really poor in spirit and smuggle into his mind the gratifying reflection, 'By jove! I'm being humble,' and almost immediately pride—pride at his own humility—will appear. If he awakes to the danger and tries to smother this new form of pride, make him proud of his attempt—and so on."*—C. S. Lewis, *The Screwtape Letters*

"For it is by grace you have been saved, through faith—and this is not from yourselves, it is the gift of God— not by works, so that no one can boast" (Ephesians 2:8-9 NIV).

The Narrow Road

"Enter through the narrow gate. For wide is the gate and broad is the road that leads to destruction, and many enter through it. But small is the gate and narrow the road that leads to life, and only a few find it" (Matthew 7:13-14 NIV).

It had been on my mind lately: the balance that has to be struck between the revelations of our desperation and weakness apart from God, our freedom and power in Jesus by his Holy Spirit to live as "God's freedmen," and the desire of God that we are living authentically as the people he made us. As I thought about it, God revealed to me that the balance I was imagining is the narrow road Jesus spoke about in Matthew, chapter 7 noted above. It is not a simple proposition by any means, and that is likely why the scripture says that **"only a few find it."** With that in mind, however, the road *is* able to be found, and God's desire (as his Word says) is that none would perish. As I continued to pray about it, the Holy Spirit quieted my heart, singing softly the song of deliverance and comfort that only God can bring. That it is near impossible for us to strike that balance on our own is a given, but for God nothing is impossible.

Three things that are the cross that Jesus calls us to carry daily if we would accept the challenge to come after him and learn from him:

1. Surrendering our will absolutely in favor of his.
2. Believing and knowing in the deep places of our heart that his grace is sufficient for us and that his strength is perfected in our weaknesses.
3. Repeat steps 1 and 2 daily.

Next God put a song in my heart, a sort of poem from his heart in me to confirm it all. I hope it blesses you.

> *"Lord, I want to walk the narrow road. I know it's more than just doin' what you're told,*

More than just humility to bear the weight of my belief, the revelation of a fallen soul.
Lord, I see the road that leads to life. I see that living's more than to be invited,
More than only being free to crucify you endlessly, a fool that's called the man you've never known.

Lord, I long to breach that open gate. I know the keys aren't born of being fake.
You desire only me, the breath of authenticity, your child renowned before creation told.
Lord, the balance seems too much to bear, for what I don't know it hardly seems fair.
In surrender, I can see you light my path and move my feet—your grace sufficient, in my weakness bold."

Prayer: *I am filled with joy and awe at your grace and favor God, that you count me worthy of your instruction and wisdom. The truth you have planted with deep roots in my heart is that everything I am begins and ends in true humility, on my knees, at the foot of the Cross where my Savior gave his life for mine. Not only so, but that I am able to be alive, to love, to see, and to breathe free air. Even my ability to be a father to my children, or to be a friend, all hinges on my recognition of the grace in which I stand, all day, every day. I worship you, Abba. You alone are God! Thank you, Lord Jesus, that your power gives me, and perfects in me, everything from you that I need for today. Thank you Lord for the honor to be counted among the foolish things of the world, since your grace given is all that bears me up and all that is my crown. Give me the strength to walk humbly before you Jesus, and the boldness to carry the impassioned light of your life into every dark place. Amen!*

Scripture: **"And he has said to me, 'My grace is sufficient for you, for power is perfected in weakness.' Most gladly, therefore, I will rather boast about my weaknesses, so that the power of Christ may dwell in me" (2 Corinthians 12:9 NASB).**

CHAPTER 4

FAITH

What is true Faith?

"Now faith is the substance of things hoped for, the evidence of things not seen" (Hebrews 11:1 NKJV).

I've given this a lot of thought over the past few years, and I believe the New King James Version of the Bible really nails what the verse means to convey. The "substance" or tangible presence of what we hope for is _____. The "evidence" or indisputable Truth of what we cannot now see is _____. You fill in the blanks. Having Faith is total surrender to, and trust in, who God is, what he says, and every good thing he does, period. Whatever you put in those blank spaces must necessarily find their beginning and their end in him.

How does true Faith come? True Faith comes by the healing and enabling work of the Holy Spirit to bring us near to God. By his grace our hearts are able to hear the words spoken about Jesus Christ, and as we hear, something wonderful happens, something inside us changes. For the first time, we are able to see him as he is, with open eyes and an unbound spirit. Sometimes it can happen all at once; sometimes it happens gradually, over many years.

"Consequently, faith comes from hearing the message, and the message is heard through the word about Christ" (Romans 10:17 NIV).

For me personally, it was the latter. I grew up going to church only on Christmas and Easter, if I went at all. I know my mother had something resembling Faith, and she did bring me up to believe in the One true God, but ours was not what you would call a "Christian" household. Faith as I know it now was a totally foreign concept until I reached the first in a series of "Rock Bottom" moments in life. Moments like these necessitated a confrontation with the reality of being utterly powerless to affect my fallen condition. For me, this began with recreational drugs, then onto alcoholism, and then addiction to prescription drugs. In the midst of it all I had also always been held captive to a poor self-image. I also had a horribly skewed and wrong-hearted view of women as sexual objects. The last thing to go, prior to an enormous breakthrough in my understanding of Faith, was my addiction to nicotine, which I eluded to in the preface of this book.

A common thread that ran throughout each individual release was my having to choose. I always hit a wall, then came to a crossroads. One path led into an absolute darkness from which there would be no escape, and the other to a Light which I can only describe as other than "me," and in that Light, a Hope of something better. You're probably thinking, *"Duh, easy choice!"* Right? Unfortunately, the choice was not as easy as you might think.

The hardest part was that choosing the Light required trust in something I could not use my five senses to prove. Once your identity is wrapped up in it, the darkness brings a powerful counterfeit to try to keep you from moving. Believe it or not, leaving behind the total comfort and familiarity of something, even when it's killing you, is almost impossible. I say "almost," because we are able, in those moments of desperation and fear, with all of our efforts exhausted, to hear the voice of God most clearly. His words to me were, *"Don't worry. I promise that when you let go I will always catch you. Don't be afraid; I will never let you fall, and I will never let go of you."* To this day, he has always been true to his words, every single one.

"Out of the depths I have cried to you, O LORD. Lord, hear my voice! Let your ears be attentive to the voice of my supplications. If you, LORD, should mark iniquities, O Lord, who could stand? But there is forgiveness with you, that you may be feared. I wait for the LORD, my soul does wait, and in his word do I hope" (Psalms 130:1-5 NASB).

So where do we get this message of Faith? And how do we know we will have it? Well, in order to understand the character of any author, you need to read their book. In this case, that book is The Bible. Sounds painless enough, eh? Sometimes not so much, so I will do my best to simplify it for you and trust that God will do the rest of the work.

"If it can be verified, we don't need faith … Faith is for that which lies on the other side of reason. Faith is what makes life bearable, with all its tragedies and ambiguities and sudden, startling joys."—Madeleine L'Engle

In the four gospels, Jesus often connected Faith and wholeness, belief and healing **(Luke 8:49-50 NKJV), (Matthew 9:21-22 NIV), (Luke 18:41-42 NIV), (Luke 17:19 NASB)**. Though it was not as important to him that we understand that he *"can"* or *"will"* make us whole when we ask. His primary concern was, and still is, that when we do ask, we *"believe"* and then secondarily it is *"what"* we believe.

"But if you can do anything, take pity on us and help us!" And Jesus said to him, " *'If you can?' All things are possible to him who believes.*" Immediately the boy's father cried out and said, "I do believe; *help my unbelief*" (Mark 9:22-24 NASB).

Is Faith, then, a belief in his willingness? Or maybe belief in his ability? Was Faith in the power of Jesus' earthly form to accomplish things a requirement, like he was some sort of rabbinical super hero? The answer is, No. Not only does placing our hope in such things fail miserably to hold any water, but when we are able to view them in the daylight, they just do not make a shred of sense. Jesus' first desire for us is that we know him and, to the degree we can, understand him. For this reason, Faith or belief that makes us whole and heals us, that understands his character, can declare only one thing:

"You are the Christ, the Son of the living God" (Matthew 16:16 NASB).

Faith and belief that is real steps back and agrees with *all* of God's promises. It *unconditionally* surrenders to his will, obeys him, and most of all, leans on him rather than our own estimation or on what we can see, touch, taste, or feel. Yes, he (Jesus) came that we might have life and life to the full **(John 10:10 NIV)**. But we do well to always remember that there can be no life at all apart from knowing the "He."

There isn't any way to apprehend the knowledge about Jesus without Faith which believes God's words, and is in turn unashamed to speak as well as do them.

"For it is with your heart that you believe and are justified, and it is with your mouth that you profess your faith and are saved. As Scripture says, 'Anyone who believes in him will never be put to shame'" (Romans 10:10-11 NIV).

What is the Faith we speak?

"But having the same spirit of faith, according to what is written, 'I BELIEVED, THEREFORE I SPOKE,' we also believe, therefore we also speak" (2 Corinthians 4:13 NASB)

What parts of us pass through heaven's lathe? What parts of us remain to be pressed and folded in the fire, trained by the Creator's masterful hammer? The very same are Faith in us withstanding each test, refreshed by the water that follows—cooled and hardened, finely sharpened by the whetstone of God's living Word.

The Refiner artfully, and with greatest care, remakes each blade's edge. We are unmistakably beholden to life in the way we are made able to confess his name, singular in precision by the manner in which we will one day reflect his light. We are most candidly his by the signature left as we are divided; he mercifully moves in us to lay bare our hearts, though we are the most obstinate of all his creatures. No thought and no intention will bring a halt to his handiwork, nor any secret obstruction bar his path. Faith will come, and it will always bear his perfect result.

"For the word of God is living and active and sharper than any two-edged sword, and piercing as far as the division of soul and spirit, of both joints and marrow, and able to judge the thoughts and intentions of the heart. And there is no creature hidden from

his sight, but all things are open and laid bare to the eyes of him with whom we have to do" (Hebrews 4:12-13 NASB).

Oh how he loves! How jealous and merciful is the abundance of grace in his eyes. He is mighty in faithfulness to save us. He is quiet and gentle as he exults over us.

Faith believes, goes, and does

When trials, storms, and attacks come into our lives—whether emotional, mental, or otherwise—they "locate" us spiritually. They test the foundation and mettle of our Faith. Real Faith knows that even when things are dry and the ground upon which we walk uneven, Jesus is still for us, and our house will yet stand. Undaunted, Faith continues to believe God in the midst of the storm, then acts, because he said so.

"Therefore everyone who hears these words of mine and puts them into practice is like a wise man who built his house on the rock. The rain came down, the streams rose, and the winds blew and beat against that house; yet it did not fall, because it had its foundation on the rock. But everyone who hears these words of mine and does not put them into practice is like a foolish man who built his house on sand. The rain came down, the streams rose, and the winds blew and beat against that house, and it fell with a great crash" (Matthew 7:24-27 NIV).

When I consider the course my life has taken until now, I can look back to the active Faith of men and women, in the way they lived out their Faith every day. I can count them on one hand, but to this day the way they "do" their Faith and the way they live out God's words are the substance of the confession and witness that reminds me who I am, and whose I am, when I am buffeted, beaten, and drowning. They are not perfect people, only a steadfast example of what God can do with imperfect people who are prepared when he says, *"Jump,"* to respond with, *"How high?"*

"Be careful how you live. You may be the only Bible some person ever reads." –William J. Toms

"What use is it, my brethren, if someone says he has faith but he has no works? Can that faith save him?" (James 2:14 NASB).

I used to answer that question with a, *"Yes,"* because there is much in scripture that seems to indicate that it can. But I have come to the conclusion that the answer is actually, *"No,"* for one reason: saving Faith. If our actions matter in the least, saving Faith is always evident by the heart of Jesus Christ and the fruit of his Sprit that accompanies it. So then, the "faith" without works that James speaks of is no Faith at all. It is only an example of vanity and false entitlement which is resident in a heart that operates by the wisdom of the world, rather than Wisdom that is from God.

"If a brother or sister is without clothing and in need of daily food, and one of you says to them, 'Go in peace, be warmed and be filled,' and yet you do not give them what is necessary for their body, what use is that? Even so faith, if it has no works, is dead, being by itself. But someone may well say, 'You have faith and I have works; show me your faith without the works, and I will show you my faith by my works.' ... For just as the body without the spirit is dead, so also faith without works is dead" (James 2:15-18, 26 NASB).

The Bible, in recounting the measure of an authentic Faith which *hears God*, *believes God*, and then <u>obeys God</u>, also harkens back to the men and women who came before us. If you take one thing from this chapter, let it be that authentic Faith, at its core, is really the combining of those three things—hearing, believing, and doing.

"By faith we understand that the worlds were prepared by the word of God, so that what is seen was not made out of things which are visible."

"By faith Abel offered to God a better sacrifice than Cain, through which he obtained the testimony that he was righteous, God testifying about his gifts, and through faith, though he is dead, he still speaks."

"By faith Noah, being warned by God about things not yet seen, in reverence prepared an ark for the salvation of his household."

"By faith Abraham, when he was called, obeyed by going out to a place which he was to receive for an inheritance."

"By faith Abraham, when he was tested, offered up Isaac, and he who had received the promises was offering up his only begotten son; it was he to whom it was said, 'IN ISAAC YOUR DESCENDANTS SHALL BE CALLED.' He considered that God is able to raise people even from the dead."

"By faith Isaac blessed Jacob and Esau, even regarding things to come."

"By faith Moses, when he was born, was hidden for three months by his parents."

"By faith Moses left Egypt, not fearing the wrath of the king; for he endured, as seeing him who is unseen."

"By faith the walls of Jericho fell down after they had been encircled for seven days."

"By faith Rahab the harlot did not perish along with those who were disobedient, after she had welcomed the spies in peace."

"And what more shall I say? For time will fail me if I tell of Gideon, Barak, Samson, Jephthah, of David and Samuel and the prophets, who by faith conquered kingdoms, performed acts of righteousness, obtained promises, shut the mouths of lions, quenched the power of fire, escaped the edge of the sword, from weakness were made strong, became mighty in war, put foreign armies to flight. Women received back their dead by resurrection."

—*All of these are excerpts from the New Testament book of Hebrews, Chapter 11 NASB*

In closing, I will leave you with the words of Saint Francis of Assisi: *"It is no use walking anywhere to preach unless our walking is our preaching."* Now who could argue with a sentiment like that?

Prayer: *Lord Jesus, I am thankful you love me enough to remind me that if I am seeking you in earnest Faith, you will reward it. I am filled up with how deeply you love me, Abba. How rich and beautiful a knowledge it is, that, as a Father with his son, you stand for me. You protect me, through my Faith you teach me, and you comfort me with a peace and an assurance that passes understanding. For these and so many other reasons, my heart cries out "Lord, you alone are holy." By Faith, my confession remains the same, just as you are the same "yesterday, today, and forever." I seek your wisdom, your correction, and even your rebuke, because by Faith I know that I am called your son and I am always confident in you. Wash me in the pure water of your Word and refine me by the fire of your Holy Spirit. I love you, Lord. In Jesus' name I pray. Amen!*

Scripture: **"And without faith it is impossible to please God, because anyone who comes to him must believe that he exists and that he rewards those who earnestly seek him"** (Hebrews 11:6 NASB).

CHAPTER 5

SALVATION

Saved from what? By whom?

"About the ninth hour Jesus cried out with a loud voice, saying, 'Eli, Eli, lama sabachthani?' that is, 'My God, my God, why have you forsaken me?'" (Matthew 27:46 NASB).

Those were the most tragically beautiful words ever spoken on earth. Oh, to be an angel in heaven at that very moment—the triumph and exultation mixed with sadness and compassion.

"He's doing it!! Right now, it's happening right now!! He's taken their curse! Rejoice! Rejoice!"

I can only suppose, as the popular hymn says, what it must have been like on *"That beautiful scandalous night."*

"For while we were still helpless, at the right time Christ died for the ungodly. For one will hardly die for a righteous man; though perhaps for the good man someone would dare even to die. But God demonstrates his own love toward us, in that while we were yet sinners, Christ died for us" (Romans 5:6-8 NASB).

"We are half-hearted creatures, fooling about with drink and sex and ambition when infinite joy is offered us, like an ignorant child who wants to go on making mud pies in a slum because he cannot imagine what is meant by the offer of a holiday at the sea. We are far too easily pleased."—C. S. Lewis, *The Weight of Glory*

The two biggest lies you will ever tell yourself, or that you will ever be told by anyone else, are these:

1. You have the power or ability to save yourself.
2. The solution to all your problems is within you.

The first statement sort of collapses in on itself. If we are able to save ourselves, why do so many of us still have need of Salvation? The wealth of evidence regarding our fallen human condition demands an autonomous Savior. The second statement, much like the first, is also self-defeating. Rhetorically speaking, if we are the solution to all of our problems, why are those problems still so plentiful and self-existent? The answer is simply that "**We**" are our biggest problem and we are utterly incapable of solving it ourselves. Rather than being the solution, we are our own worst enemy.

"I do not understand what I do. For what I want to do I do not do, but what I hate I do. And if I do what I do not want to do, I agree that the law is good. As it is, it is no longer I myself who do it, but it is sin living in me. For I know that good itself does not dwell in me, that is, in my sinful nature. For I have the desire to do what is good, but I cannot carry it out. For I do not do the good I want to do, but the evil I do not want to do—this I keep on doing. Now if I do what I do not want to do, it is no longer I who do it, but it is sin living in me that does it.

So I find this law at work: Although I want to do good, evil is right there with me. For in my inner being I delight in God's law; but I see another law at work in me, waging war against the law of my mind and making me a prisoner of the law of sin at work within me. What a wretched man I am! Who will rescue me from this body that is subject to death? Thanks be to God, who delivers me through Jesus Christ our Lord!" (Romans 7:15-25 NIV).

What would you think if you entered a room and saw a bunch of people walking on the ceiling rather than the floor? I know I'd be looking around for Rod Serling and waiting for "Twilight Zone" music to start playing. So since we're already talking "Twilight Zone," what if, once you had entered the room and begun to posit as to just how odd everyone else was, you suddenly discovered yourself stepping over light fixtures and beams, and trying to avoid the blades of a hanging fan? What if you were actually the one walking on the ceiling?

What if you had been told that what you were doing was "normal" so many times, for so many years, from so many different sources that you could no longer distinguish an imitation from reality? The good news is your next stop would *not* be The Twilight Zone. Some even better news is that a realization like this is akin to the first time a human heart is able to see with spiritual eyes. When God removes the veil of all we "think" we know, he shows us Truth, his Truth about salvation that comes through Jesus Christ. He will not, as some would say, turn your world upside down. He is, however, the only path by which you are able to finally and certainly see things right side up.

"Everyone who calls on the name of the Lord will be saved" (Romans 10:13 NIV).

We are born with the longing of eternity in our hearts, but we are at the same time separated from any knowledge to sate such a burden **(Ecclesiastes 3:10-12 NIV)**. We are born into hostility, but unable to deny an innate relation to the eternal God **(Romans 1:19-20 NIV)**. We are born both as natives to this disaffection and as sojourners without a way Home **(Psalm 119:19 NIV)**. We are spiritually naked and yearning to be clothed, knowing only in part but being fully known, empty but with an unyielding desire to be filled **(2 Corinthians 5:1-5 NIV)**.

Therein lies the tricky business of the consequence that follows rebellion against our Creator. How do we respond to this situation that is beyond our control? I don't mean what we say when we're around other people; I mean the cry of our heart in the small hours of the night when he makes certain we hear him. What will our response be then?

"And I, when I am lifted up from the earth, will draw all people to myself" (John 12:32 NIV).

We were created for fellowship, first with God and then with one another. The only answer to all of our questions and to our dilemma is a relationship with Jesus Christ.

"For there is one God and one Mediator also between God and men, the man Christ Jesus" (1 Timothy 2:5 NASB).

"Salvation is found in no one else, for there is no other name under heaven given to mankind by which we must be saved" (Acts 4:12 NIV).

In Jesus is all knowledge and all wisdom **(1 Corinthians 1:30 NASB), (Colossians 2:3 NIV)**. In him there is restoration, wholeness, acceptance, and love. Most beautifully, he is at once both the embodiment and the assurance of a way Home.

"My Father's house has many rooms; if that were not so, would I have told you that I am going there to prepare a place for you? And if I go and prepare a place for you, I will come back and take you to be with me that you also may be where I am. You know the way to the place where I am going" (John 14:2-4 NIV).

Why Salvation Lord? Why me?

"This is love: not that we loved God, but that he loved us and sent his Son as an atoning sacrifice for our sins" (1 John 4:10 NIV).

There are times when I'm reminded how easily I fall back into allowing the cares of this world to overtake me and rob me of my joy. Thankfully, I now notice these lapses more quickly, and by God's grace I'm able to come back without causing as much damage as I did before. I can surrender those things to him daily, ask his forgiveness in lieu of trying to hold burdens I was never meant to hold, and fall back into his arms. His warm embrace is immediate. That is when it is most striking to me how remarkable and loving he is in receiving me. The depth of love he must have had for me to take the punishment of the Cross, to bear what I should have rightly suffered, and give me back my life. Then it hits me again how utterly unworthy I feel to have been given such a gift, and I am broken, I am grieved. But in this love that I am still struggling to grasp, Jesus scoops me up and spreads his wings out over me.

He reassures me as no other ever could. Yes, this gift is mine. No, I could have done nothing to earn it. No, I do not deserve it. But all the same, because of what he did, I am an heir to the kingdom of heaven **(Romans 8:16-17 NIV)**. I do not always understand, but immersed in his affection and comfort, the concerns of this world begin to matter very little to me. In his light, this fretful ignorance of mine becomes just another of the burdens I was never meant to hold.

In moments like these, I can begin to imagine what the prophet Isaiah must have experienced as the Lord unraveled his heart.

"I saw the Lord seated on a throne, high and exalted, and the train of his robe filled the temple. Above him were seraphim, each with six wings: With two wings they covered their faces, with two they covered their feet, and with two they were flying. And they were calling to one another:

'Holy, holy, holy is the Lord Almighty; the whole earth is full of his glory.'

At the sound of their voices the doorposts and thresholds shook and the temple was filled with smoke.

'Woe to me!' I cried. 'I am ruined! For I am a man of unclean lips, and I live among a people of unclean lips, and my eyes have seen the King, the Lord Almighty.' Then one of the seraphim flew to me with a live coal in his hand, which he had taken with tongs from the altar. With it he touched my mouth and said, 'See, this has touched your lips; your guilt is taken away and your sin atoned for.' Then I heard the voice of the Lord saying, 'Whom shall I send? And who will go for us?' And I said, *'Here am I. Send me!'"*
(Isaiah 6:1-8 NIV)

What other response could there have been? **"Here am I. Send me!"** It doesn't matter where, for what, or for how long. But I still want to break my thoughts down a bit more, so that you know I don't just pull this stuff out of the air.

As I start asking God questions, while I am struggling to understand what he did and why he did it, somewhere between my sobs of joy and his immanent verdict, he either shows me illustrations of the truth from his Word or conveys a certain answer directly to my spirit from his. I have always been the one kid in Algebra class who asks the teacher for a philosophical answer to a simple, calculated equation. When confronted for instance with, $x = x0 + v0t + 1/2at2$, my inclination is to raise my hand and say, "*What does the v equal, and why, existentially that is?*" Thankfully God is patient, and where there is an answer I can understand, he always provides one. So then, back to my "questions" about salvation and redemption.

This is roughly how the conversation went:

Me: Am I wrong? Was I worthy?

God: **"As it is written: 'There is no one righteous, not even one; there is no one who understands; there is no one who seeks God. All have turned away, they have together become worthless; there is no one who does good, not even one'" (Romans 3:10-12 NIV)**

"...all have sinned and fall short of the glory of God" (Romans 3:23 NIV).

Me: But, but, but ...

God: " **...and are justified freely by his grace through the redemption that came by Christ Jesus" (Romans 3:24 NIV).**

(I should have let him finish)

Me: Why salvation then? Why did you bother—given what we are, what we did, and what you knew we would continue to do?

God: " **...because God is love. This is how God showed his love among us: He sent his one and only Son into the world that we might live through him. This is love: not that we loved God, but that he loved us and sent his Son as an atoning sacrifice for our sins" (1 John 4:8-10 NIV).**

Me: But why? We are not worthy of your grace or your love, Lord.

God: " ...**It is by grace you have been saved. And God raised us up with Christ and seated us with him in the heavenly realms in Christ Jesus, in order that in the coming ages he might show the incomparable riches of his grace, expressed in his kindness to us in Christ Jesus. For it is by grace you have been saved, through faith —and this not from yourselves, it is the gift of God— not by works, so that no one can boast. For we are God's handiwork, created in Christ Jesus to do good works, which God prepared in advance for us to do" (Ephesians 2:5-10 NIV).**

Me: Okay, faith, but ...

God: **"Where were you when I laid the earth's foundation? Tell me, if you understand. Who marked off its dimensions? Surely you know! Who stretched a measuring line across it? On what were its footings set, or who laid its cornerstone—while the morning stars sang together and all the angels shouted for joy?" (Job 38:4-7 NIV).**

"For my thoughts are not your thoughts, neither are your ways my ways," declares the Lord. "As the heavens are higher than the earth, so are my ways higher than your ways and my thoughts than your thoughts. As the rain and the snow come down from heaven, and do not return to it without watering the earth and making it bud and flourish, so that it yields seed for the sower and bread for the eater, so is my word that goes out from my mouth: It will not return to me empty, but will accomplish what I desire and achieve the purpose for which I sent it" (Isaiah 55:8-11 NIV).

Me: Yes, Father. But Abba ... Why me?

God: King David saw ...

"You have searched me, Lord, and you know me. You know when I sit and when I rise; you perceive my thoughts from afar. You discern my going out and my lying down; you are familiar with all my ways. Before a word is on my tongue you, Lord, know it completely. You hem me in behind and before, and you lay your hand upon me. Such knowledge is too wonderful for me, too lofty for me to attain. Where can I go from your Spirit? Where can I flee from your presence? If I go up to the heavens, you are there; if I make my bed in the depths, you are there. If I rise on the wings of the dawn, if I settle on the far side of the sea, even there your hand will guide me, your right hand will hold me fast. If I say, 'Surely the darkness will hide me and the light become night around me,' even the darkness will not be dark to you; the night will shine like the day, for darkness is as light to you. For you created my inmost being; you knit me together in my mother's womb. I praise you because I am fearfully and wonderfully made; your works are wonderful, I know that full well. My frame was not hidden from you when I was made in the secret place, when I was woven together in the depths of the earth. Your eyes saw my unformed body; all the days ordained for me were written in your book before one of them came to be" (Psalm 139:1-16 NIV).

... and so did Jesus

"Are not two sparrows sold for a penny? Yet not one of them will fall to the ground outside your Father's care. And even the very hairs of your head are all numbered. So don't be afraid; you are worth more than many sparrows" (Matthew 10:29-32 NIV).

Me: Thank you, Abba! I think I understand better now. So what would you have me do?

God: "Do not merely listen to the word, and so deceive yourselves. Do what it says. Anyone who listens to the word but does not do what it says is like someone who looks at his face in a mirror and, after looking at himself, goes away and immediately forgets what he looks like. But whoever who looks intently into the perfect law that gives freedom, and continues to do this, not forgetting what they have heard, but doing it—they will be blessed in what they do" (James 1:22-25 NIV).

"A new command I give you: Love one another. As I have loved you, so you must love one another. By this everyone will know that you are my disciples, if you love one another" (John 13:34-35 NIV).

Me: Thank you, Abba Father. I love you!

God: I love you too, son.

He sees me

I have dirt on my hands,
I have ugliness in me that makes You more sad than You will ever let me see.
My feet are often stuck in the thickest, most disgusting muck that holds me and won't let me move.
Still your hand is held out to me, and You say, *"Take it, and I can help you."*
My dirty hands grab.
My ugliness pulls.
My muck is now yours, and suddenly You are standing in it with me,
Holding me,
Comforting me,
Bearing me up in all of my filth.
Your hands now have my dirt on them.
The ugliness in me has affected your circumstance.
Your clothes are now stained as mine,
But you take my hand all the same, and we walk out together.
You give me new clothes to wear.
You wash my hands, my feet, and my heart until they are clean.

You show me a true, lighted road now to walk on.
Because You loved me, I understand love.
I am able to love because You see "me."

"Come to me, all you who are weary and burdened, and I will give you rest. Take my yoke upon you and learn from me, for I am gentle and humble in heart, and you will find rest for your souls. For my yoke is easy and my burden is light" (Matthew 11:28-30 NIV).

Each of us has a unique story and testimony about the perfect way Jesus saved us. But we all have this one thing in common: when he affected our hearts, the way he moved us was life-altering. To quote Lacy Strum from the band "Flyleaf," the moment Jesus Christ took up residence within us, we became *"something treasured, different"*—and it was tangible **(2 Corinthians 5:16-17 NASB).**

With that in mind, acceptance of God's glorious gift, the way Heaven understands it, also means humility, connectedness, and deference. Deference to others in helping them understand how special they are to God, since we understand how special we are to him **(Romans 5:8 NASB)**. God's Holy Spirit reaches our innermost parts with an eternal embrace, in a familial way. Similarly, we are now able, through Jesus, to connect with one another on a much deeper level.

Because the nature of salvation is relational, this beautiful transformation also affords us the ability to be the evidence of his love to everyone we meet. In recalling what Jesus has done for me, my light burden results in a desire to shout Jesus' love out loud from every rooftop. In remembering the way he saved me, the easy yoke upon me is to wake up and in obedience to share that joy every day until he takes me Home.

"Then Jesus came to them and said, 'All authority in heaven and on earth has been given to me. Therefore go and make disciples of all nations, baptizing them in the name of the Father and of the Son and of the Holy Spirit, and teaching them to obey everything

I have commanded you. And surely I am with you always, to the very end of the age'" (Matthew 28:18-20 NIV).

You see we were "Light." We were what God called **"very good"** before Adam fell. We were created in his likeness, to be in relationship with the Creator of the universe.

"Then God said, 'Let us make mankind in our image, in our likeness … ' So God created mankind in his own image, in the image of God he created him; male and female he created them" (Genesis 1:26-27 NIV).

We chose to forfeit the Life that is the light of all humankind when we put our own desires above obedience to God—obedience that was never for his benefit, but for our own. We were estranged, alienated from him, and spiritually dead. When evil entered the world through Adam, he and all who came after were placed under this terrible curse **(Genesis 3:14-17 NIV)**. We needed a way back home, and in his mercy God provided the Way, he revealed the Truth, and he gave us his Life in Jesus.

"For as in Adam all die, so in Christ all will be made alive" (1 Corinthians 15:22 NASB).

"So it is written: 'The first man Adam became a living being'; the last Adam, a life-giving spirit. The spiritual did not come first, but the natural, and after that the spiritual. The first man was of the dust of the earth; the second man is of heaven. As was the earthly man, so are those who are of the earth; and as is the heavenly man, so also are those who are of heaven. And just as we have borne the image of the earthly man, so shall we bear the image of the heavenly man" (1 Corinthians 15:45-49 NIV).

Faith by hearing the Word spoken about Jesus Christ now affords us the opportunity to once again be brought near, to have a right relationship with our God restored **(Romans 10:17 NIV)**.

"**But what does it say? 'THE WORD IS NEAR YOU, IN YOUR MOUTH AND IN YOUR HEART'—that is, the word of faith which we are preaching, that if you confess with your mouth Jesus as Lord, and believe in your heart that God raised him from the dead, you will be saved; for with the heart a person believes, resulting in righteousness, and with the mouth he confesses, resulting in salvation" (Romans 10:8-10 NASB).**

So do you know Jesus Christ as your Lord and Savior? If the answer is, "Yes," then praise God, and I pray that your faith is increased as you journey on into the chapters yet to follow.

If your answer was, "No," or even if it was, "Yes," but you are reading this today having fallen away from him, I believe God is stirring a desire in your heart right now to be made whole again. This chapter will be unique in that the prayer at the end will be an opportunity for you. It is a prayer for salvation and renewal. It will, if you choose, be for you a true confession of Faith in Jesus that saves your soul and changes your life forever.

Prayer: *"Father, I know that my sins have separated me from you. I am truly sorry, and now I want to turn away from my past life, and my hostility toward you. Please forgive me, and help me avoid those things that break your heart. I believe that your Son, Jesus Christ, died for me, was resurrected from the dead, is alive, and hears my prayer right now. I invite Jesus to become the Lord of my life, to rule and reign in my heart from this day forward. Please send your Holy Spirit to help me obey you and to do your will for the rest of my life. In Jesus' name I pray, Amen."*

If you prayed that prayer to receive Jesus today, or if you recommitted your life to him today, then, welcome back to God's family. You are now a new creature in Christ Jesus **(2 Corinthians 5:17 NASB)**. So as a way to grow closer to him, the Bible tells us a few ways to follow up our confession with action:

- Get baptized in water as commanded by Christ.
- Tell someone else about your newfound faith in Christ.

- Spend time with God each day. It does not have to be a long time. Just develop the daily habit of praying to him and reading his Word. Ask God to increase your faith and your understanding of the Bible.
- Seek fellowship with other followers of Jesus. Develop a group of believing friends to answer your questions and support you.
- Find a local church where you can worship God on a regular basis.

Scripture: "**For God so loved the world that he gave his only begotten Son, that whoever believes in him shall not perish, but have eternal life. For God did not send the Son into the world to judge the world, but that the world might be saved through him. He who believes in him is not judged; he who does not believe has been judged already, because he has not believed in the name of the only begotten Son of God. This is the judgment, that the light has come into the world, and men loved the darkness rather than the light, for their deeds were evil" (John 3:16-19 NASB)**

Chapter 6

The Basics

Okay, so what now?

"But the eyes of the Lord are on those who fear him, on those whose hope is in his unfailing love" (Psalm 33:18 NIV).

I had been praying regularly around a year ago for God to bring me into deeper relationship with him and give me a heart to see people the way he sees them. I wanted him to increase my sensitivity and my ability to love others the way he loves them. If I break it down, what I had really been asking is that he would take me, my fear, and my pride out of the way, so that the deepest desire of my heart would be his will for me.

I had my morning routine during that season: I would sit, read my Bible, drink my coffee, and then go to work. That got disrupted one day when a man, who was nothing more than an acquaintance from church, randomly walked over, sat down, and started talking to me. My first reaction was that I was disappointed that I was not going to have my time with God before work. However, it quickly occurred to me, by the new sensitivity to God's Spirit I'd been asking for, that this man *was* my time with God before work. So we sat and talked; mostly he talked and I listened, but it was clear to me that he needed it just then.

This situation, in addition to being not ideal, was definitely out of my comfort zone. This man was out of my comfort zone. I don't know exactly how God used me that morning, but he did. I was able to pray with him, which I could sense he needed, and God blessed me through the entire thing. Sometimes in life it's just good to know that we are not invisible, that somebody sees us, and most especially, that Abba God sees us. If being the eyes of God on this man in a way that was tangible to him was all I accomplished, then it was exactly what God intended. A beautiful little answer to prayer is often the way God works. I praise him because he always brings a response, and his beauty is always in the blessing.

"But I tell you, do not swear an oath at all: either by heaven, for it is God's throne; or by the earth, for it is his footstool; or by Jerusalem, for it is the city of the Great King. And do not swear by your head, for you cannot make even one hair white or black. All you need to say is simply 'Yes' or 'No'; anything beyond this comes from the evil one." (Matthew 5:34-37 NIV)

Sounds pretty simple right? Do not swear an oath by that which is exclusive to God, because those things are outside your control or ability to influence. If you make a promise, do all in your power to keep it. If anyone asks of you anything that requires a simple answer, "Yes" or "No" will suffice. Say what you mean, and mean what you say.

The bad news is, it is way more difficult than it sounds. If you take a moment to think about it, there really isn't anything partial about that statement. Everything in all creation is his, period **(Psalms 24:1-2 NASB)**. So as far as oaths go, think of how many times you shouldn't have but did. Think of the many things you've tried to control, that were never your burden to begin with. Finally, try to remember every time you could have just let the things you *didn't* say do the talking for you, but opted to speak instead. If you're anything like me, that list just got pretty long, and much of the time those situations did not turn out so well for you or for any of the other people involved.

The good news for us is in God's grace, and the assurance we have that he already knows our weaknesses. When Jesus came to earth, he endured everything we do on a daily basis **(Hebrews 4:15 NASB)**. He is always faithful, even when we are not; it is also impossible for God to lie **(Hebrews 6:16-20 NASB), (Romans 3:3-4 NASB)**. So if we are at least trying to live a life of love, not just by words but in the way we behave, we know we can be at rest in his presence. When our heart fails us, we need only remember that God is greater than our heart and he knows everything **(1 John 3:18-22 NIV)**.

Remind yourself daily to trust him for the big stuff and the tiny details. Keep your actions simple and your decisions true, then relax in the assurance that he will do the rest.

**"The one who calls you is faithful, and he will
do it" (1 Thessalonians 5:24 NIV)**

Why should I?

Sow to fertile ground and you harvest good fruit.
Sow to the flesh and your harvest is death.
Sow to the wind and you harvest a whirlwind.
Sow to the Spirit and your harvest is Life and Peace.

**"Whoever sows to please their flesh, from the flesh will reap
destruction; whoever sows to please the Spirit, from the Spirit
will reap eternal life." (Galatians 6:8 NIV)**

**"They sow the wind and reap the whirlwind. The stalk has no
head; it will produce no flour. Were it to yield grain, foreigners
would swallow it up." (Hosea 8:7 NIV)**

**"Still other seed fell on good soil, where it produced a crop—a
hundred, sixty, or thirty times what was sown." (Matthew
13:8 NIV)**

God showed me something relevant about "posture," mine in
particular. To begin with, I slouch way too often, I look down too
often when I walk, and I often sleep in some really awkward position.
Anyway, in context, what I heard from the Holy Spirit was, "*walk
uprightly before God."* There are plenty of reasons to do that, but I
thought it was so wonderful and cool all at the same time because he
showed me the practical as well as the heart application.

My mentor and brother in Christ, Dr. Scott is always reminding
me that the major benefit of good physical posture is that it aligns
you properly and helps to keep your spine healthy. This in turn keeps
everything operating more effectively, because the spinal cord is akin
to a transcontinental railroad of electrical impulses to the members of

your body. In the same way, when our hearts are postured correctly in walking with God and in our relationships, the result is an alignment of our hearts with his which bears good fruit in other areas. Just as with our physical posture, when we pay forward heavenly wisdom, love, joy, and hope to the people around us, there is a healthy spiritual reaction. Our social exchanges, our prayer time, etc., naturally respond to allow still more grace and glory to be poured into us. Now that is an awesome harvest!

"He stores up sound wisdom for the upright; he is a shield to those who walk uprightly; he guards the paths of justice, and preserves the way of his saints." (Proverbs 2:7-8 NASB)

"Give, and it will be given to you. A good measure, pressed down, shaken together and running over, will be poured into your lap. For with the measure you use, it will be measured to you." (Luke 6:38 NIV)

"For the Lord God is a sun and shield; the Lord gives grace and glory; no good thing does he withhold from those who walk uprightly." (Psalm 84:11 NASB)

All of us deal with an existence that is in stark contrast to these verses. From the moment our feet hit the floor each morning, the culture we live in screams from the rooftops: *"You are worth no more than your latest failure or achievement. What was the last cutting-edge class you took? The newest book you read? What is your income? Your social status? Your physical makeup? How many people like you? Are you cool enough? Are you ambitious enough? **What have you done for us lately**?"* Then we are told by this same culture: *"You are okay as long as you are happy with you, and anything divergent to that is intolerance, hate, and certainly of no real consequence; thank you very much!"* If this seems contradictory, that's because it is extremely so. If it seems impossibly empty, that's because it folds in on itself like wet paper when confronted with anything that demands an honest accounting of its veracity.

As King Solomon said, "**I have seen all the works that are done under the sun; and, behold, all is vanity and vexation of spirit**" **(Ecclesiastes 1:14 KJV).**

In considering this, also listen to Jesus' words, "**Why do you call me good? No one is good except God alone" (Luke 18:19 NASB).**

As is true with every other important facet of life, the wisdom of God is most often the antithesis of the wisdom of the world **(1 Corinthians 1:20-31 NASB)**. In short, our worth, value, and identity are found in the Love of God that is revealed through his Son Jesus Christ. God's estimation of us far outweighs that of any other, even our own. Yes, it does matter if *"you are okay with you,"* but only because that will only ever be true when you are at rest in his arms. He knows us more intimately than we could ever comprehend or imagine. He requires of us only faith and a surrendered heart, which in return paves the way for him to guide us into all the truth we'll ever need.

"Yes, my soul, find rest in God; my hope comes from him. Truly he is my rock and my salvation; he is my fortress, I will not be shaken. My salvation and my honor depend on God; he is my mighty rock, my refuge. Trust in him at all times, you people; pour out your hearts to him, for God is our refuge. Surely the lowborn are but a breath, the highborn are but a lie. If weighed on a balance, they are nothing; together they are only a breath." (Psalm 62:5-9 NIV)

"For all those who exalt themselves will be humbled, and those who humble themselves will be exalted" (Luke 14:11 NIV).

Worldly wisdom says, *"Take care of yourself first, then you will be able to take care of others."* God's wisdom says, *"Take care of others first, then trust me to care for you."* **(Philippians 2:3-4 NIV), (Proverbs 3:5-6 NASB).**

Worldly wisdom says, *"Strive and strain after everything you can get while you can get it, then you will be content."* God's wisdom says,

"Strive and strain after me. Be content in every circumstance, and I will give you the desires of your heart" **(Matthew 6:25-34 NASB), (Psalm 37:3-5 NASB).**

So, how do I?

"I will ask the Father, and he will give you another Helper, that he may be with you forever; that is the Spirit of truth, whom the world cannot receive, because it does not see him or know him, but you know him because he abides with you and will be in you. I will not leave you as orphans; I will come to you. After a little while the world will no longer see me, but you will see me; because I live, you will live also. In that day you will know that I am in my Father, and you in me, and I in you. He who has my commandments and keeps them is the one who loves me; and he who loves me will be loved by my Father, and I will love him and will disclose myself to him" (John 14:16-21 NASB).

To be Christian is to follow Christ. Literally translated it means, *"Manifesting the qualities or spirit of Jesus; Christ-like."* There are so many incorrect definitions out there, so it is really important to be crystal clear about the right one.

We Christians have this saying: *"It's not about religion, it's about relationship."* It is meant to communicate the truth that being a Christ follower is not about a set of rules, nor is it about meeting every Sunday in some stuffy building with a cross on top. To be a Christian means living a life spent pursuing intimate, daily fellowship with Jesus Christ. Think of it in the context of meeting someone, then falling in love with them. Your greatest ambition would be to spend as much time with them as possible, and to get to know everything there was to know about them. The same is true of us as believers in Jesus. Only spending time, for us, means time in prayer, and getting to know everything we can about him by regularly reading his Word.

However, this relationship we aspire to is not only a relationship with him, but with other people as well, He put us here together to love and to contend for one another. So we walk out this Faith when we hold each other up and build each other up. We strive not just to know God, but also to love him with all of our heart, mind, soul, and strength. We trust him to meet us where and when we seek him in what he says. We emulate him in what we do by our willingness to agree with his word and spend the time with him and his people.

"Dear children, let us not love with words or speech but with actions and in truth. This is how we know that we belong to the truth and how we set our hearts at rest in his presence: If our hearts condemn us, we know that God is greater than our hearts, and he knows everything. Dear friends, if our hearts do not condemn us, we have confidence before God and receive from him anything we ask, because we keep his commands and do what pleases him. And this is his command: to believe in the name of his Son, Jesus Christ, and to love one another as he commanded us." (1 John 3:18-23 NIV)

"Love the LORD your God with all your heart and with all your soul and with all your strength." (Deuteronomy 6:5 NASB)

"Trust in the LORD with all your heart and do not lean on your own understanding. In all your ways acknowledge him, and he will make your paths straight." (Proverbs 3:5-6 NASB)

My pastor is always saying it: *"We need to get around one another, get in each other's lives, and love people."* I am speaking this to myself first: Let's start today and get involved. The Lord is standing next to us screaming, *"Engage, Maverick, engage!!"* He knows it's not comfortable. He knows that getting close means possibly getting hurt or putting yourself in emotional danger, but he is also faithful to be your strength. He will always be your comfort if you get knocked around a little, or be there to patch you up when life just randomly beats the snot out of you. *"He* **lives to make intercession for** *you"* **(Hebrews 7:25 NASB)**.

"Take my yoke upon you and learn from Me" (Matthew 11:29 NASB).

To take a yoke upon you is to make a declaration. You are agreeing to bear weight, you are agreeing to do work, and you are agreeing to go where and when you are led.

The time we are given here is so very short, and every moment is such a precious gift **(James 4:14 NASB), (Psalm 139:13-18 NASB)**. All of the hustle and the din we surround ourselves with is only preoccupations and distractions. Every bit of it is designed to turn us ever more inward until we collapse on ourselves; and when there ceases to be any air around us, we can literally become a vacuum.

We fancy ourselves to be mature, but most often we have only graduated to a new and larger grade of plaything. Every facade we erect around us entices our hearts and minds away from the one thing that most matters to God—relationships **(1 Peter 4:8 NIV)**.

The yoke of Jesus is love, and his burden is a sacrifice of praise **(Psalms 116:16-18 NASB), (Hebrews 6:10 NASB)**. He continually put himself in uncomfortable situations and loved people. He ate with them, talked with them, and hung out in their homes. He was all about being in other people's lives during his earthly ministry, and he still is even now. This very moment, in fact, he stands at the door of our hearts and knocks **(Revelation 3:20 NASB)**. His example shouts above the din. Jesus left us one task. It's no coincidence that we need to be reminded to drop our guards from time to time and stop assigning value to *things*. If our desire is to learn from him, then to treasure every moment and every person he's given us is certainly a fair place to begin.

Your challenge is this: pray and ask God to put one person on your heart today to bless, love, encourage, or all of the above. Then when he does, call them, send them a note, give them a hug, speak a kind word, cook them a meal. **Loving one another as he commanded us** is simply to go be the hands and feet of Jesus for someone who needs him.

**"...encourage one another daily, as long as it is called 'Today'"
(Hebrews 3:13 NIV).**

**"This is how love is made complete among us so that we will
have confidence on the day of judgment: In this world we are like
Jesus" (1 John 4:17 NIV).**

So what am I?

To be Christian is also to be human. When you prayed and asked
Jesus to be Lord and Savior of your life, no fairy tapped you with a
wand and turned you into a newt or a ham sandwich or anything. I
don't mean to imply for one moment that you are the same human as
you were before. When you made the confession, *"Jesus Christ is Lord,"*
your spirit was made perfect and your heart was irrevocably changed.

But it's so easy to just continue *"being yourself,"* isn't it? Because
God loves us unconditionally after all, right? Though what things might
we have done or not done in the name of such a false complacency?

Sometimes, even as Christians, we can still be overly focused on
not offending anyone. We blow through the caution light to avoid the
stop. We run right through emotional and spiritual connectedness
in our headlong flight to avoid feeling uncomfortable **(Galatians
6:15 NASB), (1 Peter 1:14-16 NASB).** We are so diligently about the
business of *"being ourselves"* that we miss who God says we really are
in Christ, and we do not understand all he has given us to accomplish
his business. If being "saved" is a means to an end, apart from any
other sort of fealty, we all may as well have been taken home to heaven
the moment we confessed his Name.

To be Christian is also sometimes to fail. Contrary to the perception
of many, we will all fall short every day. This corruptible flesh we wear
still demands its daily portion, and oft times rather loudly. We are
never going to be picture-perfect while we're alive. We are going to
slip up. Our hearts will betray us, or even condemn us at times. You

can bet on it! We will still think ugly thoughts, say ugly things and emote from places we would not dare mention in polite company.

But does any of that mean we ought to casually toss the word "grace" around and congratulate ourselves? Do we then sing our own praises and crow about being so very authentic? Do we brag about being so tolerant of our own less than desirable human bits? Or should every one of us who were once lost and now found in Jesus not want to aspire to something greater?

"What shall we say, then? Shall we go on sinning so that grace may increase? By no means! We are those who have died to sin; how can we live in it any longer?" (Romans 6:1-2 NIV)

"So I say, walk by the Spirit, and you will not gratify the desires of the flesh. For the flesh desires what is contrary to the Spirit, and the Spirit what is contrary to the flesh. They are in conflict with each other, *so that you are not to do whatever you want.*" **(Galatians 5:16-17 NIV)**

What are we if not being made holy? Who are we if not a new creature? **(Hebrews 10:14 NIV), (2 Corinthians 5:17 NASB)**

"What benefit did you reap at that time from the things you are now ashamed of? Those things result in death!" (Romans 6:21 NIV).

Thankfully, we are in fact continuously being purified by God. Throughout our lives, if we have the Spirit of Jesus alive in us, we are becoming more effective Christ-imitators and Christ-pursuers daily. That is the key difference the rest of the world should see in us. It might be a slight change in the way we smile, a new confidence in the way we walk, or a light in our eyes that makes people stop and take notice. It could even be the smallest positive inflection in our voice that nobody can quite put a finger on but also can't seem to ignore when we speak. Not that we strive to be or do well under some insincere compulsion, or to arrive at some perfect adherence to an arbitrary set of rules. It's that our response to such an emphatic love for us in Jesus is a heart which naturally resounds love. We are different now. We have a choice because we are alive, and we are alive because he lives **(Hebrews 10:14 NASB), (Galatians 2:20 NASB), (Romans 8:11 NASB).**

"...you were formerly darkness, but now you are light in the Lord; walk as children of light (for the fruit of the light consists in all goodness and righteousness and truth)." (Ephesians 5:8-9 NASB)

"I believe in Christianity as I believe that the sun has risen: not only because I see it, but because by it I see everything else."—C. S. Lewis

"The Lord God has given me the tongue of disciples, that I may know how to sustain the weary one with a word. He awakens me morning by morning, he awakens my ear to listen as a disciple. The Lord God has opened my ear; and I was not disobedient nor did I turn back. I gave my back to those who strike me, and my cheeks to those who pluck out the beard; I did not cover my face from humiliation and spitting. For the Lord God helps me, therefore, I am not disgraced; therefore, I have set my face like flint, and I know that I will not be ashamed." (Isaiah 50:4-7 NASB)

That passage is a near perfect expression of how God has been using me personally. I am so humbled to think of everything he's done, and that I get to be a part of it is beyond my finest attempts to describe. Verses four to five especially, but really the entire scripture, when I read it, just popped right off the page and gut-punched me in a really good way. So two things I want to say:

If you want to be used by God, just offer your life to him every day. Seek the desire of his heart for you and he will absolutely use you. You may think you have nothing to offer, but through Jesus Christ you have the very power and love of God at work in you. There are limitless ways he can and will find to bless you and the people in your life if you are willing.

"...for it is God who works in you to will and to act in order to fulfill his good purpose." (Philippians 2:13 NIV)

The other is consistent, authentic prayer—prayer that you offer daily, asking that you would be able hear God's voice and know when he speaks to your heart. It is asking for his good courage, in thanksgiving with gratitude toward God, remembering that in Jesus' name you are gifted the ability to set your face like flint. This kind of prayer is allowing the Author and Finisher of your faith morning by morning to fill your heart of flesh, and trusting him for everything. Since you are his, he will NEVER allow anyone to snatch you from his hand. In him you will never be put to shame!

"The Lord your God is in your midst, a victorious warrior. He will exult over you with joy, he will be quiet in his love, he will rejoice over you with shouts of joy." (Zephaniah 3:17 NASB)

What we are is what God says we are, what his quiet, perfect love sings over us—period. We are not what we think about ourselves or what our friends say we are. We're not even what those people we love the most, and that love us back, esteem in us. At its pinnacle, anything they say or believe about us is just an opinion. The song of our God is the only resolute, immovable, unshakable declaration. That is why our hope in him is an anchor, and why every good and perfect gift we possess comes from him.

"My sheep hear my voice, and I know them, and they follow me; and I give eternal life to them, and they will never perish; and no one will snatch them out of my hand. My Father, who has given them to me, is greater than all; and no one is able to snatch them out of the Father's hand. I and the Father are one." (John 10:27-30 NASB)

Prayer: *Open my heart and mind, Lord Jesus, to receive your words. I offer my body to you as a living and holy sacrifice. Make me courageous to declare your name and magnify you above all else. I pray that my eyes would see, my ears would hear, and my heart discern the opportunities I have to be light in you, Lord. I have been given so very much and you are my heart's desire. Your power is made perfect in all of my weaknesses so that I would never be ashamed to shout your name and your love from every rooftop. Be my help to faithfully serve you, Abba. I will praise you Father for so many reasons; you are my greatest reward, and in Jesus you are the gate by which I am always able to get a glimpse of home when I come to you wistful or sad. Lord, thank you for your good and perfect gifts. Help me to remember what I have and who I am in you. Please give me the wisdom and strength to always choose your way, Abba. In Jesus' name, Amen!*

Scripture: "**Therefore, since we have a great high priest who has ascended into heaven, Jesus the Son of God, let us hold firmly to the faith we profess. For we do not have a high priest who is unable to empathize with our weaknesses, but we have one who has been tempted in every way, just as we are—yet he did not sin. Let us then approach God's throne of grace with confidence, so that we may receive mercy and find grace to help us in our time of need.**" **(Hebrews 4:14-16 NIV)**

CHAPTER 7

HUMILITY

The Few, the Proud, the Humbled

"It's not about you."—Rick Warren, *A Purpose Driven Life*

"For by the grace given me I say to every one of you: Do not think of yourself more highly than you ought, but rather think of yourself with sober judgment, in accordance with the faith God has distributed to each of you" (Romans 12:3 NIV).

An individual's character is defined not by their judgment of another, but by their willingness to examine themselves, and by how honestly and candidly they respond to and reflect on what they find. This is a battle that often goes unnoticed because it is a struggle of the heart and mind. It is the battle between our own pride and want of significance and our soul's deepest desire to be Christ-like.

I constantly pray that, among other things, God would give me a more meaningful "heart knowledge" of Humility. I know what it means, and there are pieces of it I genuinely understand. But I am finding true Humility, Christ-like Humility, to be akin to a multi-faceted gem that must be taken in from many angles. To view it properly, I have to approach the idea of true Humility each day with a fresh perspective and open eyes. When I do that, each time is the discovery of something I had missed at all times prior that changes the way I view my life and my faith.

"A proud man is always looking down on things and people: and, of course, as long as you are looking down, you cannot see something that is above you."—C. S. Lewis, *Mere Christianity*

"Humble yourselves, therefore, under God's mighty hand, that he may lift you up in due time. Cast all your anxiety on him because he cares for you. Be alert and of sober mind. Your enemy the devil prowls around like a roaring lion looking for someone to devour. Resist him, standing firm in the faith, because you know that the

family of believers throughout the world is undergoing the same kind of sufferings. And the God of all grace, who called you to his eternal glory in Christ, after you have suffered a little while, will himself restore you and make you strong, firm and steadfast. To him be the power for ever and ever. Amen." (1 Peter 5:6-11 NIV).

Most people skip the roaring lion part when they read that passage, and understandably so, because the previous few verses are such a comfort. But as with most everything God says, if you read only the easy parts you never get the whole story. I am learning this in my own life, and it can be painful. The first words in this passage are "**Humble yourselves**." Now I don't know how many of you have really attempted true Humility before, but I can only speak for myself in saying that it's no easy thing. It is impossible in your own power; instead it actually requires admitting that you are powerless. It necessitates seeing that you are weak, bankrupt, and bereft of anything good apart from Jesus Christ. It may also entail things like weeping and mourning, or being literally sprawled out on your face in prayer to even make a start.

This might be a depressing thought if not for God's grace. Knowing that our Savior recognizes and understands our struggles is hope, plain and simple, when we are making a go of selflessness.

"And He has said to me, "My grace is sufficient for you, for power is perfected in weakness." Most gladly, therefore, I will rather boast [a]about my weaknesses, so that the power of Christ may dwell in me." (2 Corinthians 12:9 NASB)

"For we do not have a high priest who is unable to sympathize with our weaknesses, but we have one who has been tempted in every way, just as we are, yet was without sin." (Hebrews 4:15 NASB)

An example of this in my life is that I know God wants all of me. But, alas, I am, and ever will remain, an addictive personality. My first instinct when I experience stress, joy, sadness, excitement, or really any extreme emotion, has been to try to veneer it with some counterfeit as quickly as possible. Yes, I am delivered from the bondage of drugs and alcohol. But that doesn't mean, if given the choice, I would not intentionally gravitate to some other lesser vice at times. It could be food, television, caffeine, or even sleeping too much, depending on the day.

In those weak moments, I used to find myself too often choosing quick indulgence over honest prayer as the rule rather than the exception. I would go straight for the closest one I could find rather than immediately hitting my knees and crying out to God. I can hardly express my gratitude for Wisdom from the Holy Spirit to see these moments approaching much more quickly now than in years past. This is a direct result of a desire to bring my mind and then my body into a posture of Humility before God. By his grace, I can hear him more clearly today, and prayer with a contrite heart is almost always what I run to first. Rather than in the things that give only temporary or imitation relief, in intimacy with the Source of all relief is where my soul now finds deepest rest, even when I fall. But as I said before, God still wants **all** of me.

"Do not worship any other god, for the Lord, whose name is Jealous, is a jealous God" (Exodus 34:14 NIV)

"Or do you think that the Scripture speaks to no purpose: 'He jealously desires the Spirit which he has made to dwell in us'? But he gives a greater grace. Therefore it says, 'GOD IS OPPOSED TO THE PROUD, BUT GIVES GRACE TO THE HUMBLE'" (James 4:5-6 NASB)

Even with all I understand about Humility, given the fallen part of my nature, offering him all of me is still not an instinctive response. I still mess up all the time. So my prayer continues to be that God would reveal in me that which sets itself against what he desires for me. In that way I am daily in a position to take a humble posture and set myself up to make that better choice.

So what's the big deal?

"Humility is the most difficult of all virtues to achieve; nothing dies harder than the desire to think well of self."—T. S. Eliot

The difficulty with true contrition is most aptly displayed in the way our enemy, the devil, attacks it. On the road to Humility we need to remember that we are victorious in Jesus without allowing that fact to go to our heads and puff us up. To say that achieving this balance is troublesome would be putting it mildly.

"Your patient has become humble; have you drawn his attention to the fact? All virtues are less formidable to us once the man is aware that he has them, but this is especially true of humility."—C. S. Lewis, *The Screwtape Letters*

Once we achieve Humility, we immediately begin to congratulate ourselves. As quickly as it appears, it can be lost. The only answer is in Christ and a repentant heart intentionally turned toward him. The deceiver will tell you anything to keep your focus elsewhere, but especially to keep you turned inwardly. *"This God thing, just isn't working for me."* *"Why me?"* *"Why not me?"* *"Why them and not me?"* And my personal favorite, *"I deserve/don't deserve this!"* Every last one of those are bogus; they are lies. Don't kill the messenger, but I have news for you: God owes you nothing.

"Wisdom's instruction is to fear the Lord, and humility comes before honor" (Proverbs 15:33 NASB).

Don't ever let anyone tell you Humility is anything other than a gift born of obedience. The cool thing about it is that honor does follow obedience, since the focus after being humbled is always where it should be—not on circumstances and foolishness but on the character of our God.

Wisdom instructs by pride's deference to the Truth bestowed afresh within us the way dry ground will ever need and receive new rain. It falls upon all equally since it must, though the nobility of each new harvest will never be exactly alike.

"All discipline for the moment seems not to be joyful, but sorrowful; yet to those who have been trained by it, afterwards it yields the peaceful fruit of righteousness." (Hebrews 12:11 NASB)

To bottom line it for you, Humility is not as much an action as it is an understanding. Circumstances can be humbling; people can be humbled. But Humility is one of those rare aspects of life that you'll never have until you've known it, and you'll never know until it hits you right between the eyes. Pride is its antonym for good reason. To understand Humility is to understand that your present condition is fluid and beyond your best ability to stabilize apart from God. It is realizing that despite the most self-empowering and self-affirming human antidotes imaginable, you are only ever one turn, one word, one mistake away from being reminded how completely vulnerable and fragile you are.

There is only One who is our firm foundation, *God* alone. There is only one agent that solidifies our present condition and it is his to give, *grace* alone. There is only one Word that brings Wisdom's instruction and holds us fast to the Rock and firm foundation, *Christ* alone.

"Therefore everyone who hears these words of Mine and acts on them, may be compared to a wise man who built his house on the rock. And the rain fell, and the floods came, and the winds blew and slammed against that house; and yet it did not fall, for it had been founded on the rock. Everyone who hears these words of Mine and does not act on them, will be like a foolish man who built his house on the sand. The rain fell, and the floods came, and the winds blew and slammed against that house; and it fell-and great was its fall" (Matthew 7:24-26 NASB).

Humility comes most readily to me when I consider the life of another through the loving eyes of my Savior. I say this with the full realization that all in life is relative, to a certain extent. Jesus' mercy to all and the impartial nature of grace both bear that fact out. However, our personal circumstances must always be a lens with which we view others if we have any hope at all of gaining a proper perspective. Love demands it, and honest compassion compels it.

I live in Southern California, in an upscale neighborhood with a low crime rate. I live in a country where I am free to do and be just about anything I choose, within reason. I am healthy by most standards, and I am richer than 90 percent of the world's population. I have two beautiful, heathy children. I have nightly shelter, daily provision, and in context, I lack no good thing. But if you asked me on a bad day, I could list a dozen or more things I wish I had. I could list another dozen circumstances in life that are entirely unacceptable to me. I could lament a blue streak about how much "better" my life might be … if only … if only. You can begin to see where I am headed with this.

It is all too easy for me to let my mind be dragged away to that place, and I am all too often an eager participant in that sort of self-pitying nonsense. Then God starts to bring to mind the reality that life exists beyond the borders of my small perception. That there is far more to the story than my limited understanding of the way things appear. Jesus did say, **"In this world you will have trouble" (John 16:33 NIV)**. But to be humble is to be mindful at all times of the fact that there is always somebody whose needs are greater than my own. Gratitude is thanking God for allowing me to see that I am blessed beyond measure, regardless of my circumstances. Loving him is actually stepping outside of myself and making my best effort to do something about it.

"Humble yourselves in the presence of the Lord, and he will exalt you" (James 4:10 NASB)

So I will leave you with just a few examples of the way God corrects the course of my thinking and brings me back to my right mind, along with a verse to seal it all up:

When I am hungry, he reminds me there are those who have nothing to eat. When my body aches, he reminds me there are those who can't even stand, much less walk. When I get frustrated with my children, he reminds me there are those who have either lost one or have none. When I feel lonely, he reminds me of those who are truly alone in the world and all of the people he placed around me who love me. When I feel selfish, he reminds me of the Cross. When I am tempted to be dissatisfied with my life, he reminds me that every moment I get to draw breath on this earth is a blessing. When I forget to be thankful, he reminds me why I'm here.

"Do nothing out of selfish ambition or vain conceit. Rather, in humility value others above yourselves, not looking to your own interests but each of you to the interests of the others" (Philippians 2:3-4 NASB)

Prayer: *Help me to remember that everyone lives or dies to you Lord, and give me the strength, wisdom, and compassion not to pass judgment. God show me how to walk with you in Humility. I will come on my knees with a contrite heart as many times as it takes, and until whatever strongholds in me break, because your Word, not my feelings or circumstances, is truth and a lamp to me. Stay with me and be my portion, my shelter, and my provision. You are enough for me, Father. Thank you for Humility, Lord, even when it hurts. I pray for the courage to own those things with which I struggle. I know you are faithful, Lord. Apart from you, I am blind, weak, and lost. But in you, when I am weak, then I am strong. I love you, Jesus, and my debt is to love just as you love me. You have repaid me beauty for ashes, Father; the blood of Jesus is my rescript. I receive my life in you; joy, peace, and rest are knowing you. Always stay near to me, Jesus, my Emmanuel. Guide me according to your perfect will. I pray that in every way, Lord, when I contend for you in the lives of my family, friends, and loved ones, they would see your character in me and hear your heart when I speak. In Jesus' name, Amen!*

Mark A. Luther

Scripture: " ...and all of you, clothe yourselves with humility toward one another, for God is opposed to the proud, but gives grace to the humble. Therefore humble yourselves under the mighty hand of God, that he may exalt you at the proper time, casting all your anxiety on him, because he cares for you" (1 Peter 5:5-7 NASB).

Chapter 8

Surrender

All or nothing

"For God has not given us a spirit of fear, but of power and of love and of a sound mind." (2 Timothy 1:7 NKJV).

God used the picture of a parent with their child to show me total surrender, only this time in reverse. I have two beautiful kids, and I remember when they would present something to me—like a picture or a half-broken toy. *"This is for you, daddy,"* and they would really mean it. I remember having the sense that once they handed it over they no longer made any claim to it, nor did they ever want it back. It was mine completely— without reservation and without doubt. *"Here daddy."* That is the cry of my heart by God's Grace—now and every day from this time forward.

"Then Jesus said to His disciples, 'If anyone wishes to come after Me, he must deny himself and take up his cross and follow Me'." (Matthew 16:24 NASB)

"As they were walking along the road, a man said to him, 'I will follow you wherever you go … ' Still another said, 'I will follow you, Lord; but first let me go back and say goodbye to my family.' Jesus replied, 'No one who puts a hand to the plow and looks back is fit for service in the kingdom of God'" (Luke 9:57, 61, 62 NIV)

"Peter said to him, 'We have left all we had to follow you!' 'Truly I tell you,' Jesus said to them, 'no one who has left home or wife or brothers or sisters or parents or children for the sake of the kingdom of God will fail to receive many times as much in this age and, in the age to come eternal life'." (Luke 18:28-30 NIV)

God has also laid on my heart his desire for me to understand and receive all of the good gifts he has for me through the act of surrender. As I give myself over to him, all of those wonderful things that are mine become visible. As I open my hands, letting go of the superfluous and needless things I carry around with me, I am able to more clearly see the banquet table laid out in front of me. And what's more, my surrender helps to loose an outpouring of the same onto the people around me. Through my surrender to him, God is teaching me how to be there for others, and healing the wounds that once prevented me.

I trust God with this so I'll just put it out there for you. When I shine the light of Christ on something, it drains the enemy's power to hold me in bondage any longer. I have always had trouble giving and getting real love from people for two reasons. One is the fear of them being taken away from me; the other is a fear of being taken from them. God has brought me light-years from where I was, but I still struggle with it to an extent. Another thing he has shown me through it all is that sometimes life is just going to be like that. Even when what I'm holding onto so tightly might be altogether rational and good to me, that doesn't mean it's good, right, or healthy for me according to him.

Even in the most humble circumstances, his will and command is simply *love and be loved*, so my answer and my prayer will ever be the same. *"Yes Lord, amen, finish the good work you've begun in me and show me how to let go of everything. In joy I deny myself, take up the cross you bid me bear today, and come after you. I know that there is only more freedom, rest, comfort, and assurance to gain in deference to you."*

"And God is able to make all grace abound to you, so that always having all sufficiency in everything, you may have an abundance for every good deed ... Now he who supplies seed to the sower and bread for food will supply and multiply your seed for sowing and increase the harvest of your righteousness." (2 Corinthians 9:8, 10 NASB)

I am in the habit now of praying out loud the truth of God found in his Word over my life and circumstances. In particular, I pray every morning and offer my body as a **"living and holy sacrifice, acceptable to God."** But one day as I spoke those words, God spoke to my heart: *"You don't believe that."* I thought, "What?" God again spoke to my heart, saying that though I had been mouthing it, I did not believe that my body IS, as I offer it to him, a "holy" sacrifice "acceptable" to him.

I had been believing the lie that any sacrifice I offered was far less than holy, and certainly not of any worth to God. As I considered God's whisper to me, my spirit confirmed it, and I repented for believing it. I then also renounced the lie of the enemy who spoke it. What happened next was the cool part. God showed me how and why my body offered each day is "holy" and "acceptable" to him. Here are the scriptures he showed me as I prayed:

"But if the Spirit of him who raised Jesus from the dead dwells in you, *he who raised Christ Jesus from the dead will also give life to your mortal bodies* **through his Spirit who dwells in you."** **(Romans 8:11 NASB)**

"And we know that in all things God works for the good of those who love him, who have been called according to his purpose. For those God foreknew he also predestined *to be conformed to the image of his Son,* **that he might be the firstborn among many brothers and sisters." (Romans 8:28-29 NIV)**

He predestined me to be conformed to the likeness of his Son. I am able to offer not only this body to him as a living sacrifice, but also by the sanctifying work of the blood of Jesus shed for me, to present it as a holy sacrifice acceptable to God!

"First he said, 'Sacrifices and offerings, burnt offerings and sin offerings you did not desire, nor were you pleased with them'— though they were offered in accordance with the law. Then he said, 'Here I am, I have come to do your will.' He sets aside the first to establish the second. *And by that will, we have been made holy through the sacrifice of the body of Jesus Christ once for all."* **(Hebrews 10:8-10 NIV)**

The service of worship is acceptable since the life of our physical body and of every other offering is made spiritually perfect by the blood of his Son.

"Then Jesus said to his disciples, 'Whoever wants to be my disciple must deny themselves and take up their cross and follow me. For whoever wants to save their life will lose it, but whoever loses their life for me will find it'." (Matthew 16:24-25 NIV)

As I offer the holy and acceptable sacrifice of my body to him, I agree to surrender my life. As I agree to this spiritual act of worship, I gain Christ in every moment and I am found in him. Praise God!

"But whatever were gains to me I now consider loss for the sake of Christ. What is more, I consider everything a loss because of the surpassing worth of knowing Christ Jesus my Lord, for whose sake I have lost all things. I consider them garbage, that I may gain Christ and be found in him ..." (Philippians 3:7-9 NIV)

Something to understand about total surrender is that a "loss" is no loss at all, but it is actually great gain in view of all that God promises. A life coveted or fearfully clung to apart from Christ is a dead thing not to be desired in the least. So having said all that, I will leave you with this scripture and pray that the Truth of God is renewed in and over every one of you.

"Therefore I urge you, brethren, by the mercies of God, to present your bodies a living and holy sacrifice, acceptable to God, which is your spiritual service of worship. And do not be conformed to this world, but be transformed by the renewing of your mind, so that you may prove what the will of God is, that which is good and acceptable and perfect." (Romans 12:1-2 NASB)

What about my Identity?

I have prayed hundreds of times, *"Lord, give me the desire of your heart for me"* and *"Lord, let your will for me be done, rather than my own."* But I confess there has always been a part of me that still resists.

I finish praying and move on with my day, but sometimes my actions do not reflect the precious words and heartfelt petitions that I made only a few hours prior. I am now able to see this so much more clearly, because in God's mercy and by his grace my spirit continues to be quickened. With every new appeal, with each failure, I am able to view myself more fully as the man he restored when I believed in Jesus Christ. I know this is true because the Holy Spirit whom God caused to live in me is always drawn toward deeper intimacy with him. While anything else encumbers that intimacy, I can feel the conflict and I am driven to address it. The struggle is not against God, but against my old identity. What he has always said I am is all I will ever be, but my sinful nature has other ideas.

Surrender means eliminating the struggle the moment that I realize one exists. It means declaring emphatically that I am authentically the man God always intended, then seeking to live the life God always intended for me. I am unashamedly his, in spite of the crumbs leftover from the man I once was. I've yet to completely release all of them, but I continue to pray for his Wisdom. With God's help, I will realize the freedom and the fullness of my identity in handing over every part of my life to Jesus Christ. By word and by deed, in his strength and not my own, I will stay in the race and finish well.

"Not that I have already obtained all this, or have already arrived at my goal, *but I press on to take hold of that for which Christ Jesus took hold of me.* **Brothers and sisters, I do not consider myself yet to have taken hold of it. But one thing I do: Forgetting what is behind and straining toward what is ahead, I press on toward the goal to win the prize for which God has called me heavenward in Christ Jesus." (Philippians 3:12-14 NIV)**

Nobody is beyond God's desire to love or his ability to use them. There is one catch though—total surrender to the reality that your whole identity is found in him, period. It means admitting to yourself and to God that you are powerless to do or be anything of eternal significance apart from him. It won't be easy, but I assure you he is worth it. Jesus said it, and I am a witness to it by my own former life.

My identity was in being a drunk and a drug addict. My security was in lying, selfishness, and seducing any woman who would have me. My comfort was in being a foul-mouthed, rebellious fool who dropped out of high school at age seventeen. Until the grace and love of God found me, I was a dead man.

The good news is, there is no bad news! Your life will be all the better for every ill-perceived liberty and every superfluous burden you throw off in surrender to God. There is no freedom more perfect or real than that of being a servant bound to Jesus Christ.

"I am the vine, you are the branches; he who abides in Me and I in him, he bears much fruit, for apart from Me you can do nothing." (John 15:5 NASB)

***"You are My friends if you do what I command you.* No longer do I call you slaves, for the slave does not know what his master is doing; but I have called you friends, for all things that I have heard from My Father I have made known to you." (John 15:14-15 NASB)**

Prayer: *Abba Father, I surrender all to you—my whole heart, my mind, all of my soul, and all of my strength. I exalt you above every authority in heaven, on earth, or under the earth. I come in humility to you alone, Lord, and I speak your words over my life. Lord, your Word is "**living and active**," your Spirit urges me forward and when I resist, I always feel farther from you. My prayer is that, no matter what else becomes of me, I would live every moment to see your desire for me revealed and fulfilled, and that if I am afraid to move, or reluctant to give in, you would convey to me the courage and strength to lay down my life for your sake. I find in my need for you all that I lack, knowing I can do nothing apart from you. Give me clean hands and a pure heart, Lord, so that I am able to hear your voice and trust you with total abandon. The cost is to allow every obstacle to be removed in your power. In meekness and in obedience, I am freed day by day when I remember that you are in control. I love you God. In Jesus' name, I ask it. Amen!*

Mark A. Luther

Scripture: "I am using an example from everyday life because of your human limitations. Just as you used to offer yourselves as slaves to impurity and to ever-increasing wickedness, so now offer yourselves as slaves to righteousness leading to holiness. When you were slaves to sin, you were free from the control of righteousness. What benefit did you reap at that time from the things you are now ashamed of? Those things result in death! But now that you have been set free from sin and have become slaves of God, the benefit you reap leads to holiness, and the result is eternal life. For the wages of sin is death, but the gift of God is eternal life in Christ Jesus our Lord." (Romans 6:19-23 NIV)

CHAPTER 9

SUBMISSION

We bow to no man!

"Don't you know that when you offer yourselves to someone as obedient slaves, you are slaves of the one you obey—whether you are slaves to sin, which leads to death, or to obedience, which leads to righteousness?" (Romans 6:16 NIV)

What is "idolatry," especially as it relates to us as believers in Jesus? In general, anything that you or I place above, or on the same level with, God can create a point of tension within us. In order of authority, significance, or importance, anyone or anything, other than God, that we give first place in our lives is effectually an idol. Our own intense focus makes it so; if we allow that person or interest to push God to one side and take center stage, then that is where the real trouble starts.

We may encounter many things during the course of a day. We interact with many people, confront random problems, and stumble into various circumstances. First of all, it's important to remember that just living your life is not idolatry in and of itself. However, any one of those interactions, even when totally rational, can grow into self-importance and become an idol. If we use anything as an excuse to justify our actions or inactions, we are submitting to that rather than to God. If we knowingly give in to any object, emotion, or person which then moves us beyond God's heart for us, we are obeying it as slaves. That is idolatry as plainly as I know how to explain it.

"Do not be afraid," Samuel replied. "You have done all this evil; yet do not turn away from the LORD, but serve the LORD with all your heart. Do not turn away after useless idols. They can do you no good, nor can they rescue you, because they are useless." (1 Samuel 12:20-21 NIV)

The Lord has continued to show me rocky soil in my own heart that needs overturning. For example, what does "*deny myself*" really mean?

That was one of my first thoughts. Also, what did that mean to Jesus in context? **(Luke 9:23-24 NASB)** When he was confronted with the burden of the Cross, the thought of it was abhorrent, and maybe even frightening to him, as he prayed to have God remove the weight of it.

"Abba! Father! All things are possible for You; remove this cup from Me; yet not what I will, but what You will." (Mark 14:36 NASB)

When God showed me this it became clear. If there is a Cross for me to bear, it is whatever in my life that strays beyond God's heart for me that must be nailed to it daily. Denying myself is recognizing the idol and agreeing that whatever it is will die daily. It will not be easy to look at, and to consider carrying it up my own personal hill will be even more difficult. But to go a step farther and imagine the pain in having those parts crucified is on another level entirely. If it sounds ugly, it's because it is ugly.

So what happened next with Jesus and the Cross?

"An angel from heaven appeared to him and strengthened him" (Luke 22:43 NIV)

The beginning of the good news for us is that we don't just have an angel of the Lord to comfort and strengthen us in the self-denial or the painful re-alignment on our walk up that hill. We have the LORD of Glory himself, Jesus Christ, who comes to us. He will always provide a way of escape so that we are able to bear up underneath it and find grace to endure. **(1 Corinthians 10:13 NASB)**

"Therefore, since we have a great high priest who has ascended into heaven, Jesus the Son of God, let us hold firmly to the faith we profess. For we do not have a high priest who is unable to sympathize with our weaknesses, but we have one who has been tempted in every way, just as we are—yet he did not sin. Let us then approach God's throne of grace with confidence, so that we may receive mercy and find grace to help us in our time of need." (Hebrews 4:14-16 NIV)

Mark A. Luther

Once again, let's remember that if we agree to bear a Cross at all, it must be daily if we would come after Jesus and learn from him.

"Then he said to them all: "Whoever wants to be my disciple must deny themselves and take up their cross daily and follow me. For whoever wants to save their life will lose it, but whoever loses their life for me will save it'." (Luke 9:23-24 NIV)

But let's also remember a few other things while we're at it. One is that we are called to this by God.

"Have this attitude in yourselves which was also in Christ Jesus, who, although He existed in the form of God, did not regard equality with God a thing to be grasped, but emptied Himself, taking the form of a bond-servant, *and* being made in the likeness of men. Being found in appearance as a man, He humbled Himself by becoming obedient to the point of death, even death on a cross." (Philippians 2:5-8 NASB)

And here also:

"Therefore, since Christ suffered in his body, arm yourselves also with the same attitude, because whoever suffers in the body is done with sin." (1 Peter 4:1 NIV)

Finally, it is important to remember that this reality is not a bad or depressing thing. Jesus says, " ...**but whoever loses his life for me will save it.**" That means the burdens are lifted daily! That means daily renewal! That means daily regeneration! That means daily being free! It means being rid of the terrible, ugly things that drag you down, and concurring daily that you have need of a heart submitted to God.

"You were made by God and for God and until you understand that, life will never make sense."—Rick Warren

In order to see God's victory in our lives, submission is an imperative. We need to get out of our comfort zones, get real before God every day, and put down anything that would come between us and the desire of God's heart for us. We can be filled with joy in knowing that Abba Father walks every step with us, and his reward for us is always with him. All along the paths we will tread, in every way our glory and crown is his passion for us. We bow to no man, but we do yield to one Shepherd.

"To this you were called, because Christ suffered for you, leaving you an example, that you should follow in his steps. 'He committed no sin, and no deceit was found in his mouth.' When they hurled their insults at him, he did not retaliate; when he suffered, he made no threats. Instead, he entrusted himself to him who judges justly. He himself bore our sins in his body on the cross, so that we might die to sins and live for righteousness; by his wounds you have been healed. For you were like sheep going astray, but now you have returned to the Shepherd and Overseer of your souls." (1 Peter 2:21-25 NIV)

Abba, thank you that our darkness flees from your presence. Adonai, your word is a lamp, a mirror that quickens our spirits to humility, and it is a two-edged sword that lays bare the thoughts and intentions of our hearts.

"Now as they came out, they found a man of Cyrene, Simon by name. Him they compelled to bear his cross." (Matthew 27:32 NKJV)

There is only one person I am aware of who actually carried a cross whose day did not end in death of some kind. The man, Simon of Cyrene, was compelled *(forced)* to carry Jesus' cross to the hill for him. Do you think he would have volunteered? Likely not. Do you suppose he was afraid he would be crucified by mistake? Absolutely; Scripture implies as much. But does any of that matter? The NASB version of the Bible says Simon was **"pressed into service to bear his cross."** Do you suppose this involved denying himself during that walk to

Golgotha? After all, it wasn't Simon's Cross was it? The Bible says he was come upon, put upon, and forced. Any of that sounding familiar? He was ill-prepared, ill-equipped, unfavorable, and headed the other direction. Does any of that sound familiar? He was compelled and his life was spared. Do you suppose, on the other hand, that his life was ever the same again?

Now consider yourself every morning in the place of Simon—equally as ill-prepared, equally as ill-equipped, equally as unfavorable. But you yourself are the one headed in the opposite direction, then suddenly you are being stopped. Now it IS *your* Cross to carry, now you are assured by your own spirit that it is *your* walk up that hill, now it is a part of you that will be crucified and die this day.

There is, however, a very important distinction to be made: you will not *ever* be forced, you will not ever be compelled against your will, and neither God nor any Roman soldier will *ever* press you into service. You have to choose it. So what then? When you take up that Cross, though you must ultimately bear it those last few steps, Jesus will always be your strength to drag it along the way. He will always be your courage to release and deny whatever idol must daily be put to death there.

"Submit yourselves, then, to God. Resist the devil, and he will flee from you. Come near to God and he will come near to you." (James 4:7-8 NIV)

Because Dad said so!

"The reason why many are still troubled, still seeking, still making little forward progress is because they haven't yet come to the end of themselves. We're still trying to give orders, and interfering with God's work within us."—A. W. Tozer

"The voice of the LORD twists the oaks and strips the forests bare. And in his temple all cry, 'Glory!' The LORD sits enthroned over

the flood; the LORD is enthroned as King forever. The LORD gives strength to his people; the LORD blesses his people with peace." (Psalms 29:9-11 NIV)

Critics of the one true God are always confidently asserting things like, *"Who was Lot's wife?" "What about the dinosaurs?" "There is no way a flood covered the entire earth!" "The Bible is just a collection of random books written by men!" "Does it really say there were unicorns?" "How could a loving God allow* _____*? (You fill in the blank),"* and many, many more. The origin of all the postulating is simple rebellion, pride, and an unwillingness to submit that is as old as time.

I heard a pastor say something once that was so straightforward, but at the same time it rings so true, that we all must give pause to consider it. I am paraphrasing, but his cogent point was this: *If I can agree to only one idea, "**In the beginning God** ..." (Genesis 1:1), then everything coming afterward is not only possible but totally plausible. In other words to know that God IS from the beginning makes every other contrary argument a human could make against his power, his character, or the veracity of his words moot.*

"The God who made the world and everything in it is the Lord of heaven and earth and does not live in temples built by human hands. And he is not served by human hands, as if he needed anything. Rather, he himself gives everyone life and breath and everything else." (Acts 17:24-25)

God reminded me once that we don't follow his way and submit to him because he is always good. For that we do thank him and praise him. We don't trust him completely because in everything he is our Provider. For that we are grateful, and we do remember to give him all glory. We don't agree with God because he is agreeable. For receiving his favor we are humbled and thankful that we are able to stand. We are not obedient to him because we are guaranteed a single thing; instead, for the truth in every one of his promises we rejoice and say Amen! In every way and at all times **HE IS GOD,** from everlasting to everlasting, and we move because he said, *"Move."* We say, *"Here am I"*

101

because there exists no other who could send us. The soles of our feet land on God's straight and lighted paths because there exists no other **Rock (Psalms 18:31)** besides him to bear them up.

"The Lord brings death and makes alive; he brings down to the grave and raises up. The Lord sends poverty and wealth; he humbles and he exalts. He raises the poor from the dust and lifts the needy from the ash heap; he seats them with princes and has them inherit a throne of honor. For the foundations of the earth are the Lord's; on them he has set the world" (1 Samuel 2:6-8 NIV)

Whether we like it or not, we are forced to confront *the* question. Is God who he says he is, or he is not? For this reason, and not in lieu of it, we stand or fall based on what we believe about God and whether what he promises is true. Is he really enthroned over every circumstance we could ever imagine or is he not?

The above are verses in the book of Samuel taken from "**Hannah's Song**" to God. Not surprisingly, the name Hannah in Hebrew means "Favor" or "Grace." God had created her to demonstrate these characteristics in the way she praised him and longed for him to see her. As she came each moment, pouring out all in her heart, praying to him so passionately with her spirit, God heard her. Let me say that again: He HEARD her. Why? She spoke his language: Love in utter submission. Our God is Love, our God speaks the language of Love. **(1 John 4:8 NIV)**

She gave him her whole heart, with blinders on to everything else around her, and it was there in that place of surrender that her desires were known to him. Groaning, crying, speaking spiritual thoughts to God with spiritual words, *Favor and Grace* **(1 Corinthians 2:13 NASB), (Romans 8:26-27 NASB)**. So *Favor and Grace* are what followed; God blessed her with a son, Samuel, which means *"God has heard."* She had come to God first in submission, expecting nothing but his desire for her, and desiring his expectation for her. She dedicated the blessing before it had even come to pass, the substance of what she most hoped for, and the evidence of what she could not yet see **(Hebrews 11:1 NKJV)**. From *Favor and Grace* came the reality:

God has heard. Hannah's song is an important affirmation of God's character. She spoke as though she knew it absolutely, because she did. Hannah's song is one that tells of God's justice, and she sang boldly as one who had received it, because she had. Finally, Hannah's song is one that expresses God's mercy. She shouted to all who would hear both its immediacy and its imminence, as one who knew it to be both, because she did.

Her firstborn son was dedicated to God from birth, the man of God who anointed David king over Israel, from whose line we trace the human roots of God's Word made flesh in Jesus Christ. **(Isaiah 11:10 NASB), (John 1:14 NIV)** You can hear Hannah cry out once more in this—Samuel answering **"Here I am"** to God's call. Mother and child were both foreshadowing the hope of God's coming through his only begotten Son Jesus. They are echoed through King David's prayer in the love language that only passionate longing for God's intimacy will ever breathe, and only Heaven's heart can truly hear:

"Bless the Lord, O my soul, and all that is within me, bless his holy name. Bless the Lord, O my soul, and forget none of his benefits; who pardons all your iniquities, who heals all your diseases; who redeems your life from the pit, who crowns you with lovingkindness and compassion; who satisfies your years with good things, so that your youth is renewed like the eagle. The Lord performs righteous deeds and judgments for all who are oppressed ... The Lord is compassionate and gracious, slow to anger and abounding in lovingkindness ... He has not dealt with us according to our sins, nor rewarded us according to our iniquities. For as high as the heavens are above the earth, so great is his lovingkindness toward those who fear him. As far as the east is from the west, so far has he removed our transgressions from us." (Psalms 103:1-6, 8, 10-12 NASB)

We are able to keep our hearts and allow all that we comprehend in this flesh to be dealt with, apart from any affectedness, when we understand that Jesus Christ is in control. The voice of God who spoke both the finite and the infinite into being combined that reality with a love for us so full that the whole of the universe could not contain it **(1 John 4:16 NASB)**. So then, the answer to our every question with respect to submission is spoken in his gentle voice, *"Yes, through every storm, Yes."* Breathing his comfort onto the exact point of our every pain, *"Yes, in death and in life, Yes."* Quietly in the uniqueness of a love language that will ever be our assurance of home beyond earth's imperfect veil, *"Yes, my precious one, I have you. Yes, I AM is who I say I am"* **(John 10:27-30 NASB)**

This truth should be the center, our one unassailable comfort and blessed assurance—that he, our Abba God, is enthroned over everything. Think of the most wonderful peace and rest there could ever be, let it wash over your mind and heart until you can almost touch it. Now imagine all fortuity, happenstance, and every detail of this life enfolded by that same rest and peace, literally enveloped in it. All crisis, cause, and experiential phases of our lives are swallowed up by the beauty of it. Beginning as the sun rises each morning to become our reality every day, then ebbing slowly away as night falls, his declaration is the sentinel that keeps watch over our souls and minds. This skillfully hewn shelter built up around us is able to ensure virtue, solidarity, and stability to the wellspring of our lives **(Matthew 7:24-25 NASB)**. Why? *Because Dad said so!*

"Keep your heart with all diligence, for out of it is the wellspring of life." (Proverbs 4:23 WEB)

All of our times are in his hands. We have to rely on him for everything as though every day were the same as today. We are just as desperate and reliant upon God when the world's counterfeit of good fortune is in full effect as we are when the weakness of our flesh rears up its head. We should be thankful that he is our foundation. We will have days, weeks, or even months when things just don't go our way. We should be grateful that in those moments when we grab and reach for a handhold, we lay hold of the True Vine, not a rotted, corrupted, fake that snaps and crumbles in our hands. **(John 15:1 NASB)**

"I am the Lord, and there is no other; Besides Me there is no God. I will gird you, though you have not known Me; that men may know from the rising to the setting of the sun that there is no one besides Me. I am the Lord, and there is no other, the One forming light and creating darkness, causing well-being and creating calamity; *I am the Lord who does all these.*" (Isaiah 45:5-7 NASB)

Sometimes it's hard for me to accept, and even harder to remember, that he is the One "**who does all these**." It's hard to accept because, in the smallness of my little, human fiefdom, pride would have me believe I am in full control. And it's difficult to remember because the world just keeps right on turning and I move along with it.

These, in addition to many other confused ideologies and ideas, can give the false illusion that God is either asleep at the wheel or has abandoned it, leaving us to steer the ship. It is our limited understanding of eternity, in harmony with the vastness of God, which most often blinds us to him. Total submission to the reality of an authority higher than ourselves is the only bonding agent, unwavering trust in the eternal and unseen. There are no air gaps, cracks, or holes. The parity in God's creation is complete, lacking nothing and without excess. The wonder and beauty in this miracle is that the two opposites are united together in his Son, Jesus Christ, who left us a perfect example of submission.

"During the days of Jesus' life on earth, he offered up prayers and petitions with fervent cries and tears to the one who could save him from death, and he was heard because of his reverent submission." (Hebrews 5:7 NIV)

Life is constantly happening around us; over that we have no control. We do, however, have free will to influence it, both our life and the lives of others. So while it is certainly God "**who does all these**," we seed the tornados that demand calamity as payment, and we speak the spiritual thoughts with spiritual words that bear and release his light. We choose to believe the lies and accept a counterfeit that blots out true reality. By our own agreement, we can either give death and vacancy room to spread, or allow that which is Life indeed to flourish. Finally, it is in submission by faith alone that we live out his promise of well-being, living life to the full.

We are his creation after all, and he has **good works** for us to do. I am comforted by that above all things. He already knows, and he wills to prosper us, not to harm us. We pretend at some semblance of control but only to avoid the unavoidable—our all-embracing, all-inclusive, all-encompassing reliance on him. Anyone who knows Jesus Christ as Savior today can find in that knowledge refreshing joy and freedom beyond all compare.

Reference verses: (John 1:1-5 NASB), (Ephesians 4:6 NASB), (Romans 7:21-24 NASB), (Hebrews 10:22-23 NIV), (John 1:16 NASB), (Titus 2:11-12 NIV), (1 Corinthians 2:11-13 NASB), (1 Timothy 6:18-19 NASB), (John 10:10 NASB), (Ephesians 5:8 NASB), (Jeremiah 29:11 NASB), (Revelation 1:8 NASB)

Prayer: *I pray that the light of your life, Lord Jesus, would be the abundance of my heart and my portion today. By faith I put down my flesh and all that it desires and ask that every part of my life, all of my thoughts and all of my emotions, would be at the center of your will. Thank you for your provision in times of distress, Lord, and for the answer to prayer in ways I would never expect or imagine that are unmistakably you. I am thankful for the love that you have set in the hearts of people, for the revelation of the necessity and desperation for you even in calm water. I choose total reliance upon you in the midst of good fortune and in every strong head wind of life. You alone are full of power, mercy, grace, and peace, Abba. I love you so much. I submit to your authority and to your leadership. In Jesus' name I pray, Amen!*

Scripture: **"Trust in the Lord with all your heart and lean not on your own understanding; in all your ways submit to him, and he will make your paths straight." (Proverbs 3:5-6 NIV)**

CHAPTER 10

FORGIVENESS

Why would God forgive me?

"You were bought at a price; do not become slaves of men" (1 Corinthians 7:23 NASB)

God reminded me one morning while I was praying that my life is no longer my own. It does not belong to me or anyone else; it belongs to him alone.

"...do you not know that your body is a temple of the Holy Spirit, who is in you, whom you have received from God? You are not your own; you were bought at a price ..." (1 Corinthians 6:19-20 NASB)

You see, I was usurping the forgiveness of Jesus Christ in my own life by not accepting it. By not receiving what he promised and in my own heart still condemning myself, I was making a statement. I was unwilling to believe I could be totally forgiven, and I was mistakenly assuming that it was my judgment to make in the first place.

So that I would understand, God showed me the truth in a really unique way. It was as though I was actually passing judgment on someone else. Because I am no longer my own, I am someone else's servant. I belong to Jesus Christ. These were his words that came to me as I let it all sink in:

"If we confess our sins, he is faithful and just and will forgive us our sins and purify us from all unrighteousness" (1 John 1:9 NIV)

"Who are you to judge the servant of another? To his own master he stands or falls; and he will stand, for the Lord is able to make him stand." (Romans 14:4 NASB)

To put it very plainly, if God who created the universe says I am forgiven, then I should listen to him. His Word is final, he says I *will stand*. He is my Adonai, my Master—end of story.

"So when He said to them, 'I am He,' they drew back and fell to the ground." (John 18:6 NASB)

You have to imagine Jesus pulled that punch in the Garden of Gethsemane on purpose. I used to think, *"Oh, they fell to the ground,"* like that was some huge display of his power. He was not just telling them they had found the one they were looking for, he was simultaneously declaring his sovereignty as the Christ, the Son of the living God. While they were coming to take him away to be put on trial, he was still loving them and showing them mercy. It reminds me of the book of Exodus when God's Presence was so powerful that the people were overwhelmed by him. They told Moses to do their talking for them because every word spoken from God was so powerful that they feared death with every syllable.

"Speak to us yourself and we will listen; but let not God speak to us, or we will die." (Exodus 20:19 NASB)

He had mercy then as well. He relented and allowed them to hear the Word of God spoken through Moses. Jesus does this every day in the hearts and minds of those to whom he calls. It's really poetic and beautiful, indicative of his character. Our hearts are hostile toward him but still seeking. He declares that he is the "I AM" delicately enough to draw us back and knock us over, when one word from him could as easily splinter every molecule in our bodies. He spares our lives and forgives us even as our oblivious hearts still seek to take his life. Why? I honestly can't grasp it completely myself sometimes. He created us, he understands us, and he knows our rebellion is from ignorance. Like any loving parent, he deals with us not according to the foolish things we say and do, but in perfect love because we are his. We belong with him, we are related, favored sons and daughters in his house. From before all time and creation, God's forgiveness and his mercies toward us are never ending.

"Jesus said, 'Father, forgive them, for they do not know what they are doing'." (Luke 23:34 NASB)

"God's solid foundation stands firm, sealed with this inscription: 'The Lord knows those who are his ...'" (2 Timothy 2:19 NIV)

Buttons, Paper Clips, and Pocket Lint

Has your son or daughter ever come to you in a store wanting something far beyond what they could ever afford, with absolutely no clue as to how much it costs or why? I'm sure most of you, like me, would say, *"Multiple times, yes."* If so, you will likely relate to this thing God showed me one afternoon at work.

We come by nature asking God to pay. We come as a small child to their Daddy, with our hands stretched out, proudly offering whatever we have in our pocket at that moment. Usually it's something like a button, two pennies, a paper clip, and some pocket lint. With the same discerning love that we would have when looking down at what our children bring, God also smiles down on us. That same grace is the key component to God's forgiveness in Jesus Christ—knowing it is all we have, knowing it will never be enough, but also knowing it is offered from a sincere and unaffected heart.

He just wraps us up in his arms and loves us. He gives to us without any want or hope of recompense. He takes our junk and says with joy, *"Thank you son or daughter! That is just the right amount."* Then without reservation and without us ever being aware of the true cost, our heavenly Father pays the greatest price to give the greatest gift, and we are free.

"...all our righteous acts are like filthy rags; we all shrivel up like a leaf, and like the wind our sins sweep us away." (Isaiah 64:6 NIV)

"But God demonstrates His own love toward us, in that while we were yet sinners, Christ died for us." (Romans 5:8 NASB)

"...to bestow on them a crown of beauty instead of ashes, the oil of joy instead of mourning, and a garment of praise instead of

a spirit of despair. They will be called oaks of righteousness, a planting of the Lord for the display of his splendor." (Isaiah 61:3 NIV)

Our children still come to us in the same way that we go to our Abba God. We daily ask, seek, and knock **(Matthew 7:7-10 NIV)**. Just as we do with our little ones, God always answers. We always find him, and he always opens the door when we come calling. We need comfort; he provides a comforter **(2 Corinthians 1:3-5 NASB)**. We need food; he gives us Manna **(John 6:48-51 NASB)**. We say to the mountains in our lives, *"Move,"* and he throws them into the sea for us **(Mark 11:22-24 NASB)**.

The important part is *he gives*, and *he does*. We can't do any of those things on our own, and we certainly cannot save ourselves. What a beautiful, gracious, loving, amazing Father! He is over all the vastness of the entire universe. He is in the nuclei of the tiniest atoms, and he desires intimacy with us. For this reason, when I can get out of my own way long enough, I will crawl up next to him, let him hold onto me, and receive the forgiveness in his Love every day until he takes me home.

The Family Reunion

"There is no sight like seeing the light from Calvary kiss a human face as it fills the heart with the assurance of divine forgiveness."—Gypsy Smith

"Both the one who makes people holy and those who are made holy are of the same family. So Jesus is not ashamed to call them brothers and sisters." (Hebrews 2:11 NIV)

When you get right down to it, God is all about family. The phrase *"Son of man"* or *"sons of man"* is used in all four Gospels referring to Jesus, and multiple times in the Psalms, Job, Ezekiel, and elsewhere referring to us.

"For those who are led by the Spirit of God are the children of God. The Spirit you received does not make you slaves, so that you live in fear again; rather, the Spirit you received brought about your adoption to sonship. And by him we cry, Abba, Father." (Romans 8:14-15 NIV)

It's safe to say, the manner in which we love always relates to family in one way or another because that is how we are put together. When God said in the beginning **"Let us make mankind in Our image ..." (Genesis 1:26 NIV)**, that very image we reflect—**Father, Son, and Holy Spirit**—is by design familial. His first command to us in Scripture with a promise is familial **(Ephesians 6:1-3 NASB)**. The manger gave us back our brotherhood with Jesus. The Cross gave us back our right relationship as true sons and daughters of God. His forgiveness imparted through both gave us the ability to understand *family* as he meant it, his perfect design for it.

"Now if we are children, then we are heirs—heirs of God and co-heirs with Christ, if indeed we share in his sufferings in order that we may also share in his glory." (Romans 8:17 NIV)

When God talks about loving our brothers and sisters, he means everyone. He is one God, therefore we are one family. He is deliberate in that he ties our love for him and its veracity directly to our love for each other.

"The one who says he is in the light and yet hates his brother is in the darkness until now. The one who loves his brother abides in the light and there is no cause for stumbling in him." (1 John 2:9-10 NASB)

"Love one another with brotherly affection [as members of one family], giving precedence and showing honor to one another." (Romans 12:10 AMP)

- God Forgives us like a Parent **(Luke 15:11-32 NIV).**
- God Loves us like a Parent **(Ephesians 5:1-2 NASB).**

- God Disciplines us like a Parent **(Hebrews 12:4-11 NIV).**
- God Protects us like a Parent **(John 10:28-30 NIV).**

It is no mistake then that our love for one another as brothers, sisters, sons, daughters, friends, husbands, and wives, is paramount and the center of everything Jesus was trying to teach us. More than anything, the coming of Jesus, the Christ-child, into the world was about restoring kinship. Jesus in effect says that we are *ALL* brothers and sisters to one another in a way that no DNA test will ever dispute. Sure, there are crazy uncles, deadbeat brothers, grandparents, and nephews you'd just rather not be around. Every family has them, and God's is no different. The only blood that makes it so is his blood that brought forgiveness. The only family we really are a part of is through him and by his forgiveness. We should start acting like it.

"A crowd was sitting around Him, and they said to Him, 'Behold, Your mother and Your brothers are outside looking for You.' Answering them, He said, 'Who are My mother and My brothers?' Looking about at those who were sitting around Him, He said, 'Behold My mother and My brothers! For whoever does the will of God, he is My brother and sister and mother'." (Mark 3:32-35 NASB)

The Manger and the Cross

"Forgiveness is the fragrance the violet sheds on the heel that has crushed it."—Mark Twain

"But the angel said to them, 'Do not be afraid; for behold, I bring you good news of great joy which will be for all the people; for today in the city of David there has been born for you a Savior, who is Christ the Lord. This will be a sign for you: you will find a baby wrapped in cloths and lying in a manger'" (Luke 2:10-12 NASB)

If the mystery of the Cross is Christ in us, the hope of glory **(Colossians 1:26-27 NIV)**, then the simplicity of the manger was Christ with us, who takes away the sin of the world **(Matthew 1:21-23 NIV)**. If his journey had not begun in a barn, it never could have ended with him hanging on a tree. Apart from the "**tender shoot,**" we could never have "**esteemed him stricken**" **(Isaiah 53:2-4 NASB)**. It was God's forgiveness, the answer to our dilemma. It was in a word, perfect.

The glory of the Cross cannot exist without the obscurity of the manger, just as certainly as the beauty of the manger can only properly be seen through the viciousness of the Cross **(2 Corinthians 5:21 NASB)**.

"And when they had crucified him, they divided up his garments among themselves by casting lots. And sitting down, they began to keep watch over him there. And above his head they put up the charge against him which read, 'THIS IS JESUS THE KING OF THE JEWS'." (Matthew 27:35-37 NASB)

New Wine

"His mother said to the servants, 'Whatever He says to you, do it'." (John 2:5 NASB)

This was Mary, the mother of Jesus, speaking to some servants at a wedding party in Galilee when the wine had run out. Why is what she said significant? Well, for a few reasons, but it gave me a chuckle to imagine (this being Jesus' first "public" miracle) what Mary must have been remembering when she said it. I could see a scenario where she would be standing there just grinning, knowing what was about to happen next. I can see her having to bite her lip a bit and try not to giggle some as they all looked on dubiously when Jesus asked for the six pots.

"Now there were six stone waterpots set there for the Jewish custom of purification, containing twenty or thirty gallons each.

Jesus said to them, 'Fill the waterpots with water.' So they filled them up to the brim." (John 2:6-7 NASB)

What happened next was, well, a miracle; not just because Jesus made wine from water, and not just because it was better than the choicest wine anyone had ever tasted. This event, as Scripture says, was the beginning of all the public signs and wonders Jesus did. He had not planned it **(John 2:3-4 NASB)**, and he touched nothing. Nobody knew who he was or why he was there, other than those who were with him. Yet from the servants doing what Jesus told them, right down to what the headwaiter said, all of it was perfectly orchestrated, and it all announced his arrival on the world scene as the anticipated Messiah.

"And He said to them, 'Draw some out now and take it to the headwaiter.' So they took it to him. When the headwaiter tasted the water which had become wine, and did not know where it came from (but the servants who had drawn the water knew), the headwaiter called the bridegroom, and said to him, 'Every man serves the good wine first, and when the people have drunk freely, then he serves the poorer wine; but you have kept the good wine until now'." (John 2:8-10 NASB)

It's what the headwaiter said to the bridegroom that really wraps the whole thing in a neat little, divine package. Can you imagine Mary at that moment? Eyes alive with joy, a hand to her mouth to cover her growing smile. This gathering was seeing and hearing for the first time what she had known since the evening the Angel of the Lord visited her those many years ago. The new wine had arrived! Hallelujah! Redemption, the forgiveness of sins! As with every prophet and king from the time of Adam to that moment, from the first of all promises that had been spoken about Christ to the last, the final drop of poorer wine had been exhausted, and the watered down drink now all used up. But God had saved the best of his for last, to take away the sin of the world! **(John 6:55-63 NASB), (Mark 14:22-25 NASB).**

"And the Word became flesh, and dwelt among us, and we saw His glory, glory as of the only begotten from the Father, full of grace and truth" (John 1:14 NASB)

Forgiven much?

"'So which of them will love him more?' Simon answered and said, 'I suppose the one whom he forgave more.' And He said to him, 'You have judged correctly'" (Luke 7:42-43 NASB)

If they love more who are forgiven more, it is only in their former proximity to the void, and that accompanied by perilously keen awareness of the ferocity with which it would again lay hold of them if given the chance. Still, the darkness of our enemy bears no degrees; he hates a casual dabbler as fervently as the hopelessly ensnared.

Whoever is seeking and most desperately surrounded by the darkness will more quickly recognize God's light when they see it **(Psalms 36:9 NASB)**.

The one who had lost all hope, was most utterly aware of the pit and its gravity, and who fully understood the total impossibility of escape, did ever more readily lay hold of the life-line found in God's forgiveness **(Psalms 107:17-20 NASB)**.

Those who are most poisoned and laden by the indentured nature of slavery's deep wounds do more gratefully see any deliverance from beneath the enemy's whips. They are the poor, the crippled, the blind, and the lame. They are those on the highway and along the fringes who are compelled by Jesus' love, who lead the procession to his table and most heartily eat of the feast laid before them **(Luke 14:15-23 NIV)**.

"Turning toward the woman, He said to Simon, 'Do you see this woman? I entered your house; you gave Me no water for My feet, but she has wet My feet with her tears and wiped them with her hair. You gave Me no kiss; but she, since the time I came in, has

not ceased to kiss My feet. You did not anoint My head with oil, but she anointed My feet with perfume'." (Luke 7:44-46 NASB)

Her tears are those of an unbound heart's deep understanding of the freedom in forgiveness. Her kisses are those from lips deemed long-abandoned by hope's gentle caress, though now suddenly and inconceivably they are cleansed. Her anointing is the singular compulsion of a spirit once broken and sullied beyond all recompense, now gratuitously and unaffectedly made perfect by perfect Love.

"'For this reason I say to you, her sins, which are many, have been forgiven, for she loved much; but he who is forgiven little, loves little.' Then he said to her, 'Your sins have been forgiven'." (Luke 7:47-48 NASB)

Prayer: *Thank you Lord, that I have been set free for freedom's sake. You made me free, though I could never have done anything to earn or deserve it. You poured out mercy for love's sake. You gave your life though I could never have done anything to earn or deserve it. You gave your life in humility. You died for the sake of obedience, though you never did anything to earn or deserve death. I am forgiven because you were forsaken. You knew the cost of it before you ever came. You knew the price on my head before I ever even understood the love that paid it. But you still came, Lord, and I am set free by your blood shed for me on the Cross. Lord help me to follow your example every day. Help me to humble myself and forgive in every way just as I have been forgiven. In Jesus' name I ask it, Amen!*

Scripture: **"Let all bitterness and wrath and anger and clamor and slander be put away from you, along with all malice. Be kind to one another, tender-hearted, forgiving each other, just as God in Christ also has forgiven you" (Ephesians 4:31-32 NASB)**

CHAPTER 11

FREEDOM

It's a choice. Choose wisely!

"It was for freedom that Christ set us free; therefore keep standing firm and do not be subject again to a yoke of slavery." (Galatians 5:1 NASB)

When we become free, it doesn't mean that the world, the circumstances of life, and our enemy the devil will still not do their best to convince us we are not free. I am writing this to declare that anything still holding you in bondage is a lie. I want to tell you that in Christ you have a choice. So throw off that crud and receive from God today. His plans for you are always for your good! To prepare yourself, imagine that disgusting "Edgar suit" in the first "Men in Black" movie. This is the pop culture equivalent of our old nature, our grave clothes. Here are a few Bible verses to tie it together.

"And no one puts new wine into old wineskins; otherwise the new wine will burst the skins and it will be spilled out, and the skins will be ruined. But new wine must be put into fresh wineskins." (Luke 5:37-38 NASB)

"You were taught, with regard to your former way of life, to put off your old self, which is being corrupted by its deceitful desires; to be made new in the attitude of your minds; and to put on the new self, created to be like God in true righteousness and holiness" (Ephesians 4:22-24 NIV)

We humans tend to make the huge decision in accepting Jesus Christ, then forget rather expediently that we are free and why. We say "Yes" to his love that disremembers all of the mess we used to be caught up in, but we tend to overlook the most important part of the transaction. God takes our old self and puts it to death. When we confess our sins, repent, and ask Jesus to be Lord and Savior of our lives, we are literally, inwardly crucified with Christ **(Galatians 2:20 NASB).**

"If Christ is in you, though the body is dead because of sin, yet the spirit is alive because of righteousness." (Romans 8:10 NASB)

So no more "Edgar suits," okay? That which is old cannot and should not be put on over what is new, anymore than our old nature coexists with our new one. Wow! Right? But wait; we're not done yet! What are we then called to do? And why?

"So in Christ Jesus you are all children of God through faith, for *all of you who were baptized into Christ have clothed yourselves with Christ.*" (Galatians 3:26-27 NIV)

"Rather, clothe yourselves with the Lord Jesus Christ, *and do not think about how to gratify the desires of the flesh.*" (Romans 13:14 NIV)

"...work out your salvation with fear and trembling; *for it is God who is at work in you, both to will and to work for His good pleasure.*" (Philippians 2:12-13 NASB)

In case you have yet to hear it, the story of *The Elephant and the String* makes a great point about freedom, so here goes.

On the day a new elephant is born, the training method of East Asian "mahouts" has been to tie one end of a thick rope to the elephant's neck or leg, and the other to a stake planted deeply in the ground. From birth, the young elephant struggles and fights to free itself—day after day, month after month, and year after year. But the overwhelming rope eventually conquers the young elephant, as at some point in its life, it gives up, stops resisting, and stops fighting. From that day forth, the trainer replaces the thick rope with a thin string, and the elephant continues living under the belief that it cannot defeat the rope. Whenever the elephant feels the familiar tightening of the string (albeit much softer), it is reminded of the rope and gently moves back to the center of its radius. I was fascinated upon hearing this story again, and I had to ask myself, what types of ropes do we unwittingly place around our own necks? Are there strings now placed there, out of convention, that we are completely unaware of?

120

How unfortunate a reality it must be, to live in our own captivity, without even knowing it.—Tekoa De Silva

Similarly, once we have been set free by God's grace from every bondage imaginable, we are often content to remain dressed in grave clothes. The jail door is unlocked, the jailer is long gone—a defeated foe. But for fear of losing what little comfort we have in a cold and dank cell, we are yet unwilling to get up, walk out, and live the life God intended. So always remember, your freedom in Jesus Christ is here, NOW, and it's not going anywhere!!

"So if the Son sets you free, you will be free indeed." (John 8:36 NIV)

There are even generational burdens that will keep us artificially staked down if we're not intentional about truly living out our freedom. From the very obvious burdens like addiction, vanity, and anger, to those more subtle but sometimes equally powerful things, there are layers behind the layers, and they become the afflictions that really weigh us down sometimes when we're praying. We may not even be able to name them, but they influence our decisions and intentions. By our actions and agreement to give them space in our hearts, they limit our ability to be effective for God. They rob us of joy and stifle our progress when we choose to allow them to have sway in our lives.

I would wager that if you took the time to search yourself and asked God to help you to see, at least one such burden you had otherwise completely overlooked would come to the surface. At least one thing you just can't seem to shake, that brings out the worst in you, would come to the forefront of your heart and mind. Any takers?

Well, I can tell you two things for sure. One is that if you decide to do the work, God is faithful and will do his part by removing every obstacle between you and him. The second is that, because you have a choice, you can emphatically say, NO! I don't mean just a regular response of "no." I mean you can now bring all of the power of God in Jesus Christ to bear over any situation. You have the spiritual authority to disagree with those damaged emotions and the power you may feel they have over you since you are free and walk by faith in the living, enduring Word of God **(Hebrews 4:12-13 NASB), (1 Peter 1:23 NASB).**

"For momentary, light affliction is producing for us an eternal weight of glory far beyond all comparison, while we look not at the things which are seen, but at the things which are not seen; for the things which are seen are temporal, but the things which are not seen are eternal." (2 Corinthians 4:17-18 NASB)

Expose whatever burden God reveals in you to his light; confess it! Even if it doesn't have a name you know, God does know because it has already been dealt with on the Cross. Ask him to reveal it for what it is, then pray and proclaim the freedom and deliverance that is yours **"yesterday, today, and forever" (Hebrews 13:8 NASB)** in the Lord Jesus Christ to be rid of it once and for all.

"But all things become visible when they are exposed by the light, for everything that becomes visible is light." (Ephesians 5:13 NASB)

"For by one sacrifice he has made perfect forever those who are being made holy." (Hebrews 10:14 NIV)

Keep bringing them to God, do that every day until whatever it is subsides; that is the hard part. The easy part is realizing that, even though it may seem so, generational burdens were never yours to hold. They were put upon you by birth, not by choice unless you *continue to choose them.* Release them to God, and maybe not all at once, but steadily as you do it daily, God will break them one by one. He desires that they be broken because he desires intimate relationship with you. He desires your freedom and will break every chain in your life to have you.

"Now the Lord is the Spirit, and where the Spirit of the Lord is, there is freedom" (2 Corinthians 3:17 NIV)

Our freedom really comes down to perspective. It never becomes any less real, nor is God's Word ever any less true. But the way we affirm that perspective by our choices matters. For example, *bad* is bad to the one afflicted; no matter the severity, we all experience it subjectively. A proper perspective is clarity. Not in the way that it invalidates the personal and experiential in our lives, but only relative to circumstances and the choices we make to believe God or not.

"Consider what God has done: Who can straighten what he has made crooked? When times are good, be happy; but when times are bad, consider this: God has made the one as well as the other. Therefore, no one can discover anything about their future." (Ecclesiastes 7:13-14 NIV)

Regardless of the situation, if we are honest, whether young or old, wise or foolish, male or female, rich or poor, it comes down to choice. We are, through the Holy Spirit, enabled to distinguish right and wrong by the evidence—by the fruit that is produced. We can tell the difference because we are now his. As we become more and more sensitive to what God desires for us, that which is beneficial and that which is harmful both become all the more recognizable. In the midst of our daily wanderings, that sort of choice may not always present itself in such an obvious manner. But absent the irrevocable nature of force or finality, we can be certain there will always be a choice for us to make. That is why it says that apart from him **"no one can discover anything about their future."** However, concerning our freedom and our future, that choice is always found in Jesus, we are now able to know since his Word says we can.

"But he who is spiritual appraises all things, yet he himself is appraised by no one. For WHO HAS KNOWN THE MIND OF THE LORD, THAT HE WILL INSTRUCT HIM? *But we have the mind of Christ."* **(1 Corinthians 2:15-16 NASB)**

"But when He, the Spirit of truth, comes, He will guide you into all the truth; for He will not speak on His own initiative, but

whatever He hears, He will speak; and He will disclose to you what is to come." (John 16:13 NASB)

God never tempts us, nor can he be tempted. But he does continually allow us a clear option. He always sees, he always gives us strength to carry the burden, generational or otherwise, and then shows us an exit. Lastly (*and this is important*), he never allows us to be tempted beyond what we are able. This again, in considering all that we can know, puts the weight of decision squarely on our shoulders. Why? Because we have his Spirit to guide us, his Word to fight with, and we are free to choose ... period.

"Let no one say when he is tempted, 'I am being tempted by God'; for God cannot be tempted by evil, and he himself does not tempt anyone." (James 1:13 NASB)

"No temptation has overtaken you but such as is common to man; and God is faithful, who will not allow you to be tempted beyond what you are able, but with the temptation will provide the way of escape also, so that you will be able to endure it." (1 Corinthians 10:13 NASB)

Freedom isn't free

Freedom in Christ says *"come," "rest,"* then *"go" and "do."* On the face of it, it seems like a strange dichotomy, but it really makes perfect sense. The way our heavenly Father has ordered things in the universe, everything has a cost, and freedom is no exception. We may not always see the price tag, or have to feel the sting of it personally. But if you get something for free, remember that somewhere somebody, or maybe even a group of somebodies, paid something for you to have it. For instance, the fact that Jesus came and the manner by which he came carried a cost for many, and each one of them had to choose.

"But you, Bethlehem Ephrathah, though you are little among the thousands of Judah, yet out of you shall come forth to me the One to be ruler in Israel, whose goings forth are from of old, from everlasting." (Micah 5:2 NKJV)

The journey to Bethlehem and to the manger is one of faith, obedience, and hope. Mary and Joseph, the wise Magi, and the shepherds that came in from the fields are those the Bible chose to show us as examples. They came by three very different heralds, three very different pathways, and three very different signs. Two things are certain, however: the commonality in their goal, and the inevitability of what they gave along the way.

It cost Joseph his reputation and his livelihood, and it forced him to put aside everything he believed to be right and true. It cost Mary even more; she had to face the disgrace of her family and her entire community. She sacrificed the notions of youth for the allusions and accusations of impurity and adultery. The road to Bethlehem for them was unwavering faith from beginning to end **(Luke 1:26-38 NIV), (Matthew 1:18-25 NIV), Luke 2:1-7 NIV)**.

The Magi (*wise men*) came 900 miles from Persia since they had read the prophecies about a king and his star. They were likely ridiculed by their peers and certainly beleaguered by the desert they crossed, but they listened when God said "Go," and they followed the guiding star rather than giving in to fear or giving any weight to the words of men. The road to Bethlehem for them was total obedience from beginning to end **(Daniel 2:44 NASB), (Numbers 24:17 NASB), (Matthew 2:9 NASB)**.

The shepherds were poor men of low position who understood sacrifice and humility. They were Jews who knew that God had promised them a Messiah, a Savior. So they were waiting—convinced of what God had said and patiently anticipating when it would to come to pass. Living far from the trappings of the city, they immediately recognized what was happening when a familiar silence was broken first by the voice of one messenger, and then a sky that quite literally exploded into the songs of heaven declaring an end to their long and faithful abiding. They had no good standing to lose, and their walk in from the fields was, I would expect, rather brief. The road to Bethlehem for them was an unyielding attendance to hope **(Deuteronomy 18:15 NIV), (Isaiah 9:6-7 NASB), (Luke 2:8-16 NASB)**.

As they all arrived in their own way, the Bible tells us they also exalted Jesus, each in their own way. The shepherds praised and glorified God at what they had seen. The Magi were overjoyed, and they humbled themselves before him. Joseph saw the Word of God become flesh in front of his eyes, and Mary treasured up all these things in her heart to ponder them. In these three accounts, we can be sure that by the journey to the manger and the road to Bethlehem their lives were forever changed. Surely they each sacrificed something to get there. Surely even that paled in comparison to what they saw when they first beheld the face of Jesus.

So will you make the journey? Will you travel the road? Will you count the cost and give all that is relative to you for the freedom God has given you in return?

"The people walking in darkness have seen a great light; on those living in the land of deep darkness a light has dawned." (Isaiah 9:2 NIV)

Free from what? Why?

"This is what the Lord says: 'In the time of my favor I will answer you, and in the day of salvation I will help you; I will keep you and will make you to be a covenant for the people, to restore the land and to reassign its desolate inheritances, to say to the captives, "Come out," and to those in darkness, "Be free!"'" (Isaiah 49:8-9 NIV)

What are we free from? If you know the Love of Jesus Christ, the answer, in truth is, everything.

"Therefore, if anyone is in Christ, the new creation has come: The old has gone, the new is here! All this is from God, who reconciled us to himself through Christ and gave us the ministry of reconciliation: that God was reconciling the world to himself in Christ, not counting people's sins against them. And he has committed to us the message of reconciliation." (2 Corinthians 5:17-19 NIV)

"Why freedom?" and "Why us?" Well, if you ever had any doubt, let me be the first to let you know. All of the pride that deceives you and says your life is your own, that says you are owed this time to live, walk, talk, and breath is a fabrication. The arrogance that holds your despotic will in such high esteem also sets your table with lust and calls it love. It justifies every kind of dark thing imaginable to hold you in bondage, then it calls itself freedom. But no darkness can stand in the presence of the King of kings.

Every one of you who has attempted to gratify yourself in this way knows in your heart of hearts that these words are true. When the façade is torn down and the hollow, voracious wind of vanity has accomplished its end, in that moment we see sin as sin and life as life. God in his mercy, at our weakest moments, sets the two opposites at our feet with the free will to choose. He says **"choose life,"** but he won't ever force us **(Deuteronomy 30:19 NASB)**. The apostle Paul says that a **"new creation"** is the only thing that matters **(Galatians 6:15 NASB)**. He admonishes us not to deal with anyone according to the flesh **(2 Corinthians 5:16 NASB)**. But why?

"For the love of Christ controls us, having concluded this, that one died for all, therefore all died; and He died for all, so that they who live might no longer live for themselves, but for Him who died and rose again on their behalf." (2 Corinthians 5:14-15 NASB)

So if we truly *live*, we believe the truth and live in love, with no regrets, whether by rejoicing or in sorrow. We live the life of Jesus for his glory. But equally as important to God is his desire for us to see that **"the old things"** are fake and a lie. That which once defined us is now crucified with Christ **(Galatians 2:20 NASB)**. Fear, lust, pride, anger, depression, selfishness, no longer rule, but only **"a new creation."**

Charles Stanley, a renowned pastor, once asked this question in a sermon: *Do you have any "if I'das" in your life?* His point was, what have we not done, and what won't we do that we know God is calling us to do? Or rather, what would we do if we had no fear? How would we love and speak to people? What would our goals be if we stopped viewing ourselves, others, and what we can accomplish, according to what we used to be? Since our identity and worth are now in Christ alone, and not in the opinions and judgments of the world, there is no more condemnation, no more guilt, no more shame, and no more regret **(Romans 8:1 NASB), (Philippians 4:12-13 NASB, (Colossians 3:2-3 NIV), (1 Corinthians 4:3-4 NIV)**.

"Therefore, since we have so great a cloud of witnesses surrounding us, let us also lay aside every encumbrance and the sin which so easily entangles us, and let us run with endurance the race that is set before us, fixing our eyes on Jesus, the author and perfecter of our faith." (Hebrews 12:1-2 NASB)

"In almost everything that touches our everyday life on earth, God is pleased when we're pleased. He wills that we be as free as birds to soar and sing our maker's praise without anxiety."—A. W. Tozer

"Suddenly there was such a violent earthquake that the foundations of the prison were shaken. At once all the prison doors flew open, and everyone's chains came loose." (Acts 16:26 NIV)

Where there is prayer, worshiping, and singing praises to God, his Spirit moves powerfully. When the Spirit of Jesus Christ moves, freedom happens. It is no coincidence that the one prominent Old Testament scripture Jesus read aloud in front of everyone in the congregation was this one:

"The Spirit of the Lord God is upon me, because the Lord has anointed me to bring good news to the afflicted; he has sent me to bind up the brokenhearted, to proclaim liberty to captives and freedom to prisoners; to proclaim the favorable year of the Lord." (Isaiah 61:1-2 NASB)

Captivity and affliction, like real freedom and liberty, come in many different shapes and sizes, but we will only ever buy one brand of either. Our enemy deals in death, and he peddles his wares so candidly that we would nearly miss them were it not for our familiarity with their reek. Our Father God deals in life, and he offers his freedom to us perfectly. So perfectly, in fact, that we may oft times take it for granted were it not alight and alive in such stark contrast to the artificial, ever elusive, dangling keys of the jailer. The famous are those hidden in plain sight, the infamous however unsuccessfully, just hide **(1 Corinthians 1:20, 27-29 NASB)**.

Reality is that there are many iron gates, shackles, and fortresses in the world, but there is only One who makes them level ground, removes our every bond, and causes the most rusty prison gates to swing wide. We call upon a Savior in Jesus who offers beauty for ashes. We sing with gladness to a Spirit who offers comfort and wisdom from heaven. We praise God who offers perfect peace without condition or any demand of recompense to all who seek him. Freedom is the immutable and immediate evidence of a soul once dead, now made alive. Freedom is a daily choice, because in Jesus it becomes where we have chosen to live.

"Since the children have flesh and blood, he too shared in their humanity so that by his death he might break the power of him who holds the power of death—that is, the devil— and free those who all their lives were held in slavery by their fear of death." (Hebrews 2:14-15 NIV)

"But God doesn't call us to be comfortable. He calls us to trust him so completely that we are unafraid to put ourselves in situations where we will be in trouble if he doesn't come through."—Francis Chan

"Go, stand and speak to the people in the temple the whole message of this life." (Acts 5:20 NASB)

It really is for freedom you are free. How about thinking of it this way though: It is not for your freedom alone that you are set free **(Galatians 5:1 NIV)**. *"Go," "Stand,"* and *"Speak."* To whom do we speak? To each other? To ourselves? No, to **the people**. Speak only one word? Speak only a few words? No, **the whole message of this life**. We are made free to be free, then to go and declare that freedom. Our challenge, our obligation, is just that, and it really can be challenging. Our enemy impersonates it, our flesh resists it, and the loudest voices we can hear most days are those which agree with both the impersonation and the resistance, and then call our true declaration nonsense. Since we are free, however, we are also mightily clad in heavenly armor to stand firm and speak the truth in Love, **"the whole message of this life,"** as God intended it **(Ephesians 6:10-18 NASB), (Ephesians 4:15 NASB).**

"But we have this treasure in jars of clay to show that this all-surpassing power is from God and not from us." (2 Corinthians 4:7 NIV)

Once again, this time in the context of freedom, I'll ask you to consider this idea for a moment: If our purpose on this earth were only our own salvation, the earth would be empty of all those who have trusted in Jesus until now, wouldn't it? There would be no reason for God to keep us here, would there?

"But you are a chosen people, a royal priesthood, a holy nation, God's special possession, that you may declare the praises of him who called you out of darkness into his wonderful light." (1 Peter 2:9 NIV)

Prayer: *Thank you, Lord, for the true freedom that only comes from you. I am grateful every day. I am humbled in the midst of every prayer when I consider you, Abba. Freedom, in beginnings and in endings, freedom in trials and in victory—I find it everywhere now, Father, but always as I surrender to you and trust you. It is a freedom to be authentically yours and to be the person you made me. Though I still fail and fall, my heart of hearts no longer hungers and thirsts after selfishness and satisfaction for my flesh. By the grace of Jesus Christ, I hunger and thirst for righteousness. Where my heart was once darkness that allowed hints of light to slip through, it is now light in the Lord and able by the Holy Spirit to discern and see the dark places and resist them. You have turned my heart inside out, Abba Father, and I am full with praise and adoration to you. Thank you that I am irrevocably free because you have made it so. Thank you, Lord, that as I seek your way over mine, it is your life in me that shines so that you alone receive honor and you alone are magnified by the transformed heart and mind that I am gifted in your son Jesus Christ. I love you Lord! Amen.*

Scripture: "**Now what I am commanding you today is not too difficult for you or beyond your reach. It is not up in heaven, so that you have to ask, 'Who will ascend into heaven to get it and proclaim it to us so we may obey it?' Nor is it beyond the sea, so that you have to ask, 'Who will cross the sea to get it and proclaim it to us so we may obey it?' No, the word is very near you; it is in your mouth and in your heart so you may obey it. See, I set before you today life and prosperity, death and destruction. For I command you today to love the LORD your God, to walk in obedience to him, and to keep his commands, decrees and laws; then you will live and increase, and the LORD your God will bless you ...**" (Deuteronomy 30:11-16 NIV)

"**You, my brothers and sisters, were called to be free. But do not use your freedom to indulge the flesh; rather, serve one another humbly in love. For the entire law is fulfilled in keeping this one command: 'Love your neighbor as yourself'.**" (Galatians 5:13-14 NIV)

CHAPTER 12

OBEDIENCE

Because it's just plain "better"

"For we know that the whole creation groans and suffers the pains of childbirth together until now. And not only this, but also we ourselves, having the first fruits of the Spirit, even we ourselves groan within ourselves, waiting eagerly for our adoption as sons, the redemption of our body. For in hope we have been saved, but hope that is seen is not hope; for who hopes for what he already sees? But if we hope for what we do not see, with perseverance we wait eagerly for it." (Romans 8:22-25 NASB)

These verses jumped off the page as I read them, because I realized that my spirit does groan inwardly and often. Lately my issue has been patience. It is the finest of dichotomies, in that I desire above all things to be perfectly intimate with God, but I must be *willing* to forfeit all that I desire in life to get there. I petition my Savior to see him face to face *now* and to know him as I am fully known by him *today*. But to arrive safely and in one piece, the road I travel must be his rather than mine. As I offer my own petitions, I yearn all the more with God's heart to shout his love to every ear that would hear his voice and respond. Indeed, it is because of Jesus' handiwork in my life I deeply desire to be where he is, but it is also because of his life alive in me that I always end up right where he wants me. Obedience. So in that I begin to understand why Paul says:

"For to me, to live is Christ and to die is gain." (Philippians 1:21 NASB)

I begin to understand why Jesus said:

"For them I sanctify myself, that they too may be truly sanctified." (John 17:19 NIV)

And I begin to understand the necessity in this truth that Christ proclaimed:

""If anyone wishes to come after Me, he must deny himself, and take up his cross and follow Me ..." (Mark 8:34 NASB)

I am, by obedience in love, being continually sanctified by my Lord and Savior, by the beauty in any momentary affliction I suffer for his sake. I am in that deference to his will, in his way, drawing ever nearer to perfection until the day he calls me home.

"The Spirit himself testifies with our spirit that we are God's children. Now if we are children, then we are heirs—heirs of God and coheirs with Christ, if indeed we share in his sufferings in order that we may also share in his glory." (Romans 8:16-17 NIV)

"The true follower of Christ will not ask, 'If I embrace this truth, what will it cost me?' Rather he will say, 'This is truth. God help me to walk in it, let come what may!'"—A. W. Tozer

"But if serving the Lord seems undesirable to you, then choose for yourselves this day whom you will serve, whether the gods your ancestors served beyond the Euphrates, or the gods of the Amorites, in whose land you are living. *But as for me and my household, we will serve the Lord."* (Joshua 24:15 NIV)

The debt of love and humility is obedience to God. His love that clothes us is the armor of light.

"Owe nothing to anyone except to love one another; for he who loves his neighbor has fulfilled the law ... Love does no wrong to a neighbor; therefore love is the fulfillment of the law." (Romans 13:8, 10 NASB)

The armor of light is obedience to God expressing itself through his love aptly lived out. His love in action is what it means to "put on" the Lord Jesus Christ daily.

"Do this, knowing the time, that it is already the hour for you to awaken from sleep; for now salvation is nearer to us than when we believed. The night is almost gone, and the day is near. Therefore let us lay aside the deeds of darkness and *put on the armor of light*, … But *put on the Lord Jesus Christ*, and make no provision for the flesh in regard to its lusts." (Romans 13:11, 12, 14 NASB)

I am unashamedly a willing bond-slave of Jesus Christ, a servant of God. Not because, if I step out of line, he will strike me down, or because I am afraid that he will not accept me unless I am a perfect person. I yield all to God in Christ because that love who spoke the universe into existence, who IS infinite and perfect, reaches down into my finite life and heals me every single day. I was blind; I now see. I was burdened; now I am free. I was lost; now I am found in him. So I obey, as a slave. I serve as one who owes a debt—not because I must but because he IS.

"At the Lord's command the Israelites set out, and at his command they encamped. As long as the cloud stayed over the tabernacle, they remained in camp. When the cloud remained over the tabernacle a long time, the Israelites obeyed the Lord's order and did not set out. Sometimes the cloud was over the tabernacle only a few days; at the Lord's command they would encamp, and then at his command they would set out. Sometimes the cloud stayed only from evening till morning, and when it lifted in the morning, they set out. Whether by day or by night, whenever the cloud lifted, they set out. Whether the cloud stayed over the tabernacle for two days or a month or a year, the Israelites would remain in camp and not set out; but when it lifted, they would set out. At the Lord's command they encamped, and at the Lord's command

they set out. They obeyed the Lord's order, in accordance with his command through Moses" (Numbers 9:18-23 NIV)

I read this, and it screamed simple and pure faith in who God was to the Israelites and who he is now to us. God told them through Moses to move when he moved, to stay when he stayed, and everything would be straight. Whenever they obeyed God, they were fed, clothed, and protected. Whenever they tried to go on ahead of him, they died and were lost. The weight of the above verse is really important, in that they literally traced every step God took and mimicked every move he made. If God was not going before them, they just did not go. The important thing is to see that, for Israel, it was "**in accordance with his command through Moses.**" For us today, it is not by the command of God through a person, because if we know Jesus as Savior, it is the Holy Spirit (the cloud and pillar of fire), the very presence of God that lives in us, who compels us to obedience. Why? Because it's just plain better!

"**And I will ask the Father, and he will give you another advocate to help you and be with you forever—the Spirit of truth. The world cannot accept him, because it neither sees him nor knows him. But you know him, for he lives with you and will be in you. I will not leave you as orphans; I will come to you ... But the Advocate, the Holy Spirit, whom the Father will send in my name, will teach you all things and will remind you of everything I have said to you." (John 14:16-18, 26 NIV)**

"**But when he, the Spirit of truth, comes, he will guide you into all the truth. He will not speak on his own; he will speak only what he hears, and he will tell you what is yet to come. He will glorify me because it is from me that he will receive what he will make known to you." (John 16:13-14 NIV)**

"**The wind blows wherever it pleases. You hear its sound, but you cannot tell where it comes from or where it is going. So it is with everyone born of the Spirit." (John 3:8 NIV)**

We are now "the Church." We now have the choice, we now have the Advocate, and we now have forgiveness and mercy when our desert legs and wilderness hearts fail us. Praise God for his grace in speaking so we can hear him. We develop an ear to hear him so that where he goes we should go and where he stays we should stay—no matter where, when, or for how long. In him we do not become weary and we do not grow faint. When we come into agreement with his will, we are sharpened, our faith is increased, and we begin to desire nothing but to be with him. Why? Because it's just plain better!

"Behold, to obey is better than sacrifice." (1 Samuel 15:22 NASB)

God's economy vs ours

"Jesus said to them, 'My food is to do the will of him who sent me and to accomplish his work'." (John 4:34 NASB)

Think of all the things you desire during a typical day. Let that sink in, then throw out everything you don't actually need and everything that serves only your own ends. How many essential things were you left with? If you are honest, probably not many—maybe none on your worst days.

Jesus left the above example for two reasons. The first was to point us toward the simple truth that when we turn our energy and focus to getting what we think we need, we are usually badly off course. Even if we get them, the substance is non-existent. The world's things can never fully satisfy us apart from God. The second was to remind us that what does satisfy us is spiritual food, the food that provides all we need when our aim is the desire of God's heart for us.

When our attention is focused on doing his will, the Word of God says he knows our desires. It says that all we could ever ask and more will be given to us when we put him first, when we make much of him rather than ourselves. We will never experience God's blessing more powerfully than when we make our hearts available to him in obedience. He is so full of simple, perfect love for us, if only we have eyes to see it and a heart that longs to hear from him.

"You ask and do not receive, because you ask with wrong motives, so that you may spend it on your pleasures." (James 4:3 NASB)

"But seek first His kingdom and His righteousness, and all these things will be given to you as well." (Matthew 6:33 NASB)

"I am the bread of life" (John 6:48 NASB)

"When humans should have become as perfect in voluntary obedience as the inanimate creation is in its lifeless obedience, then they will put on its glory, or rather that greater glory of which Nature is only the first sketch."—C. S. Lewis

"He who is faithful in a very little thing is faithful also in much; and he who is unrighteous in a very little thing is unrighteous also in much. Therefore if you have not been faithful in the use of unrighteous wealth, who will entrust the true riches to you? And if you have not been faithful in the use of that which is another's, who will give you that which is your own?" (Luke 16:10-12 NASB)

The **"very little thing"** is unrighteous wealth. The true riches are the **"much."** **"That which is another's"** begins for us with God's grace. Once he has shown us our sin, he affords us an opportunity in salvation that we would not otherwise have been given. He then looks on to see how we manage it, or if we pay it any mind at all.

"...work out your salvation with fear and trembling; for it is God who is at work in you, both to will and to work for his good pleasure." (Philippians 2:12-13 NASB)

We make much of the gifts, both spiritual and otherwise, which God gives us here on earth; and rightly so, since they are amazing.

However, they are only a poor reflection, a type and shadow, of the treasure he has for us in heaven. How will we then manage that which is his, that which we were born into, had squandered, and now have been given back a second time by grace?

"Do not lay up for yourselves treasures on earth, where moth and rust destroy and where thieves break in and steal; but lay up for yourselves treasures in heaven, where neither moth nor rust destroys and where thieves do not break in and steal. For where your treasure is, there your heart will be also." (Matthew 6:19-21 NKJV)

Ah, and there we come to it yet again—**your heart.** Are our hearts occupied with heaven and being about the business of our Master, or centered in earthly things of which we are but stewards, and that only for a very short while? Will we be faithful with little so that we receive much in return? Will we be faithful in pouring out his blessing so we receive that which is our own? The importance God places on these questions should be a constant reminder of our position relative to the state in which we may one day find ourselves when he returns, upon his accounting of the way we answer them.

Will it be door #1?

"His lord said to him, 'Well done, good and faithful servant; you were faithful over a few things, I will make you ruler over many things. Enter into the joy of your lord'." (Matthew 25:21 NKJV)

Or door #2?

"For to everyone who has, more will be given, and he will have abundance; but from him who does not have, even what he has will be taken away. And cast the unprofitable servant into the outer darkness." (Matthew 25:29-30 NKJV)

Mark A. Luther

The economy of God measures riches far differently than we do. The blessings are always infinitely better, and the consequences of disobedience are always the result of our choices, a matter of the heart.

Conformity is the new Rebellion

"Why do you call me, 'Lord, Lord,' and do not do what I say?" (Luke 6:46 NASB)

Wow, what a great question! Anybody have an answer? There are likely two possible answers that we need to pay real attention to and seriously consider, if we're looking for the truth. One is misunderstanding, and the other is pride.

We all begin this walk of faith believing and wanting Jesus to be a lot of things—Savior, provider, friend, King, comforter, helper, lover, protector, and the list goes on. But what if it turns out he is all those things, but not in the way we think he is supposed to be? Then what? Well, then we have a choice to make: We can get on about the business of understanding as much as we can and bringing our perception into line with his reality (Obedience), or we can walk away, both literally and spiritually, and bury our heads in the sand by continuing to trust our wisdom over his (Rebellion).

However, there exists such an overwhelming amount of grace and patience in the inexpressible Love who is our God, that he understands all of our weaknesses and all of our foolishness, along with every reason we could ever imagine for entertaining either. By his hand, we were fearfully and wonderfully made; he *gets* us. But he also understands in a way that refuses to abide anything short of life for us, real and true "living" life that is neither veiled nor diluted by ignorance or willful blindness **(Psalm 139 NIV, (Hebrews 4:12-14 NASB).**

To call him "**Lord, Lord,**" to "**believe in him,**" is to know him as he truly is and follow him even when it gets really hard. If we do this and choose him each day, his word says we will not be put to shame

(Romans 10:9-11 NASB). If not, we are left without any good excuse **(Romans 1:18-24 NASB)**.

"He who believes in the Son has eternal life; but he who does not obey the Son will not see life, but the wrath of God abides on him" **(John 3:36 NASB)**.

"I'm in Rebellion. You're just a conformist. Drunken, naked, driving around a loud motorcycle, smoking cigarettes, breaking commandments, getting pregnant outa wedlock, everyone's done that. It's so tiring. If you really wanna be a rebel, read your Bible, because no one's doing that. That's rebellion. That's the only rebellion left."—Lecrae

"Does the Lord delight in burnt offerings and sacrifices as much as in obeying the Lord? To obey is better than sacrifice ..." **(1 Samuel 15:22 NIV)**

What God gives us to do is always for good. This may twist a few people up, but in fact since the former is always true, the greatest good you or I will ever do is to obey God. He sees and knows in a wholly different manner than we do. Obedience matters most, since it is the first and only currency known to heaven.

"For My thoughts are not your thoughts, nor are your ways My ways," declares the Lord. "For as the heavens are higher than the earth, so are My ways higher than your ways and My thoughts than your thoughts." (Isaiah 55:8-9 NASB)

It could be as simple as God saying, *"Be patient and wait for me,"* which might make no sense at all to us at the time. Or it may take the form of the Holy Spirit prompting us to act in love, only not in a way we prefer, or toward a person we don't care very much for at all. The trick is keeping our eyes on God and not the thing. The *what* is never more urgent than the *who* when it comes to God. Still, unenthusiastic obedience to him in what may seem to us like the very mundane is of much greater worth than rebellion of even the noblest sort. We are all apportioned faith for this or that, some stronger, some weaker, some larger, some smaller. But we can always be sure of two things: 1) His commands to us will always fit perfectly within our ability to carry them out, they will never be burdensome **(1 John 5:3 NIV)**. 2) His commands to us will always reflect his character, they will never be condemnation nor will their fruit through us be another's judgment **(Matthew 7:1-5 NASB)**.

"The faith which you have, have as your own conviction before God. Happy is he who does not condemn himself in what he approves." (Romans 14:22 NASB)

If we closely examine both his Word and our lives, it will become wonderfully clear that God's most adamant calls for obedience almost always exist as a codicil of sorts to our faith and his most precious gifts to us. There are a lot of examples, but these are the best of all **(John 3:16), (Romans 10:8-10 NASB)**.

"Let no debt remain outstanding, except the continuing debt to love one another, for whoever loves others has fulfilled the law. ... Love does no harm to a neighbor. Therefore love is the fulfillment of the law" (Romans 13:8, 10 NIV)

Prayer: *Thank you for your Spirit, Lord, and that your command to me is not burdensome but a joy to obey. Thank you, Father, that among the many other ways, I can know I'm yours by the pruning you continue to do each day. You call me to be an imitator of Jesus, and I am grateful for the way you deal with my weakness in desiring the esteem and attention of others over yours. I am reminded that, when you came, the world did not esteem you, and that if the world hated you, there is a good chance it will hate me also. I am reminded that you admonish all who would come after you in saying that we must be willing to take up whatever cross there is to bear, to know the truth that forgoing everything save a perfect intimacy with you IS the only version of a life worth saving. Lord, you call me friend because my heart has heard and obeyed. Obedience from a desire to please you, to return your affections, from the excitement and wonder that desires to know you better and better each day. Obedience because in the presence of such a perfect love as yours, Jesus, there is no other response. In that, the currency of heaven, I receive all of my esteem from you and that is more than enough. So I will walk this line today and every day, Abba, being full of joy and your light! Father, I humble myself before the Cross and recognize that your thoughts are not mine any more than your ways are my ways. I acknowledge that there are things I will rightly never know or understand. But still I trust you and rest in you, Lord. I make nothing of myself or my deeds so that in every way all glory and honor belongs to you. Give me ears to hear the desire of your heart, Lord, which is more dear and precious beyond anything I could ask or imagine for myself. Give me grace to love what you love and the courage to be tipped and poured out even as I am filled and enveloped by your favor. In Jesus' name, Amen.*

Scripture: "**Therefore I urge you, brethren, by the mercies of God, to present your bodies a living and holy sacrifice, acceptable to God, which is your spiritual service of worship. And do not be conformed to this world, but be transformed by the renewing of your mind, so that you may prove what the will of God is, that which is good and acceptable and perfect.**" **(Romans 12:1-2 NASB)**

CHAPTER 13

TRUST

Trust but verify

"My soul, wait silently for God alone, For my expectation is from Him." (Psalms 62:5 NKJV)

God is always teaching me to rely completely on him, and to trust in him and believe for every awesome gift he has in store. I had a breakthrough in prayer at a men's group a short time ago while we were talking about being led by the Holy Spirit. The conversation turned to the question, *"How do we really know if it's God's Spirit or not?"* My two cents worth was (and I think God broke through as I heard myself say it) that the only way I know is literally to hit my knees before I do anything else in the morning. There is no better way to start a day than being totally open, transparent, and laid bare before God. So I let God do heart surgery before my day even begins, and the Great Physician's hands are always steady, his healing always sure, and wholeness always follows. In those quiet moments I can be sure it's his Spirit, because when he speaks to my heart, I know his voice **(John 10:27-28 NASB)**. I know his voice because my spirit leaps when I hear it. I can be sure, because by reading his Word, I know his character **(1 John 4:1-6 NASB)**. But all of that begins and ends with trust.

"Now faith is the substance of things hoped for, the evidence of things not seen." (Hebrews 11:1, NKJV)

"In you, Lord my God, I put my trust. I trust in you; do not let me be put to shame, nor let my enemies triumph over me. No one who hopes in you will ever be put to shame, but shame will come on those who are treacherous without cause. Show me your ways, Lord, teach me your paths. Guide me in your truth and teach me, for you are God my Savior, and my hope is in you all day long." (Psalms 25:1-5 NIV)

"There is no way to peace along the way of safety. For peace must be dared; it is itself the great venture and can never be safe. Peace is the opposite of security. To demand guarantees is to want to protect oneself. Peace means giving oneself completely to God's commandment, wanting no security."—Dietrich Bonhoeffer

"Cease striving and know that I am God; I will be exalted among the nations, I will be exalted in the earth." (Psalms 46:10 NASB)

Other versions of the Bible say, "**Be still.**" The above is from the New American Standard Bible which is considered a more literal translation. "**Cease striving**" certainly has a distinctly different ring to it. "**Cease**" covers "**Be still**" all on its own, but what about the striving part? What is it to "strive"? I looked it up and here are two of the definitions I found:

"Make great efforts to achieve or obtain something."

"Struggle or fight vigorously."

If we push that up against our daily lives, it's easy to understand what God meant to say through the psalmist. In order to be still, striving must cease, and that doesn't happen all by itself. If we are honest, our version of being still does not often include anything that resembles dropping all we're after just to be silent and remember who God is or to listen for his voice.

If you pray at all, I'm sure you've asked to hear from God and expected an answer. But have you actually stopped talking, moving, and doing long enough to hear his response? It's not as easy as you may think, even in deep prayer. But that is exactly the idea. If you desire to know God and to know he is God, such knowledge requires something of you. Professed faith by its nature pushes back on your heart and asks, *"What do you really believe?"*—right where the rubber meets the road in your life. Is he God in the trial as well as in the blessing? Will you hear him even if the answer is unpleasant or difficult to accept? The only way to know is to try it, to "**cease striving,**" and cut off all the noise. It may be the hardest thing you have ever done, but you'll be pleasantly surprised by what happens next.

"Glory in his holy name; let the heart of those who seek the Lord be glad. Seek the Lord and his strength; seek his face continually. Remember his wonderful deeds which he has done, his marvels and the judgments from his mouth." (1 Chronicles 16:10-12 NASB)

Lately God has been stirring a desire in me to more clearly see the beauty of his unchanging nature in disparity to the vacillating nature of my heart apart from him. He is, always has been, and always will be everything he declares about himself. However, on my own I am fickle, indecisive, and always wavering in one form or another. Fellowship with him, along with his instruction, is the mooring line tethering me to his omniscience and to stability in this daily walk through life. Our God who reigns, unlike humans who reign, gives his commands not to gain power (*as if he needed anything FROM me*), but to empower those who trust, follow, and obey him. This is a stark contrast, and I believe it is the reason why most people miss it, or more accurately, miss him.

God said to Moses, "I AM WHO I AM. This is what you are to say to the Israelites: 'I AM has sent me to you.'" God also said to Moses, "Say to the Israelites, 'The Lord, the God of your fathers—the God of Abraham, the God of Isaac and the God of Jacob—has sent me to you.' This is my name forever, the name by which I am to be remembered from generation to generation." (Exodus 3:14-15 NIV)

"Your word, O Lord, is eternal; it stands firm in the heavens. Your faithfulness continues through all generations; you established the earth, and it endures. Your laws endure to this day, for all things serve you." (Psalm 119:89-91 NIV)

"Jesus Christ is the same yesterday and today and forever." (Hebrews 13:8 NIV)

For many years I missed the point. It cost me, and the people around me, much lost time and a lot of pain along the way. Thanks be to God for his mercy; now I can say I am his freed man **(1 Corinthians 7:22 NASB)**.

"If any of you lacks wisdom, you should ask God, who gives generously to all without finding fault, and it will be given to you. But when you ask, you must believe and not doubt, because the one who doubts is like a wave of the sea, blown and tossed by the wind. That person should not expect to receive anything from the Lord; such a person is doubleminded and unstable in all they do." (James 1:5-8 NIV)

The very freedom we desire comes when we not only trust in, but also do, what God says. Therein lies the "mooring line" I spoke about earlier. When our hearts are firmly secured to the Rock, liberation always follows close behind.

"And He was saying to them all, "If anyone wishes to come after Me, he must deny himself, and take up his cross daily and follow Me. For whoever wishes to save his life will lose it, but whoever loses his life for My sake, he is the one who will save it.'" (Luke 9:23, 24 NASB)

He is unchanging, and his mercy is never ending. It is worth saying again: If we lack wisdom, we should certainly ask him, and he will give it to us generously, without finding fault. I am living proof of that fact.

With ALL my heart?

"Yet you do not know what your life will be like tomorrow. You are just a vapor that appears for a little while and then vanishes away." (James 4:14 NASB)

It occurs to me that if we are just a vapor, then our circumstances, problems, and afflictions, our joys, triumphs, and proud moments are only the mist that makes up that vapor. What God showed me was this: Enjoy the time you have and the people you love. "**Casting all of your anxieties on him because he cares for you**" **(1 Peter 5:7 NASB).** Don't allow the cares of this life to steal away any of the moments you've been given! God is on the throne, and he has you!

"**Do not fear, for I am with you; do not anxiously look about you, for I am your God. I will strengthen you, surely I will help you, surely I will uphold you with My righteous right hand.**" **(Isaiah 41:10 NASB)**

"**As for God, his way is perfect: The Lord's word is flawless; he shields all who take refuge in him.**" **(2 Samuel 22:31 NIV)**

A beautiful thing happened to me, and through me, in the Fall of 2013. It came in the form of revelation, as a gift from God, to a friend of mine. She is in a season of life that is testing her trust and faith in God. She is having to ask hard life questions, and sometimes the answers aren't coming in a way she wants them to come. Every time we talk I can clearly hear the pain in her voice. Her laboring to have God make sense of the things she is experiencing is palpable. God's Word says, "**'For My thoughts are not your thoughts, nor are your ways My ways,' declares the LORD.**" **(Isaiah 55:8 NASB)**

Have you ever been asked a question by, or been in a situation with, your child that required a difficult answer or explanation? Maybe it was one that came easily to you, but no matter how you tried to frame it, it would never make sense from their limited perspective. Sometimes as their parent(s), we just know that the correct answers to certain questions aren't ever going to be reasonable. They are simply beyond a child's ability to rationalize. All we can do is reassure them, gather them up in our arms, hold onto them, and love them through their pain and confusion. As his children, we confront God with those types of questions every day, because every day we live in this fallen world. Horrible, confusing, and seemingly inexplicable things consistently happen around us, to us, and to those we love.

As an example, God showed me my love and compassion for my daughter as she confronted the death of her Nana at age fourteen. It was the same love and compassion I had for my son when he was forced to confront the reality of divorce as a young boy of eight. I saw in that same moment that my friend's situations are not so dissimilar. For her, the inexplicable is dealing with the failing mental health of an aging parent, and her bewilderment is also in the helplessness of watching her family emotionally disintegrate through the realities of a broken marriage. Her heart is no less burdened than my children's were, nor is she any more able to make sense of her circumstances.

The only inequity at all is in God's love and compassion for his hurting child. His love far surpasses even the deepest I could have ever offered my children. So with that in mind, I want to say a few things to anyone reading this who may have recently been hit right where they are living, anyone who is feeling knocked down, crushed, perplexed, or abandoned by God, anyone who is having trouble trusting him because there just is no easy answer, and it hurts.

Start from here: God is always, always, always good. No exceptions. If you are not hearing any answers from him, stop for a moment and consider the question(s). Is the only answer a "Dad" or "Mom" answer that a child could never understand? Always remember that his Love is such that he feels every pang with you. He sees every tear that falls. He hears your heart scream in desperation as you try to make sense of what is happening, and he hurts with you and for you in the way that only a loving parent could. Consider the way you react when your children come running into your arms while crying. You instinctively know what to do because they are yours; you belong to them and they belong to you. Run right now with abandon into the arms of God. If he isn't answering, it may be because he can't, or if he could you'd never be able to make sense of it anyway. I promise he knows just what to do because you are his. You belong to him and he belongs to you. Trust him, and he will reassure you, gather you up in his arms, hold onto you for as long as it takes, and love you through it **(2 Corinthians 4:8-9 NASB).**

"You, Lord, hear the desire of the afflicted; you encourage them, and you listen to their cry." (Psalm 10:17 NIV)

"For he will deliver the needy who cry out, the afflicted who have no one to help" (Psalm 72:12 NIV)

"He heals the brokenhearted and binds up their wounds. He determines the number of the stars and calls them each by name. Great is our Lord and mighty in power; his understanding has no limit" (Psalm 147:3-5 NIV)

"You will keep him in perfect peace, whose mind is stayed on you, because he trusts in you" (Isaiah 26:3 NKJV)

He keeps us in perfect peace if we let him. It's really that simple. When our hearts and minds are turned toward him and toward heaven, it is natural to trust and simple to receive **(Colossians 3:2-3)**. The principle is uncomplicated, but the practical part—maybe not so much. The practical, as implied, requires intentionality and practice. To "stay" your mind requires discipline; to seek God first and to set your mind on the fruit of the Holy Spirit is purposeful **(Matthew 6:33 NASB), (Philippians 4:8 NASB), (Galatians 5:22-23 NASB)**.

Doing any of that apart from God's grace is impossible. Our utmost for him, having done all to stand, is to stand firm—clad in his heavenly armor, clothed with his love **(Ephesians 6:10-18, Galatians 3:27)**. We were far from God, but again brought near in Jesus Christ to be as he always intended, authentically his. He is always with us, and we always have his peace when we purposefully live for him.

"To the pure, all things are pure, but to those who are corrupted and do not believe, nothing is pure. In fact, both their minds and consciences are corrupted." (Titus 1:15 NIV)

"Peace I leave with you; my peace I give you. I do not give to you as the world gives. Do not let your hearts be troubled and do not be afraid." (John 14:27 NIV)

"I have told you these things, so that in me you may have peace. In this world you will have trouble. But take heart! I have overcome the world." (John 16:33 NIV)

The way things appear

"Trust in the LORD with all your heart and lean not on your own understanding; in all your ways submit to him, and he will make your paths straight." (Proverbs 3:5-6 NIV)

You've probably heard the adage, *"If it were easy everyone would do it,"* at least one time in your life. Depending on the day and the circumstance, not leaning on your own understanding of things can be as daunting a task as ever there was. However, especially in the minutia of everyday life, learning to do things God's way is not just a one-time deal. It's pretty straightforward. He's either right 100 percent of the time or he's not. With that in mind, consider that the internal origin of most mental and emotional struggles is buried somewhere within our flawed and incomplete perspective. The good news is that he constantly reads our mail and knows exactly how to respond to each one of us individually. He is always faithful, and he is always true **(Job 38:4-18 NIV)**.

"What if some were unfaithful? Will their unfaithfulness nullify God's faithfulness? Not at all! Let God be true, and every human being a liar. As it is written: 'So that you may be proved right when you speak and prevail when you judge'." (Romans 3:3-4 NIV)

Let me explain the way God showed it to me. Imagine being in an airplane, or better still, a spacecraft looking down at the earth. Now imagine sitting in your own living room, looking out the front window. These are two wholly different perspectives. Neither one is more valid than the other, but one is certainly more complete. Our heavenly Father sees all time and space rolled out like a scroll. He sees all things, at all times, all at once **(Genesis 1:1 NASB), (Psalm 90:1-2 NIV), (Psalm 139:16 NIV), (John 8:58 NASB), (Revelation 1:8 NIV).** For the most part, we see what is right in front of us, and even that vision can be easily thrown askew by the most ordinary of circumstances. What we perceive seems right to us based on our proximity to the situation. But it's hard not to agree that the way things appear to us is, to put it mildly, utterly deficient.

So when I am agitated, confused, disheartened, or feeling just plain hopeless, I will trust God. I will trust in who I know he is and in what I know his character to be. I will put my hope in this truth: 100 percent of the time my circumstances are not exactly as they appear to be. From God's perspective, everything about my life is under control; in him all things are perfectly held together.

I humble myself and pray. I bring what I can see to my Father in heaven. I ask him to lift the weight, to ease the burden, and 100 percent of the time he responds. One hundred percent of the time he is faithful, even when I am too weak to manage even one coherent thought.

"Is anyone among you in trouble? Let them pray. Is anyone happy? Let them sing songs of praise." (James 5:13 NIV)

"To You, O LORD, I lift up my soul. O my God, in You I trust, do not let me be ashamed; do not let my enemies exult over me. Indeed, none of those who wait for You will be ashamed; those who deal treacherously without cause will be ashamed. Make me know Your ways, O LORD; teach me Your paths. Lead me in Your truth and teach me, for You are the God of my salvation; for You I wait all the day." (Psalms 25:1-5 NASB)

"Because God is with you all the time, no place is any closer to God than the place where you are right now."—Rick Warren

"For God, who said, 'Light shall shine out of darkness,' is the One who has shone in our hearts to give the light of the knowledge of the glory of God in the face of Christ." (2 Corinthians 4:6 NASB)

So are you feeling yucky? Walking through dry places? Filled with wrong attitudes and intentions? Feeling like God could never use you? Unfaithful, unworthy, unlovely? Did you know that none of that matters? God said, **"Light shall shine out of darkness."** But here is the more awesome part: it's not our light at all, but the light in our hearts that is his life! It is Jesus' light unveiled through our faces, no matter how we feel. God makes it shine. All we need to do is show up and agree that he is able to navigate for us when we put our trust in him. Courage is knowing God's provision for us even when our five senses tell us otherwise and battle fiercely against such a hope. Courage is eager expectation in place of discouragement and fear. Trust in God says, *"Hope is my anchor,"* whether in this life or the one to come.

"Because God wanted to make the unchanging nature of his purpose very clear to the heirs of what was promised, he confirmed it with an oath. God did this so that, by two unchangeable things in which it is impossible for God to lie, we who have fled to take hold of the hope set before us may be greatly encouraged. We have this hope as an anchor for the soul, firm and secure. It enters the inner sanctuary behind the curtain, where our forerunner, Jesus, has entered on our behalf." (Hebrews 6:17-20 NIV)

Jesus Christ in us holds a better promise than we could ever hope for or ask of him. We confess it since we can, making much of him. We declare it by who we are and what we do, since nearness to him means obeying the truth and receiving his favor. All things are ours when we follow after him, listen to him, and trust in him.

"This is the confidence we have in approaching God: that if we ask anything according to his will, he hears us. And if we know that he hears us—whatever we ask—we know that we have what we asked of him." (1 John 5:14-15 NIV)

"Do your part to help reap a harvest, and trust God to do his part."—Katy Kauffman

"Remember your word to your servant, for you have given me hope. My comfort in my suffering is this:

Your promise preserves my life." (Psalm 119:49-50 NIV)

Our words have power for good or for evil. The things we speak set into motion our agreement or disagreement with the Spirit of God. We affect lives, events, and circumstances, especially our own **(James 3:4-5 NASB), (Proverbs 18:21 NASB)**. Consider now that the words spoken by God are always right, and, for all practical purposes, the end of the argument.

So the questions are these: What is our fear when we give it breath, our doubt in the clear light of day? What is the disdain or the self-abasement that gain entrance through our pain but the forfeiture of comfort? The refusal of hope? God has spoken so many amazing, life-giving, true and authentic words about ... well ... everything.

"I, even I, am he who comforts you. Who are you that you fear mere mortals, human beings who are but grass, that you forget the Lord your Maker, who stretches out the heavens and who lays the foundations of the earth, that you live in constant terror every day because of the wrath of the oppressor, who is bent on destruction? For where is the wrath of the oppressor?" (Isaiah 51:12-13 NIV)

Indeed our enemy's wrath is empty of power, just as surely as all of his words are empty. How much more so when we come into agreement with the words of the Lord our Maker and trust him? How much more the power released, when we set his love into motion by speaking his truth over ourselves, our lives, our families, or our circumstances?

"It is written: 'I believed; therefore I have spoken.' Since we have that same spirit of faith, we also believe and therefore speak." (2 Corinthians 4:13 NIV)

"Now we have received, not the spirit of the world, but the Spirit who is from God, so that we may know the things freely given to us by God, which things we also speak, not in words taught by human wisdom, but in those taught by the Spirit, combining spiritual thoughts with spiritual words" (1 Corinthians 2:12-13 NASB)

How are we supposed to do all that, you may ask? Be partakers with God. If we are indeed his children, then he deals with us as his own sons and daughters. He says, "All discipline for the moment seems not to be joyful, but sorrowful" (Hebrews 12:11 NASB). *Seems* is the operative word, since by what he says next we are able to deduce the meaning of all of his instruction and more; "yet to those who have been trained by it, afterwards it yields the peaceful fruit of righteousness" (Hebrews 12:11 NASB).

So we look to a better future because God promises that, no matter what we must endure, it will not be too much. We are able to bear it, and he will always see us through to the end of it, just as the worker of a field labors to realize a good harvest (1 Corinthians 10:13 NASB), (Matthew 9:36-38 NIV). Since we are called to be participants with Jesus, "weak" and "feeble" mean healing, peace, and blessing if we trust God and imitate him.

"For we have become partakers of Christ, if we hold fast the beginning of our assurance firm until the end." (Hebrews 3:14 NASB)

Jesus is the embodiment of all God promised us (his people) through Isaiah the prophet.

"...say to those with fearful hearts, 'Be strong, do not fear; your God will come, he will come with vengeance; with divine retribution he will come to save you'" (Isaiah 35:4 NIV)

Being his, belonging to him, isn't always going to be easy. He never promised that. But we can be certain of his grace to be strength for us, and we can be assured of the rewards of our endurance and hope in him. We can be comforted in the knowledge that the fog of war, the burden of death, the victory of all the ages was his alone to accept, endure, and finish **(Hebrews 12:2 NASB), (Philippians 2:6-11 NASB)**. We can be confident if we believe the truth in his Word—that the unburdened rest of a heartened sojourner is ours no matter the circumstances that life, death, or any other challenge might lay before us.

"Who shall separate us from the love of Christ? Shall trouble or hardship or persecution or famine or nakedness or danger or sword? As it is written: 'For your sake we face death all day long; we are considered as sheep to be slaughtered.' No, in all these things we are more than conquerors through him who loved us. For I am convinced that neither death nor life, neither angels nor demons, neither the present nor the future, nor any powers, neither height nor depth, nor anything else in all creation, will be able to separate us from the love of God that is in Christ Jesus our Lord." (Romans 8:35-40 NIV)

Prayer: *I trust you, Lord, because of the faith poured out in my life. I lean on your wisdom rather than mine. Wisdom from you reflects your love and your character. I trust you, Lord, since I know that your way is better than mine 100 percent of the time. Your plans for me are perfect, just as your love for me is perfect. Thank you, Abba. I don't understand so many things Lord; at times my heart is burdened by ignorance to the point of despair. But I will trust even in my doubting, at your side, rather than be satisfied to gain any counterfeit that this world would offer apart from you. Abba God, I am so filled up by this truth. I can hear your voice; you know me. I have life in you, and nothing can ever take me away from you. I love you, Lord, and I trust you with my whole heart. Thank you, my love and my everything, that you are also my help when I don't understand, my feet when I won't move, and my center when courage fails me. For that reason and so many more, I exalt you above all things, whether in heaven, on earth, or under the earth. I magnify your Name because, by your Holy Spirit, I am able, I am more than a conqueror! In Jesus' name, Amen!*

Scripture: "**Come to me, all you who are weary and burdened, and I will give you rest. Take my yoke upon you and learn from me, for I am gentle and humble in heart, and you will find rest for your souls. For my yoke is easy and my burden is light.**" (Matthew 11:28-30 NIV)

"**But we do not belong to those who shrink back and are destroyed, but to those who have faith and are saved.**" (Hebrews 10:39 NIV)

CHAPTER 14

PRAYER

Heart Songs

"Rejoice always; pray without ceasing; in everything give thanks; for this is God's will for you in Christ Jesus." (1 Thessalonians 5:16-18 NASB)

God is teaching me about worshipful submission and constant surrender through prayer. I am learning there is not one moment that goes by in a day when I can afford, in any way that matters, to be far from him. When Paul, the apostle, says **"pray without ceasing,"** he's not kidding. Prayer is where God's power is released, where bondages are broken, where there is light shined on the enemy's forgeries and lies. Prayer is the place where God's Holy Spirit falls on me and I am most wonderfully filled, protected, restored, and refreshed.

"During the days of Jesus' life on earth, he offered up prayers and petitions with loud cries and tears to the one who could save him from death, and he was heard because of his reverent submission. Son though he was, he learned obedience from what he suffered and, once made perfect, he became the source of eternal salvation for all who obey him" (Hebrews 5:7-9 NIV)

Early one morning I had the pleasure to be used by God in praying for my friend Tia. It was around 4:00 am PST, and I was just on the edge of between awake and asleep when the Holy Spirit spoke to my heart, *"Pray for Tia."* I thought, *"Okay Lord, when I wake up I will do that."* Then I rolled over and went back to sleep. To my surprise, however, no more than twenty minutes later, the Holy Spirit woke me up a second time and spoke to my heart, *"Get up and pray for Tia NOW."* This time it was adamant, urgent even. So I got out of bed, immediately hit my knees, and began to pray and intercede for her. I had no idea what to pray or how to pray for her, but as soon as I opened my mouth and said her name, God started sending what I can only describe as a flood of images, impressions, and feelings that she was in real trouble. He showed me that there was darkness all around her, and that she was in trouble and being oppressed both physically and spiritually.

With that information, I began to do battle for her as God gave me his scripture to pray over her and I let him lead my thoughts and words. I was on my knees for close to thirty minutes, but by the time I had finished, I knew that God had done something powerful through me. I could sense in my spirit that he had touched Tia and spoken to her while I prayed. I knew beyond all doubt that the spiritual realm had been shaken. It is one of the most powerful moments I have ever experienced in prayer for another person. He even put a specific verse of scripture on my heart to share with her and prompted me to get up, as soon as I had a chance to pull myself together, and send her this instant message:

"Good morning Tia! I don't know why but God woke me up at 5:00 am today with your name on my heart, and he put it on my heart to pray for you. So I did and it was really powerful and awesome. And blessed me as well. He also gave me this verse for you, I have no idea why but I am sure you will because of how adamant it was."

"For you were once darkness, but now you are light in the Lord. Live as children of light (for the fruit of the light consists in all goodness, righteousness, and truth) and find out what pleases the Lord" (Ephesians 5:8-10 NASB)

One thing I may have forgotten to mention is that Tia was living all the way across the country at the time. It took her a couple of days to get back to me. I had started to wonder whether I had imagined the whole thing, even doubting what God may have done that morning, so I wrote to her again. I wanted to make sure I had not offended her, and to apologize if I had. But despite my lack of faith, God was full of grace to give me a peek at what he had done and more. I have never doubted him or the voice of his Spirit since.

This was Tia's response to my second message:

"Not all all. It has taken me several days to process. The evening or morning you sent this, I was a bit manic and suicidal. I do not like to talk about it but just work through it. I also was up at 4:00 am, having a meltdown when you sent this. It freaked me out, but not in a bad way. My household is full of negative energy and yours was uplifting at a time I needed it. I know I am going to make it thru this but some days are harder than others. Thank you for your message, wow and wow. It was good timing. Xoxox"

Needless to say, I was filled with awe and gratitude, and I was greatly encouraged. I literally started weeping in a very public place as I was remembering every detail about how God had shown me he was in control that morning. I was reminded of how he had come alongside her, loving her through every difficult moment. I was with a friend when I read it, and I was helpless to describe my feelings. The enormity of his love had left me speechless. He did not stop there however.

Several weeks later Tia reached out to me again. We got on the phone, and she shared that not only had she been miraculously delivered out of the dark and abusive environment she was caught in at the time, but that God had been prompting her to call me so I could help her to pray and receive Jesus Christ as Savior. We talked a while, then I lead her through a simple prayer to accept him as Lord of her life. Then after a bit more encouragement that she had just made the most beautiful decision which a human heart could ever make, we hung up. I did not hear anything from her for a while after.

The next time we talked, she shared her joy in a having daily relationship with God. She told me that he was leading her to begin ministering to other women who had also experienced abuse. I say all of that to say this: Do not EVER doubt God's voice when he speaks. And do not ever doubt his ability to move mightily through you when you are obedient to pray. Whether the prayer is simple or complex, long or short, for you personally or for another, he always does something wonderful and he always answers!

Perspective ...

"Be alert and of sober mind. Your enemy the devil prowls around like a roaring lion looking for someone to devour. Resist him, standing firm in the faith, because you know that the family of believers throughout the world is undergoing the same kind of sufferings." (1 Peter 5:8-9 NASB)

"But if you do not do what is right, sin is crouching at your door; it desires to have you, but you must rule over it" (Genesis 4:7 NASB)

Prayer actively resists the enemy. With all power in the name of Jesus Christ, by prayer, sin is overruled. My heart-song is heard by God, and the spirit realm is shaken. Mountains are moved, fortresses are pulled down, and even the mightiest winds are stilled by a single word spoken in sincere faith that aligns with his will.

"Truly I tell you, whatever you bind on earth will be bound in heaven, and whatever you loose on earth will be loosed in heaven." (Matthew 18:18 NASB)

"Every good and perfect gift is from above, coming down from the Father of the heavenly lights, who does not change like shifting shadows." (James 1:17 NASB)

The Lord only gives good gifts, and his will is that we enjoy everything he has created for us. Be so lost in your love for God and in seeking him, that the deepest desires of your heart become his deepest desires for you. Then when you ask, it is always according to his will, for his glory, and there is no downside. God's great love for us means that he wants the best for us—his best. Get a good strong picture of the most amazing life you could ever imagine for yourself. Now let this sink in: the least of what God desires for you is more perfect than anything you could ever imagine for yourself.

"Whatever you ask in my name, that will I do, *so that the Father may be glorified* in the Son. If you ask me anything in my name, I will do it." (John 14:13-14 NASB)

*"Delight yourself in the L*ORD*; and He will give you the desires of your heart. Commit your way to the L*ORD*, trust also in Him, and He will do it." (Psalm 37:4-5 NASB)*

Our prayers are a tapestry of the most intimate moments we will ever spend with God. They are a human soul's beautiful, individual, and secret resounding song to the adoring Composer of all things. A mosaic of every single joy, affliction, exultation, and thought, they are the authentic picture of our reflected love arrayed in God's splendor.

"Deep calls to deep at the sound of Your waterfalls; all Your breakers and Your waves have rolled over me. The LORD will command His lovingkindness in the daytime; and His song will be with me in the night, a prayer to the God of my life" (Psalm 42:7-8).

Where we find him

"But to each one of us grace was given according to the measure of Christ's gift. Therefore it says, 'When he ascended on high, he led captive a host of captives, and he gave gifts to men'." (Ephesians 4:7-8 NASB)

One of those gifts is prayer. We get to be in the presence of God anytime, anyplace, for any reason, and we are able to speak with him in confidence as we would to a dear friend.

"In the morning, Lord, you hear my voice; in the morning I lay my requests before you and wait expectantly. ... But I, by your great love, can come into your house; in reverence I bow down toward your holy temple." (Psalm 5:3, 7 NIV)

Notice in the Psalm it says **"requests."** That word is used another time as a command that we make them known to God **(Philippians 4:6 NIV)**. He not only wants to hear them, he delights to hear them.

"...the prayer of the upright is His delight." (Proverbs 15:8 NASB)

"The Lord has heard my supplication, the Lord receives my prayer." (Psalm 6:9 NASB)

Never doubt the power of prayer or for a moment ever believe that God does not answer. He always answers, even if it is not in the way we expect, want, or think he should. Since that is true, remember it and never stop praying, asking, and seeking. He always knows. He always sees. He always cares.

"God is able to do far more than we could ever ask for or imagine. He does everything by his power that is working in us." (Ephesians 3:20 NIVR)

"The prayer of a righteous person is powerful and effective." (James 5:16 NIV)

"So I say to you: Ask and it will be given to you; seek and you will find; knock and the door will be opened to you. For everyone who asks receives; the one who seeks finds; and to the one who knocks, the door will be opened." (Luke 11:9-11 NIV)

There is something very powerful that happens when you open your mouth and speak your heart out loud to God. First of all, you can know beyond all doubt that he hears **(Psalm 69:33 AMP)**. Think about that, "**I AM,**" who willed the DNA of the entire universe with his voice **(Genesis 1:1 NASB)**, hears yours every time you reach out with your faith and use your mouth to say something to him.

"But You, O Lord, are a shield about me, my glory, and the One who lifts my head. I was crying to the Lord with my voice, and He answered me ..." (Psalm 3:3-4 NASB)

As if that were not enough to grab hold of, when you decide to drop what you're doing and say *"Hello,"* he listens. It does not matter what you say to God. What matters to him is that you make the effort and care enough to seek his counsel. Whatever your heart of hearts cries out for in that moment interests him, and he will not be silent.

"...He is a rewarder of those who seek him." (Hebrews 11:6)

Finally, and most incredibly, when you speak out loud the cry of your heart and know that he not only hears but also reciprocates, he is pleased by it and moves the course of your life. He protects you, he guides you, he gives you good gifts, and he helps you. When you worship him in that way, he lifts your head and changes you. He changes your circumstances because he desires more than anything to be in relationship with you. It literally pleases him.

"Or what man is there among you who, when his son asks for a loaf, will give him a stone? Or if he asks for a fish, he will not give him a snake, will he? If you then, being evil, know how to give good gifts to your children, how much more will your Father who is in heaven give what is good to those who ask him!" (Matthew 7:9-11 NASB)

You might say, *"How can I possibly expect any of that from a holy God?"* Because of Jesus Christ! He has given you everything you need, if only you would believe that he is, and that he really does reward all those who seek after him with a sincere and surrendered heart **(1 Peter 5:6-7 NASB), Romans 10:11 NASB).**

So what should your response be to such a wonderful truth? Wake up every day, hit your knees, open your mouth, and speak! Talk with him at work, in your car, while you exercise. Anytime is the right time, and anywhere is a perfect place.

"Through him then, let us continually offer up a sacrifice of praise to God, that is, the fruit of lips that give thanks to his name." (Hebrews 13:15 NASB)

"Prayer is not asking. Prayer is putting oneself in the hands of God, at his disposition, and listening to his voice in the depth of our hearts."— Mother Teresa

"Sing to God, O kingdoms of the earth, sing praises to the Lord. *Selah*. To Him who rides upon the highest heavens, which are from ancient times; Behold, He speaks forth with His voice, a mighty voice." (Psalm 68:32-33 NASB)

God's voice is always mighty, to be sure. The curious thing is that each of us in our own way hear it through all of the many filters we've plugged our ears with. Even the whisper of God is like a crack of thunder to the human heart. His still small voice reaches even the deepest places.

"The Lord said, 'Go out and stand on the mountain in the presence of the Lord, for the Lord is about to pass by.' Then a great and powerful wind tore the mountains apart and shattered the rocks before the Lord, but the Lord was not in the wind. After the wind there was an earthquake, but the Lord was not in the earthquake. After the earthquake came a fire, but the Lord was not in the fire. And after the fire came a gentle whisper." (1 Kings 19:11-12 NIV)

To the prophet Elijah, the Lord was not in the wind, the fire, or the earthquake. But the mighty wind went forth nonetheless, as did the fire and the earthquake. Still Elijah heard only a **"still small voice."** Why? Because he was weary, he was afraid, he was running and hiding. Jesus' disciples, on the other hand, had an entirely different experience.

"And suddenly there came from heaven a noise like a violent rushing wind, and it filled the whole house where they were sitting. And there appeared to them tongues as of fire distributing themselves, and they rested on each one of them." (Acts 2:2-3 NASB)

"And when they had prayed, the place where they had gathered together was shaken, and they were all filled with the Holy Spirit and began to speak the word of God with boldness." (Acts 4:31 NASB)

The mighty wind blew, the fire came, and the earth shook. For them, God was not only in those things, he *was* those things. They were his power and his voice in response to their prayers. The difference was in the hearts of the people praying, not in the heart of God to respond with the full weight of his glory. The way they heard him was unique and personal, intended to meet them right where they were. For Elijah, God's glory was compassion and mercy in a **"still small voice"** to reassure, revive, and prepare him to do what came next. For the disciples, it was power and boldness to accomplish the task at hand.

The filters are only our minds, in a finite way, attempting through the everyday things of life to process the brilliance of the sovereign and infinite. Regardless, in his love and desire that we should know him even now, God speaks. One of my favorite radio pastors, Alistair Begg, has a saying: *"The main things are the plain things and the plain things are the main things."* That is to say, in whatever circumstance, pray. Inquire, search, grope, and God's answer, however we may perceive it, will always come and will always be mighty, full of his glory.

"The voice of the LORD is over the waters; the God of glory thunders, the LORD thunders over the mighty waters. The voice of the LORD is powerful; the voice of the LORD is majestic." (Psalm 29:3-4 NIV)

Prayer: *Let the cry of my heart be to you every moment, Lord. When I speak the thoughts of my heart aloud, may every one of them become a prayer and petition to you, the God of my life, Lord of heaven and earth. Thank you that you meet me in that place, Abba, however I may come. You are in all of my moments and all of my tears. You, Lord, are all of me. May my heart always be such that I am found in you alone, and my mind such that every thought is captive to your love. Thank you, Adonai, that you work in me to will and to act according to what pleases you, that your desire for me is life to the full. I exalt you, Lord Jesus, and I magnify your name. I ask all of this by your power alive in me to trust and to stand. In the matchless name of Jesus Christ I pray, Amen!*

Scripture: "**In the same way the Spirit also helps our weakness; for we do not know how to pray as we should, but the Spirit Himself intercedes for us with groanings too deep for words; and He who searches the hearts knows what the mind of the Spirit is, because He intercedes for the saints according to the will of God. And we know that God causes all things to work together for good to those who love God, to those who are called according to His purpose.**" (Romans 8:26-28)

CHAPTER 15

GIFTS, PROMISES, AND PROVISION

For me?!

"For we are God's handiwork, created in Christ Jesus to do good works, which God prepared in advance for us to do." (Ephesians 2:10 NIV)

God has filled my heart with a love of his beauty in the expression of the gifts he gives so uniquely. When I consider things like music and dance, painting, and poetry, I am filled with awesome wonder that he has given gifts this great, and even greater, to every one of us. For example, I bet if you thought a moment, you could come up with at least one thing that nobody else can do as well or in exactly the same way as you.

God relishes seeing you use your gift, and he smiles down at you like a proud parent. Just as our own children sometimes inherit our talents and traits, that particular gift of yours is a reflection of his character expressed through you. Be filled each morning, feel God's pride and favor, knowing that every one of us is his, and that we are wonderfully made—just as he intended, his very own workmanship.

"...be alert and of sober mind so that you may pray. Above all, love each other deeply, because love covers over a multitude of sins. Offer hospitality to one another without grumbling. Each of you should use whatever gift you have received to serve others, as faithful stewards of God's grace in its various forms. If anyone speaks, they should do so as one who speaks the very words of God. If anyone serves, they should do so with the strength God provides, so that in all things God may be praised through Jesus Christ. To him be the glory and the power for ever and ever. Amen." (1 Peter 4:7-11 NIV)

God has been showing me what humility is, as I am realizing how much I need to rely on him moment by moment. In particular, the realization that anything I can do and am able to accomplish is in the gifting he provides. How ridiculous my way looks when I compare it to his! Our Lord has an amazing sense of humor and an inexhaustible forbearance. Because of that, he lovingly abides with our attempts to stumble around on our own. It's kind of comical really.

"The cautious faith that never saws off a limb on which it is sitting, never learns that unattached limbs may find strange unaccountable ways of not falling." —Dallas Willard

"If you are insulted because of the name of Christ, you are blessed, for the Spirit of glory and of God rests on you. If you suffer, it should not be as a murderer or thief or any other kind of criminal, or even as a meddler. However, if you suffer as a Christian, do not be ashamed, but praise God that you bear that name." (1 Peter 4:14-16 NIV)

People take pride in being called a lot of things, each for their own reasons and with their own motives. But very few people I am acquainted with would agree with the sentiment conveyed in the above verse, or if they did, they probably wouldn't admit it anyway. As for me, I do praise God that I **"bear that name."**

"But we have this treasure in jars of clay to show that this all-surpassing power is from God and not from us. We are hard pressed on every side, but not crushed; perplexed, but not in despair; persecuted, but not abandoned; struck down, but not destroyed. We always carry around in our body the death of Jesus, so that the life of Jesus may also be revealed in our body. For we who are alive are always being given over to death for Jesus' sake, so that his life may also be revealed in our mortal body." (2 Corinthians 4:7-11 NIV)

In the first several verses, the *"are"* things and the *"but not"* things are negatives. The latter are all implied positives of course, but God prompted me to go a lot further. If we are NOT crushed then *we are expanded and gifted* by God!

"When you go into your land, I will force your enemies out of that land. I will expand your borders—you will get more and more land." (Exodus 34:24 ERV)

If we are NOT in despair then *we are gifted the fullness of God's hope*!

"We have this hope as an anchor for the soul, firm and secure. It enters the inner sanctuary behind the curtain, where our forerunner, Jesus, has entered on our behalf." (Hebrews 6:19-20 NIV)

"Therefore, having been justified by faith, we have peace with God through our Lord Jesus Christ, through whom also we have obtained our introduction by faith into this grace in which we stand; and we exult in hope of the glory of God." (Romans 5:1-2 NASB)

If we are NOT abandoned, then *we are grafted in and gifted adoption into the family of almighty God*!

"For you have not received a spirit of slavery leading to fear again, but you have received a spirit of adoption as sons (*and daughters*) by which we cry out, 'Abba! Father!' (Romans 8:15 NASB)

"But when the set time had fully come, God sent his Son, born of a woman, born under the law, to redeem those under the law, that we might receive adoption to sonship. Because you are his sons, God sent the Spirit of his Son into our hearts, the Spirit who calls out, 'Abba, Father'." (Galatians 4:4-6 NIV)

If we are NOT destroyed, then *we are being built up and our gifting is multiplied by God*!

"And coming to him as to a living stone which has been rejected by men, but is choice and precious in the sight of God, you also, as living stones, are being built up as a spiritual house for a holy priesthood, to offer up spiritual sacrifices acceptable to God through Jesus Christ." (1 Peter 2:4-5 NASB)

"So then you are no longer strangers and aliens, but you are fellow citizens with the saints, and are of God's household, having been built on the foundation of the apostles and prophets, Christ Jesus Himself being the corner stone, in whom the whole building, being fitted together, is growing into a holy temple in the Lord, in whom you also are being built together into a dwelling of God in the Spirit" (Ephesians 2:19-22 NASB)

As Paul, the apostle says, "**I will boast all the more gladly about my weaknesses, so that Christ's power may rest on me.**" Amen! How many of you knew that fragility was actually a superb, divinely appointed present?

"**Here is a trustworthy saying that deserves full acceptance: Christ Jesus came into the world to save sinners—of whom I am the worst. But for that very reason I was shown mercy so that in me, the worst of sinners, Christ Jesus might display his immense patience as an example for those who would believe in him and receive eternal life.**" (1 Timothy 1:15-16 NIV)

Wisdom and Knowledge

"**Who among you is wise and understanding? Let him show by his good behavior his deeds in the gentleness of wisdom.**" (James 3:13 NASB)

Praise God for the promise of real wisdom. Knowing a lot of things or a lot about a particular thing is awesome. *"Knowledge is power."* Right? Or so they say. However, whomever "they" are, they are wrong at least in this context. Real power is knowledge combined with heavenly wisdom. On its own, raw knowledge is hollow and only useful to the one who "knows." It takes that extra ingredient, the wisdom that only God can provide, to impart life and give it a soul. Then we see power.

"'We all possess knowledge.' But knowledge puffs up while love builds up." (1 Corinthians 8:1 NIV)

Being knowledgeable is a state in which we may or may not find ourselves, based on what things we learn or don't learn. Godly wisdom, however, has his character. It has a personality, and it contains real beauty.

"But the wisdom from above is first pure, then peaceable, gentle, reasonable, full of mercy and good fruits, unwavering, without hypocrisy." (James 3:17 NASB)

Pure: **Freedom from anything that contaminates or pollutes; carefully correct.**

Peaceable: **Disposed to peace, not contentious or quarrelsome, quietly behaved, free from strife or disorder.**

Gentle: **Considerate or kindly in disposition; amiable and tender. Not harsh or severe; mild and soft.**

Reasonable: **Not extreme or excessive; moderate and fair. Possessing sound judgment.**

Full of Mercy: **Showing compassion or forbearance when circumstances demand otherwise. Charity stressing benevolence and goodwill shown in broad understanding and tolerance.**

Unwavering: **Not wavering or hesitant; resolute. Marked by firm determination; not shakable.**

Without hypocrisy: **Upright; righteous as a consequence of being honorable and honest. Being fully trustworthy as according with fact; worthy of acceptance or belief.**

Think of the greatest minds of our time, or really any time in history. From those intellects, select a few of your favorites. The goal of knowledge has always been the building up and prosperity of societies, culture, families, or individuals. Compare those on your list whose attempt at the impartation and use of knowledge was successful in that regard with those to whom we credit only selfishness, despair, and destruction—on any level, in any or all of the same categories.

Ultimately they were separated by only one thing. Life, as only God can define it, along with the inherent value God places upon life that trumps all other ambition or motivation and develops every part of the fruit by which his wisdom combined with knowledge then becomes mature **(John 1:4 NIV)**. The promise of heavenly wisdom is a gift from God, and his Holy Spirit gives it freely to all who ask **(John 14:26 NASB)**.

"The beginning of wisdom is this: Get wisdom. Though it cost all you have, get understanding." (Proverbs 4:7 NIV)

"And the seed whose fruit is righteousness is sown in peace by those who make peace." (James 3:18 NASB)

How awesome is this place?!

"This stone, which I have set up as a pillar, will be God's house, and of all that You give me I will surely give a tenth to You" (Genesis 28:22 NASB)

God came to Jacob in a dream. And though Jacob didn't realize it at the time, God made a declaration and promise that the man Jacob (Israel) would be his dwelling place.

"Behold, I am with you and will keep you wherever you go, and will bring you back to this land; for I will not leave you until I have done what I have promised you." (Genesis 28:15 NASB)

God promised Jacob many things that night. One was that in him all the families of the earth would be blessed. God kept this promise through Jesus who came in perfect love to "save" and "take away the sin" of the world **(John 3:16-17 NASB), (John 1:29 NASB)**. Jacob was so awestruck by what he had seen in his dream that the first thing he did when he woke up was to make some declarations of his own.

"Surely the Lord is in this place, and I did not know it." He was afraid and said, "How awesome is this place! This is none other than the house of God, and this is the gate of heaven." (Genesis 28:16-17 NASB)

Looking backward to that day and all that has happened between then and now, it's difficult not to agree with him and say, "**How awesome is this place!**" What God had just shown him were the fulfillments of promises—our foundation in faith and the mysteries of the salvation of all people. Jesus Christ would be the bridge to restoring right relationship between God and humankind **(Genesis 28:12 NASB), (John 1:51 NASB), (Galatians 3:28-29 NASB), (1 Timothy 2:5 NASB)**. What God showed Jacob that night and what Jacob said and did also foreshadowed three things that are all now firmly established as proven and true.

"You are the Christ, the Son of the living God." (Matthew 16:16 NASB)

"...and upon this rock I will build my church; and the gates of hell shall not prevail against it." (Matthew 16:18 KJV)

"The kingdom of God does not come with observation; nor will they say, 'See here!' or 'See there!' For indeed, the kingdom of God is within you." (Luke 17:20-21 NKJV)

"...you also, as living stones, are being built up as a spiritual house for a holy priesthood, to offer up spiritual sacrifices acceptable to God through Jesus Christ" (1 Peter 2:5).

"He (Jacob) called the name of that place Bethel ..." (Genesis 28:19 NASB).

"Bethel," means literally *"House of God."*

"I will put my law in their minds and write it on their hearts. I will be their God, and they will be my people. No longer will they teach their neighbor, or say to one another, 'Know the Lord,' because they will all know me, from the least of them to the greatest," declares the Lord. "For I will forgive their wickedness and will remember their sins no more." (Jeremiah 31:33-34 NIV)

"Do you not know that you are a temple of God and that the Spirit of God dwells in you?" (1 Corinthians 3:16 NASB)

We are all part of the *"Bethel,"* if we know Jesus Christ, and our hearts are the tablet upon which God, through him, pens a continual love letter to all the earth **(2 Corinthians 3:3 NASB).** Promises? Gifts? Provision? Amen! ***This is our God!***

Prayer: *Heavenly Father, I pray that you would take all of me. All of your promises are true, every one, no matter how many. These are the days, now is the time of your favor. How wonderful are your mercies! When I seek your will and your desires ahead of my own, you lift me up and give me abundantly more than I could ever ask or imagine. Your Holy Spirit is my counselor that leads me and guides me into all Truth and Wisdom. Concerning your good gifts, all day long I am thankful for and thinking about family—marriages, relatives, relationships, and close friends. You call me your family, I'm so thankful that you left me so many examples in your Word. For me, these are a special expression of your love, Abba. Praise you Jesus, my only benchmark, my only plumb line. Apart from you I am only stumbling in the dark, but walking where you walk, stepping where you step, my paths are lighted and straight. By no other avenue than the gift of your grace am I able to succeed one moment at a time. Over every high peak and through every low valley, I hem myself to you and fix my eyes squarely on the road down which only you can lead. You are my portion, my shelter, my provision, and my sufficiency. I declare it all by your power. I ask and pray in the perfect name of Jesus, Amen!*

Scripture: "**I will plant her for myself in the land; I will show my love to the one I called 'Not my loved one.' I will say to those called 'Not my people,' 'You are my people'; and they will say, 'You are my God'.**" (Hosea 2:23 NIV)

"**For no matter how many promises God has made, they are 'Yes' in Christ. And so through him the 'Amen' is spoken by us to the glory of God.**" (2 Corinthians 1:20 NASB)

CHAPTER 16

TRIALS AND TESTING

Bad things and good people

"In this world you will have trouble. But take heart! I have overcome the world." *(John 16:33 NIV)*

As a tree grows, it adds a new layer to its trunk for each year that passes. Every single one represents a unique season in the life of the tree. By counting them, you can find its age. If you bother to look more closely, you can see that some rings are wider than others, some are darker, and some are lighter. Look even closer, and you will see imperfections or scars from serious wounds. Some scars have healed over time and others have not and likely will not ever completely heal because they run so deep.

Much like a tree, our souls have layers that similarly represent the seasons, conditions, and events in our lives. Their abundance and strength show our age, and maybe wisdom gained along the way. Their colors and widths are akin to times of prosperity and refreshing, or times of famine and drought. When the Ax falls, when Lightning strikes, when Wild Fires scorch, and the Winds of life blow, they leave behind their marks. They test our foundation and our resolve. These trials can be disfiguring and scarring. But alternatively, we can allow God, just as he sustains a tree and carries it through the ages, to transform them into beauty and strength, badges of courage and character.

If we stick close to God, soaking up the living water of his Word, no root can turn bitter. If we are nourished by his healing warmth, we are made able to grow tall and resilient. If we seek shelter in him, trusting his desire and ability to sustain us, the storm is rendered void. Any power to affect us is drained when we come daily and allow ourselves to be open and laid bare, exposed to the light of Jesus Christ.

"But blessed is the one who trusts in the LORD**, whose confidence is in him. They will be like a tree planted by the water that sends out its roots by the stream. It does not fear when heat comes; its**

leaves are always green. It has no worries in a year of drought and never fails to bear fruit." (Jeremiah 17:7-8 NIV)

"Iron, till it be thoroughly heated, is incapable to be wrought; so God sees good to cast some men into the furnace of affliction, and then beats them on his anvil into what frame he pleases."—Anne Bradstreet

The first thing you must know is this: Trouble and hard times are not God punishing us. He will never reach down from heaven and personally *"cast"* you anywhere that you have not already asked or decided to go on your own. However, he cannot cease to be God any more than the perfect way he has ordered the universe can relent to accommodate our whims and failings.

"When tempted, no one should say, 'God is tempting me.' For God cannot be tempted by evil, nor does he tempt anyone; but each person is tempted when they are dragged away by their own evil desire and enticed." (James 1:13-14 NIV)

I'm reminded of God's patience with me. Often times I picture a new-born moose—all legs, no real balance, stumbling around trying to find its footing. It keeps sliding around and falling while the parent watches, only intervening when necessary. Even though they would never allow harm to come to their child, they know there are things a child just needs to figure out on his or her own.

So I consider that today—as my Savior is patient with me, ever watchful and certainly concerned with every step I take, allowing me the freedom to fall then gently but firmly nudging me back to my feet and saying, *"It's okay son, try again, now this way."* Each time I try, my spiritual legs become more stable, and through each humbling experience, I become more wise and full of faith. Assured by God's patience, in his love and grace I learn to stand and walk properly. I learn my own legs by accepting his correction, listening to the Holy Spirit when he speaks, and, with lots of practice, imitating the way that Jesus walked.

"It is for discipline that you endure; God deals with you as with sons; for what son is there whom his father does not discipline? But if you are without discipline, of which all have become partakers, then you are illegitimate children and not sons. Furthermore, we had earthly fathers to discipline us, and we respected them; shall we not much rather be subject to the Father of spirits, and live? For they disciplined us for a short time as seemed best to them, but he disciplines us *for our good*, so that we may share his holiness. All discipline for the moment seems not to be joyful, but sorrowful; yet to those who have been trained by it, afterwards it yields the peaceful fruit of righteousness. Therefore, strengthen the hands that are weak and the knees that are feeble ..." (Hebrews 12:7-12 NASB)

So why do bad things happen to "good" people? I can assure you they are not the result of the divine Thumb of God reaching down and pressing us to the floor until we break. That would be against his nature. They are mostly, as they have been from the beginning of time, the consequence of our unfortunate choices. They result from one choice in particular—the fall of Adam in the garden **(Genesis 3:1-20)**. Unless we start from there, it becomes very easy to blame God for any number of disasters and general calamities, even to see him as vindictive, uncaring, or indifferent. But those things could not be farther from the truth. God's discipline is the perfect result of an always good, always loving Father allowing his children the free will to act. We go our own way, we grumble against him, we do the opposite of what he knows is best for us, and the result is always some sort of nonsense or chaos. He does not make bad things happen to us, he merely steps back and says quite literally, **"as I live, declares the Lord, *I will do to you the very thing I heard you say*"** **(Numbers 14:26-28 NIV)**. It absolutely **"seems not to be joyful but sorrowful"** at the time, but as the scripture says, if we *allow ourselves to be trained by it*, better things always follow.

"The great thing, if one can, is to stop regarding all the unpleasant things as interruptions of one's 'own,' or 'real' life. The truth is of course

that what one calls the interruptions are precisely one's real life—the life God is sending one day by day: what one calls one's 'real life' is a phantom of one's own imagination."—from a letter to Arthur Greeves, December 20, 1943

Frequently I find myself wanting for things—like the strength to surrender or the courage to submit. I thought I understood it, but God showed me otherwise. How complete a fallenness is ours which can see us one moment immersed in Jesus' love to the omission of all else, then in the next instant choosing to be mired down in burdens and the desires of our flesh. We are turned inwardly, sometimes too suddenly or subtly even to recognize this. My best estimation of life up to now, however, is that we are always being tested, always being refined. As I draw nearer and nearer to God, I continually experience pieces of the old me that have been hanging around a bit too long. If trials are heat, the testing of my faith is pressure. Let endurance have its perfect result so that this vessel comes out displaying every facet, just as God imagined me before time began.

"Your eyes saw my unformed body; all the days ordained for me were written in your book before one of them came to be." (Psalm 139:16 NIV)

How does that make you "feel"?

I had probably seen it a thousand times, but this one particular morning it stuck out to me like never before. The social media website, Facebook, wanted to know: "How are you feeling?" *(Chuckle)*. Well my answer that day, had I taken the bait, would've been, *"Not particularly great at the moment, woke up feeling real crummy in fact."* More importantly though is what occurred to me next; that "How are you feeling?" was the wrong question entirely. The right one would've been, *"What do I know?"* So I answered that one instead.

It went something like this: "I know a hope, a love, and a peace that pass human understanding. I know an assurance, a grace, a forgiveness, and a salvation that is **Joy** incarnate. Not a feeling, but a firm foundation when the waves hit me and the wind blows harder than I can bear. The Word of God calls it "**inexpressible,**" "**glorious,**" and it is both of those things. Inasmuch as the One, Jesus Christ, who pours them into me daily embodies the two, I am filled with this "**Joy**" in intimacy with him. All of this is true because he came, all happenstance is irrelevant because my Redeemer lives!"

"Praise be to the God and Father of our Lord Jesus Christ! In his great mercy he has given us new birth into a living hope through the resurrection of Jesus Christ from the dead, and into an inheritance that can never perish, spoil, or fade. This inheritance is kept in heaven for you, who through faith are shielded by God's power until the coming of the salvation that is ready to be revealed in the last time. In all this you greatly rejoice, though now for a little while you may have had to suffer grief in all kinds of trials. These have come so that the proven genuineness of your faith—of greater worth than gold, which perishes even though refined by fire—may result in praise, glory, and honor when Jesus Christ is revealed. Though you have not seen him, you love him; and even though you do not see him now, you believe in him and are filled with an inexpressible and glorious joy, for you are receiving the end result of your faith, the salvation of your souls." (1 Peter 1:3-9 NIV)

"It is the Spirit who gives life; the flesh profits nothing; the words that I have spoken to you are spirit and are life" (John 6:63 NASB)

God has placed a burden on my heart to be authentic, with no pretenses. That means constant change in my heart and my mind acting in concert with the humility to desire his way more than my own comfort. I've given up a lot of things in my lifetime, but for some reason I always seem to fall into one of two categories. I either begin to believe that for even a moment I'm finally refined enough to be done growing *(Ignorance)*, or else I imagine that the next time God allows me to be stretched for some reason it will be easier *(Foolishness)*.

Thanks be to God, I have come to realize that both are lies, and I praise God that he will never be finished doing that sort of business with me while there is still breath in my body. The next time, just as with the last and with the many still to come, I will be emotionally, mentally, and spiritually divided from the inside out. I know that each push heavenward will certainly be painful, at least temporarily. But I know that God will also certainly sustain me by his grace. He will continue through every step ahead, in every inch of growth, to be the fountain from which I am pouring over with living water onto everyone and everything I touch.

"Therefore, having been justified by faith, we have peace with God through our Lord Jesus Christ, through whom also we have obtained our introduction by faith into this grace in which we stand; and we exult in hope of the glory of God. And not only this, but we also exult in our tribulations, knowing that tribulation brings about perseverance; and perseverance, proven character; and proven character, hope; and hope does not disappoint, because the love of God has been poured out within our hearts through the Holy Spirit who was given to us" (Romans 5:1-5 NASB)

"Blessed be your name, on the road marked with suffering. Though there's pain in the offering, blessed be your name. Every blessing you pour out I'll turn back to praise. When the darkness closes in Lord, still I will say, blessed be the name of the Lord."—Matt Redman, "Blessed be Your Name"

"See what great love the Father has lavished on us, that we should be called children of God! And that is what we are! The reason the world does not know us is that it did not know him." (1 John 3:1 NIV)

He does know us though; be certain of that today. I have been moved very deeply to consider a father's love—Father God's love.

Most directly, in comparing the way my Abba Father loves me with the way I am able, in all of my failings, to love my own children. How short I fall in word and deed to be even a fraction for them of what my heavenly Father is to me. My prayer is always for the confidence, compassion, and wisdom that is from heaven, to be a good steward of this incredible gift I have been given by God. I want to do more good than harm as for this short time I care for the beautiful girl and boy he gave me. I know that I will always fall short, but by grace I am able to trust God to be the love of Jesus for them, through his love in me.

In pondering all this, he has also given me a glimpse of the way he must feel when, as his children, we ignore his wisdom and direction, when we ask him for advice; then no matter his answer, we still choose to go our own way. I begin to understand, in this love I have for my kids, God's desire to just scoop us up and put us on the right path **(Luke 6:46 NIV), (Luke 13:34 NIV)**. But I also see that for our own good, sometimes he cannot, that in the necessity for us to know the sting of failure and welcome the balm of wisdom's healing voice, he does not. For love's sake, so we will grow and possibly draw nearer to him in the offering, he will not. How great indeed is Father God's love.

"We love because he first loved us" (1 John 4:19 NIV)

It's about perspective

"I have proclaimed glad tidings of righteousness in the great congregation; Behold, I will not restrain my lips, O Lord, You know. I have not hidden Your righteousness within my heart; I have spoken of Your faithfulness and Your salvation; I have not concealed Your lovingkindness and Your truth from the great congregation. You, O Lord, will not withhold Your compassion from me; Your lovingkindnes and Your truth will continually preserve me" (Psalms 40:9-11 NASB).

I have learned so much over the last three years; it's hard to let it all soak in and begin to apply it. In the times of refining, God is always my assurance that everything is in his time and according to his will. When I am surrendered to that truth, I can trust him and what he desires for me. It's not easy, because attacks always come. The storms always reveal both the weakness and the strength in the way I live out my faith.

Tearing certain things down and beginning to rebuild, or allowing God to rebuild, has not been an uncommon experience. Old wounds, some I wasn't even aware I still had, can allow destructive patterns that have developed over many years to again rear their ugly head. Whether in the thoughts and intentions of my heart or in the way I speak and act toward people, since my whole heart is open and laid bare before him, nothing is off limits.

The deceiver (Satan) would have us believe every mole hill is *the* mountain and that there is a final rainbow beyond each one. To chase after these lies can only lead to failure and despair. In reality, however, the *test* is the mountain, and the mountain is truly the span of our natural lives. God's perfection is joy all along the way. He delights to be our strength, and he rewards our fealty and trust as we climb.

There is no ultimate victory, save that which we have in Jesus Christ, but we rejoice since we have that victory every day! He has overcome the world, period. What that means is until he returns all we long for and all our hearts desire can be in the tiniest of details. The "**day of small things**" **(Zechariah 4:10 NASB),** urges us every moment to look around and see beauty, listening and living for God, receiving his good gifts not in lieu of trials but in the thick of them.

"For we will surely die and are like water spilled on the ground which cannot be gathered up again. Yet God does not take away life, but plans ways so that the banished one will not be cast out from him." (2 Samuel 14:14 NASB)

In this statement is Faith. When we hear it, we are hearing words spoken about Jesus Christ **(Romans 10:17 NASB).** How many times have we felt like water spilled out that could not be gathered up again? The truth is, we were all once exactly that until Jesus took the burden of every banished one and said, *"Take my burden instead"* **(Matthew 11:28-29 NASB)**. Is his word any less true for you and me today than when we first believed? No! Through every sadness, through every disappointment, through every sickness, and through every pain, God does not take away life; he gives it. There is one who does desire to take away life; he lies, he accuses, and he would put a boot across our throats to bring so much calamity that the voice of God is drowned out. But even as faith comes by hearing the Word about Jesus Christ, our enemy can only affect circumstances in our lives if we agree with him **(2 Corinthians 1:20 NIV), (John 10:10 NIV)**. Otherwise, the most Satan can do is lie, accuse, and try to frighten us. God's ways are power that is always in our favor, if only we take hold of them and use them!

"We are destroying speculations and every lofty thing raised up against the knowledge of God, and we are taking every thought captive to the obedience of Christ" (2 Corinthians 10:5 NKJV).

So then our obligation is to the truth. We say "yes" and "no" by our actions; there is no middle ground. As surely as if we sow the wind, the whirlwind will be soon to follow, we are going to be given what we ask for when we pray according to God's will in our time of need.

"But the vessel that he was making of clay was spoiled in the hand of the potter; so he remade it into another vessel, as it pleased the potter to make." (Jeremiah 18:4 NASB)

We are being continually sanctified and remade into the image of Jesus as it pleases God to allow the circumstances of life to mold and shape us.

"For not from the east, nor from the west, nor from the desert comes exaltation; but God is the Judge; He puts down one and exalts another." (Psalms 75:6-7 NASB)

Though our actions do matter **(Jeremiah 18:7-8 NASB)**, he desires vessels that he can use. His desire for us is Love, Peace, and Joy! Life is what Jesus brought, and that so we would live it to the fullest! Recognizing and addressing that every stronghold, every fortress either in front of us or built up around us needs to be dealt with, torn down, and taken captive to the obedience of Christ is our victory! And this is not in our own power, but in his divine power. Wearing his heavenly armor, we do so much more than just survive. We overcome so that our lives are filled with and reflect his **(Romans 14:17-18 NASB), (John 10:10 NIV), (2 Corinthians 10:3-5 NASB), (Ephesians 6:10-16 NASB), Hebrews 10:39 NASB), (Ephesians 5:8-13 NIV).**

What an awesome thing!

"...thanks be to God! He gives us the victory through our Lord Jesus Christ" (1 Corinthians 15:57 NIV)

Tears in his bottle

"You have taken account of my wanderings; put my tears in Your bottle. Are they not in Your book? Then my enemies will turn back in the day when I call; this I know, that God is for me. In God, whose word I praise, in the Lord, whose word I praise, in God I have put my trust, I shall not be afraid. What can man do to me?" (Psalms 56:8-11 NASB)

"There is no pit so deep that God's love is not deeper still."—Corrie ten Boom

In times of adversity and weariness, it seems as though giving in to the current of this world and all its rumblings is not only easy but even a wise thing. On those days and in those moments, our hope, our encouragement, our strength to stand, and the courage to obey our deepest knowing from Jesus by his Spirit speaking life to us is in remembering—remembering who we are, whose we are, and most important of all who he IS.

"Praise be to the name of God for ever and ever; wisdom and power are his. He changes times and seasons; he deposes kings and raises up others. He gives wisdom to the wise and knowledge to the discerning. He reveals deep and hidden things; he knows what lies in darkness, and light dwells with him." (Daniel 2:20-22 NIV)

If we do more than just read his words, we let the Living Word **(John 1:1 NASB), (1 Peter 1:23 NIV)** rise up from within our spirits and involve God. He will always stand in our stead as adversity's Master and as the Conqueror of weariness saying, *"This one is mine and nothing will ever snatch them from my hand"* **(John 10:27-30 NIV)**. When we remember that God turns the hearts of all those who either commend or oppose us, we are assured that all of our times are in his hands. When we remember that every hair on our heads is numbered, and that, in perfect love, every day of our lives were written in his book before one of them ever came to be, there is perfect peace **(Proverbs 16:1-2 NASB), (Psalms 31:15 NIV), (Matthew 10:28-31 NASB), (Psalm 139:16 NIV)**. When we remember him, there is conviction and a promise that if he is for us, then whatever would stand against us must deal with "I AM," our Creator God, before it ever gets anywhere near our lives. His love for you and me is so immense, so great and deep and wide, that it could never be measured by any means we know **(Romans 8:31-39 NASB)**.

"Yes, my soul, find rest in God; my hope comes from him. Truly he is my rock and my salvation; he is my fortress, I will not be shaken. My salvation and my honor depend on God; he is my mighty rock, my refuge." (Psalms 62:5-7)

I am smiling to myself as I write this last paragraph for a couple of reasons. One of which is the amusing irony that I've been beaten with a knotted plow line from a spiritual perspective through writing the entire chapter called "Trials and Testing." Secondly, I know God's grace is enough to cover it all. He teaches and reminds me of so much in these experiences that I know my enemy has gained nothing from the effort or from my failings. So remember when you ask God to prune, winnow, and remove the things in your life that hinder his blessing and his purpose, don't expect it to be easy … Just sayin'.

Prayer: *Lord, when I'm tempted to falter, you help me to lean into the trial and rejoice in the knowledge that I have a Savior who knows, who suffered and died for me. My strongest defensive weapon is not my will to resist, but in humility remembering that when I submit and I'm broken, you resist for me. My weapons are your truths spoken over me in power. My agreement to take them up and use them is my victory. Thank you that, even when my heart fails me, you are greater than my heart and able to make me stand. Thank you Lord, that even when my faith is not strong, your faithfulness remains immovable and unfailing. Thank you that your revealed truth is separate from me and does not depend on me! I thank you, Abba, that the darkness must flee in your presence when I am bold to approach your throne and remember that I belong to you. Thank You for comfort and peace that are joy from you. Thank you for reminding me that it's not in the calm waters apart from total dependence upon you that I find those things. But as I am found red-faced, with aching knees, crying out from the deepest places of my soul, knowing I am wrapped tightly in your arms of love that they are most pure and candid to me. You speak the truth only a desperate and seeking heart can receive, Abba, so I can say, "It is well with my soul." In Jesus' mighty name, Amen!*

Scripture: **"Consider it pure joy, my brothers and sisters, whenever you face trials of many kinds, because you know that the testing of your faith produces perseverance. Let perseverance finish its work so that you may be mature and complete, not lacking anything" (James 1:2-4 NIV)**

CHAPTER 17

COMFORT AND JOY

Strangely dim

"And he said to them, 'Why is it that you were looking for me? Did you not know that I had to be in my Father's house?'" (Luke 2:49 NASB)

Isn't it such a sweet and awesome thing to always know where he'll be? It is comfort beyond measure to know there is an open door to where the lover of every soul waits for us and bids us to come **(Hebrews 4:16 NASB)**. In this world we have so many troubles, but he is far above all those troubles and he makes them all okay **(John 16:33 NASB)**. When all about us, for a time, in any particular trial, seems too huge to hold, he says, *"I can hold that for you."* When nights are cold and worry presses in, he holds out his arms of assurance and enfolds us in warmth. When we haven't the strength even to stand, he clothes us and puts the new robes of his strength around us. He says, *"Nothing will ever separate us and nobody will ever snatch you from my hands"* **(Matthew 11:28 NASB), (Romans 8:27 NASB), (Romans 8:37-39 NASB), (John 10:27-28 NASB)**. Oh, that these fragile and breakable vessels we are given would always find fair use in his house by day and a place of honor and safety by night.

"For a day in Your courts is better than a thousand outside. I would rather stand at the threshold of the house of my God than dwell in the tents of wickedness." (Psalms 84:10 NASB)

Nothing else can compare. Of course he had to be in his Father's house. His Spirit knows, so that we know he could be found there then, and he will be now or whenever we seek him. He is near to each of us if ever we cry out **(Luke 17:20-21 NKJV), (Acts 17:27 NIV)**—as near as our knees to the floor, as near as a tear that meets the air and with our spirit prays, *"Abba, I need you more than all on this earth; help,"* as near as his perfect name to our lips. Forever desiring the possible and the intimate, his Spirit is as near to us as our own. When we allow the noise of the world to fade away, the din of our flesh is overcome by his peace that cannot be explained and will not be moved **(Philippians 4:7 NASB), (James 1:17 NASB)**. Oh what a beautiful, wonderful Comforter! Oh what an indescribable wholeness we have in Jesus!

"And I will pray the Father, and He will give you another Helper that He may abide with you forever— the Spirit of truth, whom the world cannot receive, because it neither sees Him nor knows Him; but you know Him, for He dwells with you and will be in you." (John 14:16-17 NKJV)

Since he is so close at hand, we can seek him as a friend, a companion, a brother, a counselor, and a refuge. When all else seems to fall poorly and terribly short of home, he can always be found in his Father's house, always in our midst **(Colossians 1:19-20 NASB)**.

"But now in Christ Jesus you who formerly were far off have been brought near by the blood of Christ. For He Himself is our peace ..." (Ephesians 2:13-14 NASB)

"...you also, as living stones, are being built up as a spiritual house for a holy priesthood, to offer up spiritual sacrifices acceptable to God through Jesus Christ." (1 Peter 2:5 NASB)

Where the rubber meets the road, we don't really have any choice but to be as transparent as possible, so that we are always honest, even when it's hard. Today may even have started off as a hard day. As a matter of fact, we may have had many weeks that were filled with the most profound, intimate revelations from God, and they were then followed, for a few days at least, with times of struggle and battle. This is a common thing; the wisest people I know, who have been walking with God a lot longer than I have, told me so, and I believe them. Scripture bears it out as well **(1 Kings 18 and 19 to begin with, and there are many others)**.

But my only purpose in saying that is to ask you all this question, *"Are you happy right now?"* The answer may be Yes or No, but that is really irrelevant. The only important thing to know is that in any condition we can be firmly established in joy. We can be content, not because our circumstances warrant it or because they don't, and not because of our frame of mind or our sensations are at a high or low point, but because the position from which we always begin depends on God alone who is in all things, who was before all things, and the one through whom everything that *is* has its being. He is enough—without anything or anyone else, whether the abundance of what he created is to our favor at the moment, or it is in some way, due to our weakness or whatever else, all stripped away. What we are left with, or rather what we began with, where all things begin, is our foundation in intimate love and relationship with God our Savior. That is infinite, unfailing, and constant—in other words, pure joy!

"...I have learned to be content whatever the circumstances. I know what it is to be in need, and I know what it is to have plenty. I have learned the secret of being content in any and every situation, whether well fed or hungry, whether living in plenty or in want. I can do all this through him who gives me strength." (Philippians 4:11-13 NIV)

Lit up and Salty

"For everyone will be salted with fire. Salt is good; but if the salt becomes unsalty, with what will you make it salty again? Have salt in yourselves, and be at peace with one another." (Mark 9:49-50 NASB)

All who have faith in Jesus Christ as Savior are called to be seasoned with the Holy Spirit **(Matthew 3:11 NASB)**. Our hearts surge again to life with a chorus of love from the very multitudes of heaven, crying, *"Holy, Holy, Holy."* Our eyes alight with new birth, with the warmth and comfort of God's amazing love and grace. We have the finest spices that our Abba Father affords his beloved with which to both sanctify and be sanctified, all for his Kingdom purposes. But sometimes we let the light in our eyes grow dim; we allow the urging of a gratitude that remembers the depths from which we were grasped to be crowded out. We may even forget, if only momentarily, the voice of the One who called down to us, the feel of his hand that laid hold of us, and his strength by which we made solid ground at all. Do not allow doubt to take root, as one fell swoop is often more than enough to waste the good fruit borne of a lifetime. A single moment can be long enough to render ineffective a far piece of narrow road traveled and hewn in sincere faith **(James 3:2-18 NASB)**.

The warnings Jesus gives are solemn and to be ever heeded.

"The eye is the lamp of your body; when your eye is clear, your whole body also is full of light; but when it is bad, your body also is full of darkness. Then watch out that the light in you is not darkness. If therefore your whole body is full of light, with no dark part in it, it will be wholly illumined, as when the lamp illumines you with its rays." (Luke 11:34-36 NASB)

So also are his exhortations made all the more weighty by the importance of our focus and where it lands from thought to intention, and from intention to action. Comfort must never become complacency in us, lest we be deprived a proper understanding of authentic joy. Being immediately and intentionally present in *the joy of his salvation* is central to our ability as God's kids to stay lit up and salty **(Luke 12:35-36)**. Thanks be to God for his tender mercy, his ceaseless answer to our prayers, and his faithfulness to sustain us with a willing spirit when we cry out for help.

"Create in me a clean heart, O God, and renew a steadfast spirit within me. Do not cast me away from Your presence and do not take Your Holy Spirit from me. Restore to me the joy of Your salvation and sustain me with a willing spirit" (Psalms 51:10-12 NASB).

The Gardener

"Joy is the infallible sign of the presence of God."—Pierre Teilhard de Chardin

"For I know the plans I have for you," declares the Lord, "plans to prosper you and not to harm you, plans to give you hope and a future." (Jeremiah 29:11 NIV)

One time, not too long ago, when I was feeling very dry spiritually, I happened to be walking by a tree that had just been pruned and cut back. It was bare, with no leaves, and empty, with missing branches everywhere. As soon as the thought crossed my mind that this tree looked how I felt, God showed me a picture of the way that he tends to me spiritually, as a gardener would tend to that tree during the different seasons of a year. I'll try to explain it as best I can.

"I am the true vine, and my Father is the gardener. He cuts off every branch in me that bears no fruit, while every branch that does bear fruit he prunes so that it will be even more fruitful." (John 15:1-2 NIV)

There are times we resist the pruning part because, really, who wants to feel barren and leafless with a bunch of cutoff branches anyway? The problem is, if we do resist for too long, while we may be okay for a while, there are places that will become overgrown and need to be cut back so that we can grow and bear more fruit. If we continue to resist God's trimming process, those overgrown parts remain and eventually become like overheavy branches that break off anyway. Only when that happens, whether to a good fruit-bearing branch or to one that just needed cutting off, healthy parts also fall along with it.

Thankfully, he tends to us perfectly. God never allows too much to be cut off, and he never leaves too much behind. When the new growth begins, and the seasons continue to change, we receive just the right amount of all he has in just the right places. He sees the finished product, and he lovingly shapes us accordingly.

Here are three things God showed me in this:

1. Pruning is absolutely imperative for growth. Whether it is a healthy branch or one that needs to go altogether, each branch needs tending in order for us to become the healthy, vibrant tree that God sees.

2. Resisting the process only hurts us and those around us. It may take surrender and submission to accept our lives being cut back and trimmed a bit, but even though it looks and feels funky, God knows what he is doing.

3. Remember it is only a season. Just as there will be times of testing and growth, there will also always follow times of refreshing joy and comfort flourishing under God's loving hand of direction.

"Weeping may last for the night, but a shout of joy comes in the morning." (Psalms 30:5 NASB)

"Therefore we do not lose heart. Though outwardly we are wasting away, yet inwardly we are being renewed day by day. For our light and momentary troubles are achieving for us an eternal glory that far outweighs them all. So we fix our eyes not on what is seen, but on what is unseen, since what is seen is temporary, but what is unseen is eternal." (2 Corinthians 4:16-18 NIV)

Straight and lighted pathways

"Your word is a lamp for my feet, a light on my path. I have taken an oath and confirmed it, that I will follow your righteous laws. I have suffered much; preserve my life, LORD, according to your word. Accept, LORD, the willing praise of my mouth and teach me your laws." (Psalms 109:105-108 NIV)

I would rather spend an eternity navigating the uneven ground of a path illumined by God's Word than one moment stumbling around on a level and broad path shrouded in darkness apart from him. The Holy Spirit reminds me of this each morning when I begin relying too heavily on created things for comfort and joy in place of God. It isn't a scolding, finger-wagging sort of reminder, only a tap on the shoulder, along with a loving and furtive look as if to warn me again, firmly but gently. This helps me remember how finite and breakable I am apart from seeking daily and straining toward God.

"So, if you think you are standing firm, be careful that you don't fall! No temptation has seized you except what is common to mankind. And God is faithful; he will not let you be tempted beyond what you can bear. But when you are tempted, he will also provide a way out so that you can endure it." (1 Corinthians 10:12-13 NIV)

God reminded me that he rewards those who earnestly seek him **(Hebrews 11:6)**, that I am accepted, loved, forgiven, comforted, and held firmly in the arms of joy no matter what else may come. Right this moment, "**I am my beloved's and my beloved is mine ...**" **(Song of Songs 6:3 NIV)**, and the reverse cannot ever be so again **(Romans 8:35-39 NASB)**. He brought to my mind that I am running a race with a goal that requires my attention and focus, then he assured me that I am able to stand in his power, clad in his armor **(Ephesians 6:10-18 NASB)**.

God also gave me a picture of this: He made everything, he is everything, he is in everything, and he is through everything **(Ephesians 4:6 NASB), (Colossians 1:16-17 NASB)**. What we humans do is attempt to avoid a confrontation with this fact, and in so doing we put up all manner of created things in place of the esteem that God alone was meant to hold. We do this to mask pain, gain temporary relief, distract ourselves from reality, and generally just to keep from having to admit even a hint of the truth that is our unassailable need for a restored love relationship with the only One who matters, God. He made the world and everything in it for us, but apart from him any of it is only a shadow, a cheap imitation of what he intended it to be. Our enemy (Satan) will use that fact in whatever form he can whenever we allow him.

"Therefore Jesus said again, 'Very truly I tell you, I am the gate for the sheep. All who have come before me are thieves and robbers, but the sheep did not listen to them. I am the gate; whoever enters through me will be saved. They will come in and go out, and find pasture. The thief comes only to steal and kill and destroy; I have come that they may have life, and have it to the full'" (John 10:7-10 NIV).

Also check out these scriptures if you want to go a little deeper: **(John 1:4 NIV), (John 6:48 NASB), (1 John 5:12 NIV), (John 5:35-40 NIV), (Colossians 1:16 NASB), (John 15:5-8 NASB).**

For those of you who like word pictures, accepting the quick fixes and counterfeits could be compared to the feeling of desperation you used to get the morning after a sleepover with your best friend when you realized they would be gone soon and you would again be alone. Seeking first after God is conversely like the same morning, but with the added warmth and consistent love of a family that remains long after the friend has gone. This allows you the true joy of knowing that, while the prior night's fun is now past, you can be confident it will come again. In the meantime, you are secure and safe because your foundation is in enduring love, not in the emotion or feeling of the moment. They both have a distinct beginning and a certain end—the former from selfishness to despair, the latter from selflessness to fulfillment.

"Trust in the LORD with all your heart and do not lean on your own understanding. In all your ways acknowledge Him, and he will make your paths straight." (Proverbs 3:5-6 NASB)

"But seek first his kingdom and his righteousness, and all these things will be given to you as well." (Matthew 6:33 NIV)

Enter his gates

"Shout joyfully to the Lord, all the earth. Serve the Lord with gladness; come before him with joyful singing. Know that the Lord himself is God; it is He who has made us, and not we ourselves; *we are His* people and the sheep of His pasture." (Psalms 100:1-3 NASB)

We are his.

Those have got to be three of the most beautiful words ever formed into a sentence. They are beautiful because they are full of joy. And what is joy if not our knowing who he is and who we are (Psalms 135:3 NASB). There is a gladness in saying, *"Yes Lord!"* There is a confidence that goes beyond all of the uncertain days ahead of us and all of the now spent past to which we so often return. We can know by our praises to him and through our declarations about him, that we are held in the arms of God's love as it will be, as it is now, and as it was before all time or creation (Psalms 136:12 NIV), (Psalms 139:1-18 NIV). Our hope in this life and for eternity is made secure by his living Word, Jesus Christ (Mark 10:29-30 NIV), (John 11:25-26 NASB). We are cosseted and certain by his gentle hand upon us, by his watchful eyes that always see us, and by his familiar voice that entreats us to be always where he is, and to enter his gates with a thankful heart and rest.

Our God will never falter. He will never give us up nor leave us behind. In plenty or in want, in deep pain or the merriest of happenstance, we will yet praise him (Psalms 42:5 NIV), (Philippians 4:11-13 NASB), (1 Thessalonians 5:16-18 NASB). He is immovable, unshakable, unchanging; the pinions of his mighty wings are a safe refuge around us (Nahum 1:7 NASB), (Psalms 91:4 NIV).

How awesome is our God, worthy of all glory, honor, and praise in every circumstance of our lives! For these reasons and so many more, we are not dismayed, never overcome, and forever victorious. We are filled with a light and power that can never be snuffed out, never be diminished **(Revelation 4:11 NASB), (1 Peter 1:3-5 NASB)**. No, we are not our own. In comfort, with a solace that no human intellect can touch, we are gratefully and forever his.

"Enter His gates with thanksgiving and His courts with praise. Give thanks to Him, bless His name. For the Lord is good; His lovingkindness is everlasting and His faithfulness to all generations." (Psalms 100:4-5 NASB)

Prayer: *Thank you God for reminding me of your deliverance and hope spoken over me. It is like healing water poured out on my head. The deepest part of me is able to stand by your mercy, in your strength, and for your glory. But not only so, I also take up whatever cross you bid me bear today, and in fullness of joy I choose to come after you. Praise your holy name! When I consider all you have done, all that you are doing, and all of the amazing things beyond comprehension that you will yet do, they are more than I could ever ask or imagine. My spirit rises up within me to join all creation and declare, "You, O God, are HOLY, HOLY, HOLY! Hallelujah!" I will speak out your praise in my home, and from every rooftop I will declare: "Our God is exalted high above all the earth!" In Jesus' name, Amen!*

Scripture: **"You will make known to me the path of life; in Your presence is fullness of joy; in Your right hand there are pleasures forever." (Psalms 16:11 NASB)**

CHAPTER 18

WARFARE AND THE ENEMY

Yes, he does exist

Whether we like it or not, we do have an enemy who is the devil, or Satan. As surely as God is light, our adversary is darkness (the absence of light). In fact, if you consider everything that makes up God's character, Satan has fashioned a counterfeit to mimic it (however poorly). Firstly, I want you to know that our greatest offensive weapon against him is to do everything we can to be like Jesus Christ and imitate his character. The only sure way to know the character of God is to learn about him from his Word, and by your faith in action, he will put light on all of the darkness and counterfeits of the enemy.

"Consequently, faith comes from hearing the message, and the message is heard through the word about Christ" (Romans 10:17 NIV)

Below I have listed a few scriptures that clearly show God's character and what it looks like to be Christ-like. Yes, that means you've got to crack a Bible open and do some reading, but trust me when I say it'll be well worth your time. First battle the darkness by being the light of Jesus and by choosing to walk in the light every day.

(1 John 4:7-20 NIV), (1 Corinthians 13 NASB), (1 John 1:5 NASB), (Galatians 5:22-23), (Philippians 2:1-11 NASB), (2 Peter 1:3-9 NIV), (Colossians 3:1-3 NASB), (Ephesians 5:8 NIV)

Having said that, I also want to say that, in life, not everything that comes against you is from the enemy. In Christian circles people say, *"Don't look for a demon under every doily."* If we are earnestly seeking, God meets us right where we are **(Hebrews 11:6 NIV)**. If there is any kind of spiritual or other darkness in your life, bring it out into the open, pray about it, or tell somebody about it. The enemy's first aim is to keep you and your issues isolated from God, your family, and your friends. He cannot operate any longer once things are exposed and in the light.

"...God is light; in him there is no darkness at all." (1 John 1:5 NIV)

"But all things become visible when they are exposed by the light, for everything that becomes visible is light." (Ephesians 5:13 NASB)

Be accountable for your own actions. Confess your sin to God and to another when you know you should, then ask him for forgiveness. Doing this is, to Satan, the spiritual equivalent of drawing poison from a wound since God's response is definitive and immediate.

"If we confess our sins, He is faithful and righteous to forgive us our sins and to cleanse us from all unrighteousness." (1 John 1:9 NASB)

"...the devil doesn't come dressed in a red cape and pointy horns. He comes as everything you've ever wished for ..."—Tucker Max

"He has shown you, O man, what is good; And what does the Lord require of you? But to do justly, to love mercy, and to walk humbly with your God" (Micah 6:8 NKJV)

Most people believe Satan and his attacks to be overt, and it may seem so in some instances. But his most destructive, most powerful attacks are those that begin and fester in our hearts and minds. They are subtle, to say the least, and invisible until their most potent damage is done.

A tree will either flourish or die at its root, so Satan attacks the root. First he goes after the heart and mind of the individual, then the family, and on out from there. But knowing all of this, I still fall every day. Even being conscious of, as the verse above says, " ...**what is good,**" I still sometimes fail to do it. Yes, we can earnestly repent and ask God's forgiveness, being certain that by his grace we have it. But what I want to make most clear to you is the importance of understanding that spiritual darkness comes not as some big, scary boogeyman, but instead as a thought, an emotion, or even a word from someone you love, and who loves you. It comes in the form of ignorance, innuendo, and wrong assumptions all along the footpaths of pride; so be alert and aware, remembering what we already know.

"You were taught, with regard to your former way of life, to put off your old self, which is being corrupted by its deceitful desires; to be made new in the attitude of your minds; and to put on the new self, created to be like God in true righteousness and holiness.

"Therefore each of you must put off falsehood and speak truthfully to your neighbor, for we are all members of one body. 'In your anger do not sin': Do not let the sun go down while you are still angry, and do not give the devil a foothold. Anyone who has been stealing must steal no longer, but must work, doing something useful with their own hands, that they may have something to share with those in need.

"Do not let any unwholesome talk come out of your mouths, but only what is helpful for building others up according to their needs, that it may benefit those who listen. And do not grieve the Holy Spirit of God, with whom you were sealed for the day of redemption. Get rid of all bitterness, rage and anger, brawling and slander, along with every form of malice. Be kind and compassionate to one another, forgiving each other, just as in Christ God forgave you" (Ephesians 4:22-32 NIV)

"Above all, keep fervent in your love for one another, because love covers a multitude of sins." (1 Peter 4:8 NASB)

God's Word says the enemy is cunning **(2 Corinthians 11:3 NIV)**. I take that to be an admonition, meaning that he is more cunning than me and too much for me to handle apart from the power of Jesus Christ. I find that he most fiercely attacks me when I take my eyes off of God and put them on my own circumstances. But the good news is he is defeated and powerless. The only power he has, beyond the ability to bring lies, fear, and accusations, is that which we allow him. Satan and his demons can yammer on all they like, but unless we come into agreement with them, they are mostly helpless to affect our lives.

I laugh sometimes when people put Satan on the same level with God like they are two heavyweight boxers squaring off in the battle for all humanity and creation. Our enemy the devil is a created being and no more able to meet God on level ground in battle than a thatch hut is able to withstand a tidal wave. So he is left to prey on those weaker than he is, and to take up scraps wherever he can get them. We are not able to stand up to him alone, but if we stand firm in our identity through Jesus Christ, he is little more than an afterthought. If you know Jesus as your Savior today, know also that you are free and victorious as long as you stay alert and sober-minded. With your eyes turned toward the Cross and what God did for you there, you are clad in the armor of heaven and **"no weapon fashioned against you shall prosper"** (Isaiah 54:17).

"Be well balanced (temperate, sober of mind), be vigilant and cautious at all times; for that enemy of yours, the devil, roams around like a lion roaring [in fierce hunger], seeking someone to seize upon and devour.

Withstand him; be firm in faith [against his onset—rooted, established, strong, immovable, and determined], knowing that the same (identical) sufferings are appointed to your brotherhood (the whole body of Christians) throughout the world." (1 Peter 5:8-9 AMP)

"Finally, be strong in the Lord and in his mighty power. Put on the full armor of God so that you can take your stand against the devil's schemes. For our struggle is not against flesh and blood, but against the rulers, against the authorities, against the powers of this dark world and against the spiritual forces of evil in the heavenly realms. Therefore put on the full armor of God, so that when the day of evil comes, you may be able to stand your ground, and after you have done everything, to stand. Stand firm then, with the belt of truth buckled around your waist,

with the breastplate of righteousness in place, and with your feet fitted with the readiness that comes from the gospel of peace. In addition to all this, take up the shield of faith, with which you can extinguish all the flaming arrows of the evil one. Take the helmet of salvation and the sword of the Spirit, which is the word of God. And pray in the Spirit on all occasions with all kinds of prayers and requests. With this in mind, be alert and always keep on praying for all the saints" (Ephesians 6:10-18 NIV)

"The weapons we fight with are not the weapons of the world. On the contrary, they have divine power to demolish strongholds. We demolish arguments and every pretension that sets itself up against the knowledge of God, and we take captive every thought to make it obedient to Christ." (2 Corinthians 10:4-5 NIV)

Amen! God keeps bringing to my mind that we "**do not wage war as the world does.**" Most of our weaponry is "armor," but know this: "**the sword of the Spirit, which is the word of God,**" the word about Jesus Christ spoken out loud or prayed in sincere faith, whether over your life or someone else's, causes the darkness to scatter and the enemy to run in the opposite direction.

"Then I heard a loud voice in heaven say: 'Now have come the salvation and the power and the kingdom of our God, and the authority of his Messiah. For the accuser of our brothers and sisters, who accuses them before our God day and night, has been hurled down. *They triumphed over him by the blood of the Lamb and by the word of their testimony* ...'" (Revelation 12:10-11 NIV)

The shield of our faith is both an offensive and defensive weapon. As I said though, the sword of the Spirit that is the very Word of God (*both the spoken Word of God and Jesus Christ the living Word of God*) is "**the**" weapon. Put most plainly, love. Jesus Christ IS the love of God that spoke life into all creation, and as we strike every blow with that mighty sword, no foul spirit will be able to stand. Again, Jesus left us one command, and as his word is flawless **(Proverbs 30:5 NIV),**

(Psalms 12:6 NIV), (Psalms 18:30 NIV), that command is left for us so every ear that hears is called to action and truth.

"A new command I give you: Love one another. As I have loved you, so you must love one another." (John 13:34 NIV)

Nothing the enemy can bring against you will ever stand against that declaration of God's love lived out, and poured out into your life and into the lives of everyone he puts around you.

Who is he?

"The thief comes only to steal and kill and destroy; I came that they may have life, and have it abundantly." (John 10:10 NASB)

When Jesus was asked this, **"Teacher, which is the great commandment in the Law?" (Matthew 22:36 NIV),** he responded: **And he said to him, "'You shall love the Lord your God with all your heart, and with all your soul, and with all your mind.' This is the great and foremost commandment. The second is like it, 'You shall love your neighbor as yourself.' On these two commandments depend the whole Law and the Prophets" (Matthew 22:37-40 NASB).**

So if those commandments are the greatest and all of God's law and prophecy depend on them, Satan seeks their counterfeit to the end of destroying all that is of God and all those who are for God.

If loving God with all of our heart, soul, and mind is his word to us, then the enemy's counterfeit is not overt hatred of God, but rather that which has its conception, birth, and maturity in complacency and total indifference toward God and his desire.

If loving our neighbor as ourselves is his word for us, then the enemy's counterfeit is not an overt hatred toward our neighbor or of ourselves, but rather an unnatural vanity and love of self so extreme as to have its conception, birth, and maturity in an utter disregard for anything, save our own gratification.

The terrible and destructive result of each then is self-absorption on a level that renders both God and our neighbor not only unimportant to us, but also totally irrelevant.

"The beginning of wisdom is this: Get wisdom. Though it cost all you have, get understanding." (Proverbs 4:7 NIV)

"...Satan himself masquerades as an angel of light." (2 Corinthians 11:14 NIV)

Realizing that our enemy is not only crafty but also subtle in the darkest way imaginable is to prepare our minds for action, as God's word says:

"Therefore, with minds that are alert and fully sober, set your hope on the grace to be brought to you when Jesus Christ is revealed at his coming." (1 Peter 1:13 NIV)

Our enemy desires our deception and confusion at all times in every circumstance; he desires it insatiably. Remember Jesus' words about him:

"He was a murderer from the beginning, and does not stand in the truth because there is no truth in him. Whenever he speaks a lie, he speaks from his own nature, for he is a liar and the father of lies." (John 8:44 NASB)

But be encouraged and thank the Lord today for wisdom that is from him. Thank him for humility and the grace that saves us from the enemy's schemes. Your Savior Jesus Christ has given you power to use both his Word and his love that is alive in you as weapons of light and life. He has given you the ability to stand and fight, and he is the One who always goes before you into battle.

"And He said to them, 'I was watching Satan fall from heaven like lightning. Behold, *I have given you authority* to tread on serpents

and scorpions, and *over all the power of the enemy*, and nothing will injure you. Nevertheless do not rejoice in this, that the spirits are subject to you, but rejoice that your names are recorded in heaven'." (Luke 10:18-20 NASB)

"But He gives a greater grace. Therefore it says, 'God is opposed to the proud, but gives grace to the humble.' *Submit then to God. Resist the devil and he will flee from you."* (James 4:6-7 NASB)

Prayer: *Lord, may your commands and your admonitions strengthen all who hope in your Word today. I thank you for instruction and for the Cross that stole away the victory of death, triumphed over the grave, and took away Satan's power! Glory to you God! Help me to keep your Word and your love at the center of my ranks in battle, Lord. I will not allow the enemy to steal or rob me of my peace today in the name of Jesus! Lord, I thank you that you alone are my confidence. You clad me in the finest and strongest armor of heaven and make my life an offence to the darkness. In you I am a sentry and a mighty warrior captain in your service. I shout the name of JESUS, name above all names and declare the authority of Most High God over my life and my household, over all of the saints of God that are being menaced by a defeated enemy. I declare victory in the name of Jesus! I take authority over the enemy of God and I declare, "You have no power over any of God's chosen." I pray the light of Christ into every dark place and declare that every counterfeit of the enemy is exposed and scattered in the name of Jesus! I declare in the name of Jesus that the gates of hell will not prevail. In the name of Jesus, I take back every inch of ground that Satan has stolen from the hearts and minds of God's people. I pray all this through the power and authority that is found in the name of Jesus, Amen!*

Scripture(s): "**How you have fallen from heaven, O star of the morning, son of the dawn!**

You have been cut down to the earth, you who have weakened the nations! But you said in your heart, 'I will ascend to heaven; I will raise my throne above the stars of God, and I will sit on the mount

of assembly in the recesses of the north. I will ascend above the heights of the clouds; I will make myself like the Most High.' Nevertheless you will be thrust down to Sheol, to the recesses of the pit." (Isaiah 14:12-15 NASB)

"Both the one who makes people holy and those who are made holy are of the same family. So Jesus is not ashamed to call them brothers and sisters. He says, 'I will declare your name to my brothers and sisters; in the assembly I will sing your praises.'

"And again, 'I will put my trust in him.'

"And again he says, 'Here am I, and the children God has given me.'

"Since the children have flesh and blood, he too shared in their humanity so that *by his death he might break the power of him who holds the power of death—that is, the devil—* and free those who all their lives were held in slavery by their fear of death." (Hebrews 2:11-15 NIV)

CHAPTER 19

SIN AND MERCY

The punishment that brought us peace

"...for all have sinned and fall short of the glory of God, and all are justified freely by his grace through the redemption that came by Christ Jesus." (Romans 3:23 NIV)

Whenever I fall hard, it reminds me of what God teaches us about sin: Not only that in Christ all of it is forgiven and the debt paid once for all **(Hebrews 10:14 NIV)**, but also that sin's consequences and God's mercy are mutually exclusive. When we hurt other people, there are consequences; when we make bad decisions, there are consequences **(Romans 6:21-22 NIV)**. Jesus Christ died once for all for the forgiveness of sins, but that will never make sin's effect any less ugly and detrimental every time we choose it over what we know is right **(Romans 6:16 NIV)**.

"If anyone, then, knows the good they ought to do and doesn't do it, it is sin for them." (James 4:17 NIV)

Nothing but total contrition and humility before the Lord and Savior of our lives can make any of those consequences "okay," or take the burden of them from a human heart. So every attempt we make in our own power, or by any other means to fix things, only piles them up ever higher. The most foul and destructive lie the enemy will ever tell any man or woman is as old as creation: *"You are fine on your own, and there is no need to repent because there is nothing to confess."* He will do his best to convince you that you are an island, for lack of a better term, and that all of your poisonous emotions, desires, problems, and shortcomings are supreme so that there is no demand for the supremacy of God. Satan's appeal to our pride is a counterfeit to top all counterfeits.

"Now the serpent was more crafty than any of the wild animals the Lord God had made. He said to the woman, 'Did God really

say, "You must not eat from any tree in the garden"?' The woman said to the serpent, 'We may eat fruit from the trees in the garden, but God did say, "You must not eat fruit from the tree that is in the middle of the garden, and you must not touch it, or you will die."' 'You will not certainly die,' the serpent said to the woman. 'For God knows that when you eat from it your eyes will be opened, and you will be like God, knowing good and evil.' When the woman saw that the fruit of the tree was good for food and pleasing to the eye, and also desirable for gaining wisdom, she took some and ate it. She also gave some to her husband, who was with her, and he ate it." (Genesis 3:1-5 NIV)

God is so full of mercy and grace to love us in spite of it all. The reality of the Cross, of why Jesus had to die for us to be free, brings tears of joy and grief whenever I consider it. The eternal nature of his justice and compassion that orders the universe touches the most tender places of every wounded soul. His love is so delicate and personal that even as our hearts break to know the pain we've caused, they are instantaneously convinced of the righteousness which made us undeniably and irrevocably his.

Don't be deceived

"A man by his sin may waste himself, which is to waste that which on earth is most like God. This is man's greatest tragedy and God's heaviest grief."—A. W. Tozer

"My people have committed two sins: They have forsaken me, the spring of living water, and have dug their own cisterns, broken cisterns that cannot hold water." (Jeremiah 2:13 NIV)

The two most common mistakes we make are turning away from God and ceasing to believe what he says, then turning to ourselves and our wisdom by beginning to believe we have things all figured out. We fall into the trap of believing we are waterproof and airtight all on our own, when in reality we are leaky and all full of holes **(Revelation 3:17 NIV).**

Thankfully there are three ways we can walk out our faith. These all give God permission to plug up the holes or, more accurately, to make us into the vessels he can use. The apostle John gives us some BIG hints in **(1 John 2:12-15 NASB):**

"I am writing to you, little children, because your sins have been forgiven you for His name's sake."

Approach God as a child. His Word says, " …**the kingdom belongs to such as these.**," because the condition of their hearts is pure. In the way they approach him, they are highly favored **(Luke 18:16 NASB)**

"I am writing to you, fathers, because you know him who has been from the beginning."

God calls us all to be elders, in part—mature in a faith that comes from the pursuit of him and his Word. Living as "**wise not as unwise**," brings us deeper and makes us more effective **(Ephesians 5:15-17 NASB), (Hebrews 5:14 NASB)**.

"I have written to you, young men, because you are strong, and the word of God abides in you, and you have overcome the evil one."

God calls us to be vigorous and fervent, and to receive the strength he gives in his living Word, to do battle in the world and be victorious *by magnifying his name and giving his Word first place in our hearts* **(1 Corinthians 9:24-27 NIV).**

We are to be as John the Baptist and Isaiah the prophet: " …**a voice of one crying in the wilderness, 'Make straight the way of the Lord'" (John 1:23 NASB), (Isaiah 40:3 NKJV)**. It is then God's perfect way. As we choose faithfulness and obedience daily, he is faithful to respond daily with forgiveness and the fulfillment of all of his promises.

"For no matter how many promises God has made, they are 'Yes' in Christ. And so through him the 'Amen' is spoken by us to the glory of God." (2 Corinthians 1:20 NIV)

Going through changes

"As surely as the Lord lives, the man who did this must die! He must pay for that lamb four times over, because he did such a thing and had no pity." Then Nathan said to David, *"You are the man!"* (2 Samuel 12:7 NIV)

REBUKE
CONVICTION
GRIEF

At one point, every human being will confront that stinging reality and see it come into full view. If you don't believe me, take a look at the hammer and nails we all hold, then hear the voices of every soul under heaven, including your own, that screamed, *"Crucify him!"* and sent Jesus to the Cross.

Then David said, "I have sinned against the Lord." Nathan replied, *"The Lord has taken away your sin. You are not going to die.* But because by doing this you have shown utter contempt for the Lord, the son born to you will die." (2 Samuel 12:13-14 NIV)

FORGIVENESS
GRACE
CONSEQUENCES

David's response to God is important since it acknowledges the one undeniable thing every one of us has in common—sin. God's response to David is important since it models Jesus to us under the same circumstances—mercy. That our actions ripple widely and will produce affectedness is important to recognize, since they distinguish God's intentional grace from sin's unintentional but inevitable ramifications.

"David pleaded with God for the child. He fasted and spent the nights lying in sackcloth on the ground. The elders of his household stood beside him to get him up from the ground, but he refused, and he would not eat any food with them." (2 Samuel 12:16-17 NIV)

WRESTLING WITH GOD
MOURNING
REPENTANCE

Once we realize, like David did, the futility of trying—and we always try—to get the "crap back in the goose," we rightly mourn and repent. So we can be sure of this: that these are not only very necessary steps, but also that God sees and hears when we take them.

"'Is the child dead?' he asked. 'Yes,' they replied, 'he is dead.' Then David got up from the ground. After he had washed, put on lotions and changed his clothes, he went into the house of the Lord and worshiped." (2 Samuel 12:19-20 NIV)

ACCEPTING
RECEIVING
WORSHIPING

God most often allows our punishment to be the havoc we've caused. He treats us as sons and daughters in this for *our* good and to *his* glory. David's response here is important since it models an acknowledgement of both as, in the immediate aftermath of deep pain, his choice is to go and worship.

"Then David comforted his wife Bathsheba, and he went to her and made love to her. She gave birth to a son, and they named him

Solomon. The Lord loved him; and because the Lord loved him, he sent word through Nathan the prophet to name him Jedidiah." (2 Samuel 12:24-25 NIV)

FAVOR
SALVATION
MERCY

Our Abba Father is always willing and able to redeem us from whatever pit we've fallen into. The affirmation of his perfect love for David is also the unshakeable hope we have in Jesus, our merciful Savior. In showing that he is both willing and able to bring unequaled beauty from even the most tangled ugliness that our weakened flesh may produce, we see God's true character, sovereign over all creation as both Adonai (Lord and Master) and Emmanuel (God ever with us).

"The Lord's mercy often rides to the door of our heart upon the black horse of affliction."—Charles H. Spurgeon

"Let us hold unswervingly to the hope we profess, for he who promised is faithful." (Hebrews 10:23 NIV)

When confronted with the character of Jesus, a human soul will have one of two reactions. A saving faith runs toward perfect love unbound and without reservation, being clothed in God's light and peace that surpasses our ability to express. For those who would allow themselves to be deceived into a state of shame and guilt, despite all knowledge to the contrary, the beauty is repellent, since they remain unconvinced that Jesus' work on the Cross was truly enough to take away their sin. Like the twin to an opposite polarity magnet, agreement with their sin nature can only resist God. However unnecessarily, it refuses the only outstretched arm which has any ability or authority to draw it into the light.

"What a wretched man I am! Who will rescue me from this body that is subject to death? Thanks be to God, who delivers me

through Jesus Christ our Lord! So then, I myself in my mind am a slave to God's law, but in my sinful nature slave to the law of sin." (Romans 7:24-25 NIV)

If we're honest, there is a bit of both in every one of us. Thankfully, since he is who he is, God always finds a way to ensure more of the former and even an eventual ruin of the latter, though we would all do well to be occasionally reminded of the contrast.

When it becomes clear to me that nothing in me will ever be enough to hold real weight, my only option is to stop trying in my own strength. What happens then is nothing short of a miracle. God shows me his love, faithfulness, and mercy so that there can be no doubt in my mind. The only thing that makes any sense is that he allows me to come to the end of myself (the former), so that, in recognizing his love, faithfulness, and mercy, I am compelled to see him as the only trustworthy source of permanence and strength in my life (the latter).

"Blessed are the meek, for they will inherit the earth." (Matthew 5:5 NIV)

Most people don't know this, but there is a big difference between biblical meekness and weakness, as the world views it. There are times I am remiss to remember the power of the One to whom I belong, Jesus Christ. Sometimes it can be confusing, because the same God who says his power is made perfect in weakness also says that his Spirit and his name are power! The same God who says, " ...apart from me you can do nothing," also says through the Apostle Paul, "I can do all things through him who strengthens me." The same God who says, "Blessed are the meek, for they will inherit the earth," also says, " ...let the weak say, I am strong."

The answer is: in my own power, on my own, I am weak and have nothing, no strength. But as I surrender to God and exchange my life for his, my will for his, day by day his power becomes more and more alive in me. I need to remember the end of **Matthew 5:5** every day and walk in meekness, which is true power under control **(2 Corinthians 12:9 NASB), (2 Timothy 1:7 NIV), (John 15:5 NIV), (Philippians 4:13 NASB), (Joel 3:10 NKJV).**

221

Prayer: *Lord Jesus, it is so easy for me to get off track and get focused on the petty things of this life, too focused on those things that I would say are important. I lose my perspective and focus on the creation rather than the Creator. I pray that in your mercy I have forgiveness for those things and that sin's lie is crushed under the weight of your love, in the name of Jesus. I pray that by your Holy Spirit I am made strong even in weakness, every time I turn to you, no matter how or when. You enable me to be and do everything through you, Lord. Your power living in me enables me to cease being conformed to the world's terms. It is only in your power that I am able to be transformed and discern your will. In every facet of my life, shine today Lord Jesus! Let your power be shone through my weaknesses. Be glorified in me Abba. Amen!*

Scripture(s): **"You see, at just the right time, when we were still powerless, Christ died for the ungodly. Very rarely will anyone die for a righteous person, though for a good person someone might possibly dare to die. But God demonstrates his own love for us in this: While we were still sinners, Christ died for us." (Romans 5:6-8 NIV)**

"Praise be to the God and Father of our Lord Jesus Christ! In his great mercy he has given us new birth into a living hope through the resurrection of Jesus Christ from the dead, and into an inheritance that can never perish, spoil or fade—kept in heaven for you, who through faith are shielded by God's power until the coming of the salvation that is ready to be revealed in the last time." (1 Peter 1:3-5 NIV)

CHAPTER 20

THE WORD AND THE SPIRIT

Small moves Ellie

Have you ever said or heard someone else say, *"A loving God would never (_____),* or, *"I could never believe in a God that (_____),"* totally independent of any real knowledge about who God is or what his Word says he would or wouldn't do? I have. And what's more, to my shame, there was a time when I was guilty of sentiments like this—even as a Christian. Where the will of imperfect people encroaches upon the sovereign territory of God's revealed will (his Word), chaos always follows.

"Every man's way is right in his own eyes, but the Lord weighs the hearts." (Proverbs 21:2 NASB)

"There is a way which seems right to a man, but its end is the way of death." (Proverbs 14:12 NASB)

God's way is right, period. His Word is flawless; his justice is love, no matter what form it takes, no matter how we feel about it. Because his way is perfect, in his presence we are undone but for his Grace in the ability to approach everything trusting in him and in his Word **(Isaiah 6:5-8 NASB)**. We would be unable to come to him, not only unconcerned with our own nakedness **(Genesis 2:25 NIV)**, but as he ever intended—like little children **(Matthew 18:3 NIV)** totally ignorant of our condition and unaffected in the shelter of his wings **(Psalm 36:7 NIV)**.

Carl Sagan wrote a novel called *Contact* that eventually got made into a movie by the same name around the year 1997. In the novel, mankind receives a design, a blueprint, from a higher species of being to construct a means by which they would travel to places unknown and somehow connect with these higher species. During the process, particular emphasis is put on the question: Should they precisely follow the plans as they were given? Or, for very noble and reasonable purposes, should they modify the design according to what they thought it should be?

Dr. Eleanor Arroway: *"The transmitted specs never said anything about a chair, or a restraining harness, or survival gear. I mean **why can't we just trust the original design**?"*

Launch Engineer: *" ...we have determined that the design impact is negligible. The bottom line is we're not putting anyone aboard this machine without some sort of minimal protection ..."*

Yeah, protection. No harm in that, right? But the problem was the same in the story as it is with us in real life—the design impact was NOT negligible. Deviating from the original plan just a little was unnecessary, and it almost killed the passenger. The real bottom line is that there is no flaw in God's original design either. He has no need of our help and no use for our input **(Acts 17:24-25 NASB)**. Just as in the movie, when we trust in the instructions as written, there is protection, safety, assurance, and peace. The more that we try to add our ideas of "how things should be" to God's Word, and the more of our debris that we bring into his presence, the larger the chance of harm and deception.

The entire movie actually ended up making a very compelling argument for the sovereignty of a personal God and the excellence of his revealed Word. As is always the case with our arrogance, the strength with which we humans oppose God is dwarfed only by the contrast of our fallibility against the backdrop of his faultlessness. Total deference to God in every area of life is the only reasonable choice. As the Apostle Paul says:

"For this reason I kneel before the Father, from whom every family in heaven and on earth derives its name ..." (Ephesians 3:14-15 NIV)

Beyond the love of the Cross and God's living Word Jesus Christ, there is no further grace to be given to us. If we wantonly refuse to believe God, we are in danger of being assigned a place which is quite literally the darkest and deepest of voids, and being left, in utter futility, left to our own devices **(Romans 1:20-25 NIV)**.

"For the word of God is alive and active. Sharper than any double-edged sword, it penetrates even to dividing soul and spirit, joints and marrow; it judges the thoughts and attitudes of the heart. Nothing in all creation is hidden from God's sight. Everything is uncovered and laid bare before the eyes of him to whom we must give account." (Hebrews 4:12-13 NIV)

"It is impossible for those who have once been enlightened, who have tasted the heavenly gifts, who have shared in the Holy Spirit, who have tasted the goodness of the word of God and the powers of the coming age and who have fallen away, to be brought back to repentance. To their loss they are crucifying the Son of God all over again and subjecting him to public disgrace." (Hebrews 6:4-6 NIV)

I can only imagine how God, because of his deep love for us, must feel deep sadness when we reject him by following our own ways. Every bit of our goodness, righteousness, truth, compassion, and any altruism we could ever claim at all, is from God, through God, and for God. Despite any knowledge we think we have, every rusted crown we claim when coming into his presence only weighs us down. Whatever justification we may use to elevate a flawed version of truth over the Truth in his Word cries out and convicts us, our every word even bearing witness against us.

"...We know that 'We all possess knowledge.' But knowledge puffs up while love builds up. Those who think they know something do not yet know as they ought to know." (1 Corinthians 8:1-2 NIV)

"What if some were unfaithful? Will their unfaithfulness nullify God's faithfulness? Not at all! Let God be true, and every human

being a liar. As it is written: 'So that you may be proved right when you speak and prevail when you judge'." (Romans 3:3-4 NIV)

"Woe to those who are wise in their own eyes and clever in their own sight. Woe to those who are heroes at drinking wine and champions at mixing drinks, who acquit the guilty for a bribe, but deny justice to the innocent. Therefore, as tongues of fire lick up straw and as dry grass sinks down in the flames, so their roots will decay and their flowers blow away like dust; for they have rejected the law of the Lord Almighty and spurned the word of the Holy One of Israel." (Isaiah 5:21-25 NIV)

I say all of these things first to myself as a Christian and through God's conviction in my own heart. I have too many times found myself at the wrong end of this loaded weapon, noticing the smoking hot barrel only after I had shot myself or someone else square in the face. But thanks be to God! He always lovingly pushes us back into the light if we are willing to see, turn, and follow him there. Whether intentionally or not, whenever we use God's principles as a vehicle to deny God or to add or subtract the bits of him and his words that make us uncomfortable, we choose death and the curse. So then all "**heaven and earth**" plainly testify against us. With each forged inference, we presume to have a more refined understanding of God and the character of God than the one true God has of himself.

"'Vanity of vanities,' says the Preacher, 'All is vanity.'
"And moreover, because the Preacher was wise, he still taught the people knowledge; yes, he pondered and sought out and set in order many proverbs. The Preacher sought to find acceptable words; and what was written was upright—words of truth. The words of the wise are like goads, and the words of scholars are like well-driven nails, given by one Shepherd. And further, my son, be admonished by these. Of making many books there is no end, and much study is wearisome to the flesh.
"Let us hear the conclusion of the whole matter: Fear God and keep his commandments,

"For this is man's all. For God will bring every work into judgment, including every secret thing, whether good or evil." (Ecclesiastes 12:8-14, NKJV)

"I call heaven and earth to witness against you today, that I have set before you life and death, the blessing and the curse. So choose life in order that you may live, you and your descendants, by loving the Lord your God, by obeying His voice, and by holding fast to Him." (Deuteronomy 30:19-20 NASB)

Now, so much more than before, I see clearly the depth of Jesus' grief and compassion as he got ready to enter Jerusalem.

"Jerusalem, Jerusalem, who kills the prophets and stones those who are sent to her! How often I wanted to gather your children together, the way a hen gathers her chicks under her wings, and you were unwilling. Behold, your house is being left to you desolate! For I say to you, from now on you will not see me until you say, 'Blessed is he who comes in the name of the Lord!'" (Matthew 23:37-39 NASB)

Jesus was God's living Word who became flesh for them (John 1:14 NASB). On that day so long in coming, the first day that he was to be announced publically as Messiah, he wept for them (and for us) because he knew so many would not "see" him. Their eager expectation to witness his coming was perverted, their hearts were darkened by pride. They missed it because they ignored the Truth and viewed him through the lens of wisdom from the world rather than through the words of God.

I believe that the author, C. S. Lewis, puts this into context and makes the point well in his book *The Four Loves*. To paraphrase, just as Lucifer—a former archangel—perverted himself by pride and fell into depravity, so too can love—commonly held to be the arch-emotion (or any other of God's attributes alive in us for that matter) —become corrupt by presuming itself to be what it is not.

That statement could apply to any of God's qualities within us that have become so marred by pride that we presume them to be what they are not and deny his true character.

In conclusion, however, we are left most graciously by God with hope in the comforting reality that our salvation is not merely a postage stamp, nor is it a letter opener at the end of our life's journey. It is rather most perfectly realized (again by his design) through every precious moment gifted to us in between the two.

"Therefore, since we have so great a cloud of witnesses surrounding us, let us also lay aside every encumbrance and the sin which so easily entangles us, and let us run with endurance the race that is set before us, fixing our eyes on Jesus, the author and perfecter of faith, who for the joy set before Him endured the cross, despising the shame, and has sat down at the right hand of the throne of God." (Hebrews 12:1-2 NASB)

Fruity?!?

"Earthly wisdom is doing what comes naturally. Godly wisdom is doing what the Holy Spirit compels us to do."—Charles Stanley

"And I will ask the Father, and he will give you another advocate to help you and be with you forever— the Spirit of truth. The world cannot accept him, because it neither sees him nor knows him. But you know him, for he lives with you and will be in you. I will not leave you as orphans; I will come to you. Before long, the world will not see me anymore, but you will see me. Because I live, you also will live. On that day you will realize that I am in my Father, and you are in me, and I am in you" (John 14:16-19 NIV)

"But the fruit of the Spirit is love, joy, peace, patience, kindness, goodness, faithfulness, gentleness, self-control ..." (Galatians 5:22-23)

Jesus calls us his branches **(John 15:5 NASB)**. Paul the apostle goes a step further and rightly calls us engrafted branches **(Romans 11:24 NASB)**.

Both verses are clear that we received the Holy Spirit of God when we believed in Jesus Christ as Savior. If, then, his Spirit is in us, if our deepest longings are for the desires of his heart over our own, we must in turn produce good fruit. Whether for better or worse, it is clear the way people will know us—by the kind of fruit we produce **(Matthew 7:16-20 NASB)**. So what is the good fruit that is listed in **Galatians 5:22-23**?

Love—*Agape, the covenant love of God for us, as well as our reciprocal love for God; this also necessarily extends to the love of one's fellows.*

Joy—*The result of a right relation with God. It is not something people can create through their own efforts. We distinguish joy from pleasure since true joy rarely has anything to do with simply being happy or feeling happy. Its origin and substance are God so that joy is present in the midst of trouble; it cannot be extinguished by mere circumstance.*

Peace—*The peace of God; it bears that name since he is the author of peace. It is neither temporary nor circumstantial, and is available at all times. God's peace passes our ability to understand because it thrives most perfectly in the midst of chaos not in lieu of it.*

Patience—*Suffering long for something or someone, enduring pain or difficulty without complaint or want of recompense. Consider the patience of God with us; in his mercy it bears all things and allots us time we have not earned and leeway we do not deserve.*

Kindness—*A genuine concern for the needs of others above our own. Jesus modeled this perfectly when he said,* "**Whoever forces you to go one mile, go with him two. Give to him who asks of you, and do not turn away from him who wants to borrow from you. You have heard that it was said, 'You shall love your neighbor and hate your**

enemy.' But I say to you, love your enemies and pray for those who persecute you" (Matthew 5:41-44 NASB).

Goodness—*The goodness God's people exhibit shows itself in various moral qualities, notably kindness toward others. Many words describe the specific characteristics and behaviors of good people, including justice, righteousness, and purity. If goodness is the general term, these other specific terms show what goodness means in daily living.*

Faithfulness—*This is the exhibition of our Abba Father's steadfast love, a walking in the way of truth. Faithfulness from a human heart filled up with the Spirit of Jesus that imitates him, stands firm with and holds fast to even the soul of the faithless one, or in the face of faithlessness itself.*

Gentleness—*Sensitivity of disposition and of behavior, founded on strength and prompted by deepest concern for the comfort of another. To be gentle is to look through the masks we use to shield ourselves from one another and make Jesus' first order of business our own in the way we deal with one another, find the pain, become a comforter, and love others.*

Self-Control—*More accurately, temperance. Webster defines self-control as "control of one's feelings, desires, or actions by one's own will; the power of controlling one's external reactions, emotions; equanimity." Roget lists as synonyms: restraint, self-discipline, willpower, mettle, resolve, and composure. These are all correct but for one crucial mistake: temperance by God's Spirit is only possible, not in the control or mastery of anything by one's own will, but in absolute and total surrender to God's will. Herein, we actually see the possibility of "good fruit" and our ability to manifest every other quality that brings it forth. It can be no coincidence that this one was the book end of them all.*

Peter, the disciple of Jesus, tells us this:

"For if these qualities are yours and are increasing, they render you neither useless nor unfruitful in the true knowledge of our Lord Jesus Christ." (2 Peter 1:8 NASB)

For the short time we are given here on earth we are afforded only two real, though relatively small, glimpses of heaven **(1 Corinthians 13:12-13 NASB)**. First, through the kingdom of God alive in us when by his grace we are inexpressibly moved and changed as we look full into the reality of his affection turned toward us **(Luke 17:20-21 NKJV)**. Secondly, and most tangibly by his perfect design, reflected through the eyes of our faith expressing itself in his love poured out into the lives of those God places in our paths each day **(Matthew 22:37-40 NASB), (Matthew 25:39-40 NIV)**.

"The only thing that counts is faith expressing itself through love." (Galatians 5:6 NASB)

Except by the Spirit

"The presence of the Holy Spirit is the keystone of all our hopes."—John Nelson Darby

"You know that when you were pagans, you were led astray to the mute idols, however you were led. Therefore I make known to you that no one speaking by the Spirit of God says, 'Jesus is accursed'; and no one can say, 'Jesus is Lord,' except by the Holy Spirit." (1 Corinthians 12:2-3 NASB)

I've never cared for the word "pagans" or the word "Gentiles," since they both seem to evoke a certain emotion that usually distracts from a larger point being made in the text. But while the words themselves are ambiguous in reference to actual people at times, the meanings of the words are not. For our purposes they both boil down to meaning those who either do not know the one God, or those who are without God entirely.

"But you have an anointing from the Holy One, and all of you know the truth. I do not write to you because you do not know the truth,

but because you do know it and because no lie comes from the truth." (1 John 2:20, 21 NIV)

When we were without God, we were led into all kinds of things, but we did allow ourselves to be led. Therein lies the larger point; we heard the spiritual equivalent of *"Jesus is accursed"* and followed anyway. We heard *"Jesus is Lord"* and went the other direction. Paul the apostle says, **"Therefore I make known to you"** in the context of spiritual ignorance but he also warns us against a form of spiritual arrogance that blinds us even when we are weak and allow it to happen.

For this reason, remember at all times that anyone or anything which either speaks directly or even by subtle implication, *"Jesus is accursed,"* does in no way seek anything other than our confusion, deception, and destruction. Conversely, anyone or anything that is able directly or by implication to sincerely say, *"Jesus is Lord,"* speaks from God and necessitates our attention. In other words, know the difference, since if you are not without God you actually can know the difference. Be alert and aware of who speaks to you and moreover what they are saying; it really does matter.

"I have many more things to say to you, but you cannot bear them now. But when He, the Spirit of truth, comes, He will guide you into all the truth; for He will not speak on His own initiative, but whatever He hears, He will speak; and He will disclose to you what is to come. He will glorify Me, for He will take of Mine and will disclose it to you. All things that the Father has are Mine; therefore I said that He takes of Mine and will disclose it to you." (John 16:12-15 NASB)

Prayer: *Help me today, Lord, to delight in your instruction; give me eyes to see and ears to hear your voice. Thank you, Holy Spirit, for helping me remember that it's not only casting off the things of this world, but also allowing you to fill me up each day and receiving the fullness I have in Jesus that matters most. I am filled with gratitude and awe for the intimate way that you know me, Lord. That is to say, some days* *it is difficult not to hold onto things that were never mine to hold, but having the assurance of you and everything in your Word brings me back. Knowing that you don't just hold all of those things in your hand, but that in your mercy you also hold me up and hold onto me as well. **"Such knowledge is too wonderful for me ..." (Psalm 139:6 NASB).** I worship you, Father. I praise you Jesus my Christ, lover of my soul. In your perfect name and in agreement with every word that comes from you, I pray. Amen!*

Scripture(s): **"For there are three that bear witness in heaven: the Father, the Word, and the Holy Spirit; and these three are one. And there are three that bear witness on earth: the Spirit, the water, and the blood; and these three agree as one." (1 John 5:7-8, NKJV)**

"The Spirit and the bride say, 'Come.' And let the one who hears say, 'Come.' And let the one who is thirsty come; let the one who wishes take the water of life without cost." (Revelation 22:17 NASB)

CHAPTER 21

WORSHIP AND GIFTING

In Spirit and Truth

*"Always remember to worship God unashamedly
and with a full heart in everything you do!"*

"Sing to the Lord, all the earth; proclaim his salvation day after day. Declare his glory among the nations, his marvelous deeds among all peoples. For great is the Lord and most worthy of praise; he is to be feared above all gods. For all the gods of the nations are idols, but the Lord made the heavens." (1 Chronicles 16:23-26 NIV)

This is a part of what King David's worship team sang and played along with him after the Ark of God was carried back to Jerusalem. It's pretty cool to imagine what that must have sounded like.

Exuberant, unrestrained, and jubilant are the words that come to mind. A passion turned wholly toward exultation and praise that didn't bother with who was watching or what they might think. King David knew that what he brought to God was pure spirit and truth, and he was recompensed in joy for his adoration and praise.

Authentic worship is, to the heart who hears and responds, a redirection of focus from earthly things to heavenly things. It is to the heart who offers and brings it, surrendering to holiness, an unfettered march ahead in thanksgiving and celebration in agreement with God's declaration of victory.

"He appointed some of the Levites as ministers before the ark of the LORD, even to celebrate and to thank and praise the LORD God of Israel: Asaph the chief, and second to him Zechariah, then Jeiel, Shemiramoth, Jehiel, Mattithiah, Eliab, Benaiah, Obed-edom and Jeiel, with musical instruments, harps, lyres; also Asaph played loud-sounding cymbals, and Benaiah and Jahaziel the priests blew trumpets continually before the ark of the covenant of God.

Then on that day David first assigned Asaph and his relatives to give thanks to the LORD" (1 Chronicles 16:4-7 NASB)

Our flesh would have us improperly carry the dwelling place of God's glory on an ox cart, maybe even tweak its position a bit so it doesn't fall **(2 Samuel 6:6-10 NIV)**. Our flesh would also likely have us looking down on God's cheerful procession, despising the leaping and celebrating worshipers and their leader **(2 Samuel 6:16 NIV)**.

The Holy Spirit is the one who examines our hearts **(1 Corinthians 2:10-16 NASB)**. If we enter the Lord's gates with gladness and turn our eyes toward heaven, then we are blessed whenever we come into his courts to worship him; he fills us from the inside out. In those holy moments our posture before him is unaffected adoration to the exclusion of all else, whether in the giving or the receiving **(Psalm 100 NASB)**.

"Splendor and majesty are before him; strength and joy are in his dwelling place. Ascribe to the Lord, all you families of nations, ascribe to the Lord glory and strength. *Ascribe to the Lord the glory due His name; bring an offering and come before Him. Worship the Lord in Holy array."* (1 Chronicles 16:27-29 NASB)

Everything that has breath

"You were designed to worship God and if you fail to worship him, you will create other things (idols) to give your life to."—Rick Warren

"Praise the LORD! Praise God in His sanctuary; praise Him in his mighty expanse. Praise Him for his mighty deeds; praise Him according to His excellent greatness. Praise Him with trumpet sound; praise Him with harp and lyre. Praise Him with timbrel and dancing; praise Him with stringed instruments and pipe. Praise Him with loud cymbals; praise Him with resounding

cymbals. Let everything that has breath praise the Lord. Praise the Lord." (Psalm 150:1-6 NASB)

Worship is an amazing thing. Our Lord Jesus has given us all good gifts, and as we discover those and use them, God blesses every moment spent. The best part is, it could be anything. Take a few minutes to think about the times you've felt most consistently in tune and connected with God. Now try to remember what you were doing in those moments. Whether it's one thing or five, or even fifteen, those are yours, individually and perfectly from him and for him. One of the most beautiful aspects of worship is that it's multi-faceted. So many different things can be going on simultaneously when we find that niche and begin to groove with our Abba Father. It is really quite breathtaking. In the midst of our hearts being locked into his and surrendered to bringing him glory and praise, he meets us there.

In the midst of that communion of exultation, our gifts are often in operation to build up those around us, or to lead his procession by playing an instrument. It may be in service, helps, or prayer. They could be spiritual in nature and result in healings or prophecy. No matter what, one thing is for sure: when we operate in those special places, for his special purposes, the miraculous takes place. In those instances, time becomes immaterial, the veil is lifted off, and we get a rare glimpse of home. As I feel it while I am writing, I know there is no way to use mere words to do such an intimate experience justice. All I can say is, if you've felt this before, you are nodding your head and know exactly what I mean. If you haven't yet, you will, and you will recognize it immediately when you do because the Holy Spirit will be right at the center leading you on.

"God has given each of you a gift from his great variety of spiritual gifts. Use them well to serve one another. Do you have the gift of speaking? Then speak as though God himself were speaking through you. Do you have the gift of helping others? Do it with all the strength and energy that God supplies. Then everything you do will bring glory to God through Jesus Christ. All glory and power to him forever and ever! Amen." (1 Peter 4:10-11 NLT).

"We have different gifts, according to the grace given to each of us. If your gift is prophesying, then prophesy in accordance with your faith; if it is serving, then serve; if it is teaching, then teach; if it is to encourage, then give encouragement; if it is giving, then give generously; if it is to lead, do it diligently; if it is to show mercy, do it cheerfully." (Romans 12:6-8 NIV)

"Now there are varieties of gifts, but the same Spirit. And there are varieties of ministries, and the same Lord. There are varieties of effects, but the same God who works all things in all persons. But to each one is given the manifestation of the Spirit for the common good. For to one is given the word of wisdom through the Spirit, and to another the word of knowledge according to the same Spirit; to another faith by the same Spirit, and to another gifts of healing by the one Spirit, and to another the effecting of miracles, and to another prophecy, and to another the distinguishing of spirits, to another various kinds of tongues, and to another the interpretation of tongues. But one and the same Spirit works all these things, distributing to each one individually just as he wills." (1 Corinthians 12:4-11 NASB)

Hand to the plow

In the way many institutions, and by proxy their congregants, approach worship and worship services, too often the production and the agenda end up taking first place over seeing God's Spirit move. Our churches are so busy thinking up a perfect mission statement, following a timeline, or trying to get everyone in and out before lunchtime that the heart of God gets lost somewhere in the mix.

God fills all in all **(Ephesians 1:22-23 NASB)**. If we believe he is "I AM" then we know that we can trust him unequivocally for everything. If all things were created by him, for him, and through him **(Colossians 1:16 NASB), (Romans 11:36 NASB),** then he and his desire should be at the genesis and foundation of all that we are and all that we do as "the Church," his Bride. God's heart is for revival, restoration, " **...that all would come to repentance." (2 Peter 3:9 NASB).**

The cry of our hearts, from those who have been called and appointed all the way down to the average every day believer, should be to wait upon his Holy Spirit until there is breakthrough. From Pentecost, to Azusa Street, to the Great Wall of China, in our history, one common thread connecting the most powerful works of God is that they have taken place when his people have waited on him in worship, meditation, and prayer—to the exclusion of all else. Yes, that means homes, jobs, finances, sports, errands, funerals, to-do lists, leisure time, weddings, television, etc. I have heard countless calls and questions from the pulpit of *"Imagine what would happen if ..."* or *"What would the Church look like today if we all ...,"* but then the Sunday service ends and for the most part, however heartfelt, they are merely words when all is said and done. No revival happens, no significant change occurs, no follow-through is made. I know these are hard words, but until we lay all the distractions in our lives at the foot of the Cross where they belong and our actions reflect to Abba Father, *"We trust you for everything, period,"* we should not expect that he will respond in the way we desire.

Abraham believed what God said so deeply that he tied his only son to a stone altar and raised a knife to slaughter him **(Genesis 22:8-13 NASB), (James 2:21-23 NASB).** God who says, **"Cease striving,"** also says, **"Test me now in this."** This same God then says, when his Word lives in us and we truly live in him, **"ask whatever you wish, and it will be done for you."** It takes courage to look into the perfect law of the Spirit of life and remain, to see not only God's perfect estimation of us but also the despotic nature of our hearts apart from him **(James 1:23-25 NASB), (Romans 8:1-2 NASB).** It takes courage to say, *"Yes Lord, let it begin with me." "To the exclusion of all else, I give you and what you desire first place in my heart and my life."* But in that place of worship, that place where we say, *"Yes"* with confidence and then with trust and perseverance wait to see his glory fall, miraculously and powerfully, HE MOVES!!

"These all with one mind were continually devoting themselves to prayer, along with the women, and Mary the mother of Jesus, and with his brothers." (Acts 1:14 NASB)

"When the day of Pentecost had come, they were all together in one place. And suddenly there came from heaven a noise like a violent rushing wind, and it filled the whole house where they were sitting. And there appeared to them tongues as of fire distributing themselves, and they rested on each one of them. And they were all filled with the Holy Spirit." (Acts 2:1-4 NASB)

"And when they had prayed, the place where they had gathered together was shaken, and they were all filled with the Holy Spirit and began to speak the word of God with boldness." (Acts 4:31 NASB)

Three thousand people were saved in one day because a dozen or so men and women believed God, obeyed God, sought God, trusted God, prayed to God, and then patiently waited on him because they knew he would show up. That is true worship!

"But about midnight Paul and Silas were praying and singing hymns of praise to God, and the prisoners were listening to them; and suddenly there came a great earthquake, so that the foundations of the prison house were shaken; and immediately all the doors were opened and everyone's chains were unfastened" (Acts 16:25-26 NASB)

"...in early April, 1906 a massive spiritual awakening erupted at Azusa Street, Los Angeles. The event was so great that the after-shock waves have been felt throughout the world for almost a century, impacting almost every nation of the world. A new Pentecost had come. God had opened up his heavenly portals again and had sent great power to his people once more ...

"...Growth was quick and substantial. Most sources indicate the presence of about 300 to 350 worshipers inside the 40-by-60-foot

whitewashed, wood-frame structure, with others mingling outside before the end of summer, including seekers, hecklers, and children. At times it may have been double that. By summer, crowds had reached staggering numbers, often into the thousands. The scene had become an international gathering. One account states that, 'Every day trains unloaded numbers of visitors who came from all over the continent.'"

**—William Seymour and the History
of the Azusa Street Outpouring**

"I would have despaired unless I had believed that I would see the goodness of the LORD in the land of the living. Wait for the LORD; be strong and let your heart take courage; yes, wait for the LORD." (Psalms 27:13-14 NASB)

"Another also said, 'I will follow you, Lord; but first permit me to say goodbye to those at home.' But Jesus said to him, 'No one, after putting his hand to the plow and looking back, is fit for the kingdom of God'." (Luke 9:62 NASB)

This is happening right now:

"China is thriving," says Freddie Sun of the nation's faithful. He estimates there are 150 million Protestants and Catholics, compared with 60 million communist party members. "Every day, 30,000 people believe in Jesus—even communist party members. It's the greatest revival in church history."

"By all accounts, the Holy Spirit is moving in unprecedented ways in the world's most populous nation."

—*The Biggest Revival In History,* by Ken Walker

"I wait for the LORD, my soul does wait, and in His word do I hope. My soul waits for the Lord more than the watchmen for the morning; indeed, more than the watchmen for the morning." (Psalms 130:5-6 NASB)

"Peter said, 'Behold, we have left our own homes and followed you.' And he said to them, 'Truly I say to you, there is no one who has left house or wife or brothers or parents or children, for the sake of the kingdom of God, who will not receive many times as much at this time and in the age to come, eternal life'." (Luke 18:28-30 NASB)

You might be asking yourself about now: *"What does God have to say about all this?"* Well then, all we need do is ask him.

Q. *Lord, how should we love you?*
A. "You shall love the LORD your God with all your heart and with all your soul and with all your might. These words, which I am commanding you today, shall be on your heart. You shall teach them diligently to your sons and shall talk of them when you sit in your house and when you walk by the way and when you lie down and when you rise up. You shall bind them as a sign on your hand and they shall be as frontals on your forehead. You shall write them on the doorposts of your house and on your gates." (Deuteronomy 6:5-9 NASB)

"Or do you think that the Scripture speaks to no purpose: 'He jealously desires the Spirit which He has made to dwell in us'?" (James 4:5 NASB)

Q. *Lord, why should we trust you with everything?*
A. "Trust in the LORD with all your heart and do not lean on your own understanding. In all your ways acknowledge Him, and He will make your paths straight." (Proverbs 3:5-6 NASB)

"Heaven and earth will pass away, but My words will not pass away." (Matthew 24:35 NASB)

"Trust in the LORD forever, for in GOD the LORD, we have an everlasting Rock." (Isaiah 26:4 NASB)

Q. *Lord, will you take care of us no matter what?*

A. **"Are not two sparrows sold for a penny? Yet not one of them will fall to the ground outside your Father's care. And even the very hairs of your head are all numbered. So don't be afraid; you are worth more than many sparrows." (Matthew 10:29-31 NIV)**

"For this reason I say to you, do not be worried about your life, as to what you will eat or what you will drink; nor for your body, as to what you will put on. Is not life more than food, and the body more than clothing? Look at the birds of the air, that they do not sow, nor reap nor gather into barns, and yet your heavenly Father feeds them. Are you not worth much more than they? And who of you by being worried can add a single hour to his life? And why are you worried about clothing? Observe how the lilies of the field grow; they do not toil nor do they spin, yet I say to you that not even Solomon in all his glory clothed himself like one of these. But if God so clothes the grass of the field, which is alive today and tomorrow is thrown into the furnace, will he not much more clothe you? You of little faith! Do not worry then, saying, 'What will we eat?' or 'What will we drink?' or 'What will we wear for clothing?' ... for your heavenly Father knows that you need all these things. But seek first His kingdom and His righteousness, and all these things will be added to you." (Matthew 6:25-34 NASB)

"For no matter how many promises God has made, they are 'Yes' in Christ. And so through him the 'Amen' is spoken by us to the glory of God." (2 Corinthians 1:20 NIV)

I would say that about sums things up! Thank you Jesus!

So whatever way God has given you in which to worship him, whatever gift you have to help others or to bring the Lord praise, do those things for him and to him that make your heart leap, and exult to see him smile down on you. No matter what they are, he loves to watch you. He loves to commune with you there, and he is proud of you. Acknowledge every one of them and do them all unto him, to the exclusion of all else. Taste and see that he is always good! **(Psalms 34:8 NIV)**

"...whatever you do, do it all for the glory of God." (1 Corinthians 10:31 NIV)

"Whatever you do, work at it with all your heart, as working for the Lord ..." (Colossians 3:23 NIV)

Prayer: *Abba Father, I fall on my face before you in worship and adoration. I give you my whole heart, all of my mind, soul, and strength. I clothe myself with Jesus Christ and set Jesus Christ apart in my heart as Lord. I offer my life today through Jesus as a sacrifice of praise, with lips that continually profess your name. I trust you with all of my heart. I lean not on my own understanding, but in all of my ways I submit to you, and I pray that you would please make straight paths for me. I humble myself before your mighty hand because you alone are able to lift me up at the right time. I humble myself, casting all of my anxiety upon you because you care for me. I come to you weary and heavy burdened and receive rest. Jesus, you are gentle and humble in heart, and I take your yoke upon me to learn from you because your burden to love is light and your yoke to obey is easy. I choose to take up the cross that is mine today and every day. I lose my life for your sake and for the sake of spreading the gospel. I worship you, Abba, because you alone are my shelter, my sustenance, my treasure, my joy, my comfort, and my song. I worship you, being your workmanship created in Jesus for every good thing you prepared beforehand for me to do so that I would be equipped to walk in your ways. I worship you because I am fearfully and wonderfully made, and because you alone work in me to will and to act according to your good pleasure. I come into agreement with your Word that never returns to you void without accomplishing every purpose for which you sent it. I ask and pray all of these things in the matchless name of Jesus Christ, Amen!*

Scripture: **"But an hour is coming, and now is, when the true worshipers will worship the Father in spirit and truth; for such people the Father seeks to be His worshipers. God is spirit, and those who worship Him must worship in spirit and truth." (John 4:23-24 NASB)**

Epilogue

I'm going to get pretty transparent and let you all know that I shed tears in putting the finishing touches on the final chapter of this book. It has been kind of a time-machine journey for me as I was remembering all that God has done and all of the ways he has dealt with me over my lifetime. It would be impossible for me to list the number of tangible blessings that have accompanied his gentle Spirit's work of overturning all of the rocky soil in my heart to get me where I am today, much less to tell you all the little things he does every day that I never even see. So it is "today" in his comfort, and today for me is rest. But today is also thankfully the constant heating, folding, and pressing of being sanctified. Today is the moment by moment joy and humility of sojourning, of surrendering to the sure, steady hands of the Master Potter at his wheel.

Wisdom

The soft and melancholy melody of aural memories
Peaceful and warm
Clothe me in the sudden comfort of reflection
Bitter and assuring
Lost in thought's alluring sea
My entranced heart silently sings, meekly,
"What is man that you are mindful of him?" Oh, Lover of my soul.

The unyielding and joyful song of olfactory memoirs
Chaotic and cold
Reticently entreat me, intuitively declaring
Sweet and irresolute

247

Myriad episodes of existent immersion
My enraptured soul silently sings, deeply,
"Such knowledge is too wonderful for me," Oh, my Abba Father.

I have cried the kind of tears that only Mercy can truly see
That only Heaven's perfect adoration can wipe away.
I have paid a toll to Love's own maven
To realize the Truth in being lain completely bare before another
I am left now with only two options:
To consider the potential folly in asking,
To ponder the complexity in the way She answered me.

"I, wisdom, dwell together with prudence; I possess knowledge and discretion. To fear the LORD is to hate evil; I hate pride and arrogance, evil behavior and perverse speech. Counsel and sound judgment are mine; I have insight, I have power. By me kings reign and rulers issue decrees that are just; by me princes govern, and nobles—all who rule on earth. I love those who love me, and <u>those who seek me find me</u>." (Proverbs 8:12-17).

When I began this book my hope was that you would receive what I did in every revelation of scripture, every story, and every prayer. I still hope those things, but having come from there to here, I would like to impart one final thing that God showed me along the way before I say, *"So long for now."*

A Love Letter

"My beloved responded and said to me, 'Arise, my darling, my beautiful one, and come along. For behold, the winter is past, the rain is over and gone. The flowers have already appeared in the land; the time has arrived for pruning the vines, and the voice of the turtledove has been heard in our land. The fig tree has ripened its figs, and the vines in blossom have given forth their

**fragrance. Arise, my darling, my beautiful one, and come along!'"
(Song of Solomon 2:10-13 NASB)**

This is a beautiful love letter, a love poem even, between two betrothed—just as in Jesus Christ we are now betrothed to God. Jesus died to present us to God as his Bride. We are raised up to life with him and made ready for God when we confess our faith.

"Then I heard what sounded like a great multitude, like the roar of rushing waters and like loud peals of thunder, shouting: 'Hallelujah! For our Lord God Almighty reigns. Let us rejoice and be glad and give him glory! For the wedding of the Lamb has come, and his bride has made herself ready'." (Revelation 19:6-7 NIV)

In context, if you read it with a lover's heart, the entirety of the Bible is God's love letter to humanity, his people, made in his image. The hardness of our hearts, because he can never deny his nature, demands the swiftness of his response and comes neither from his desire nor by his intention to harm us. Rather, the whole of what those who choose to turn away from both his written and living Word will ever site as their validation for doing so, originates in humankind's fallen nature and its ripple effect throughout time. Whether in the Bible or in life, our perversion of God's perfect love, to suit some end that is absolutely other and separate from his, can account for any and every reason or calamity skeptics give for not receiving him and allowing themselves to be immersed in his love. We are without any excuse.

God knew this, which is why he sent his Son in the form of perfect love, clothed with flesh, also knowing full well what we would do to him. Why? Because the coming, persecution, life, death, and resurrection of Jesus Christ was and still is the only answer to our dilemma. We had to murder Love to really understand both his grace and our own depravity apart from him. Praise God for his mercy that we now have a choice. Choose Life. God loves us unequivocally.

"Therefore if anyone is in Christ, he is a new creature; the old things passed away; behold, new things have come. Now all these

things are from God, who reconciled us to himself through Christ and gave us the ministry of reconciliation, namely, that God was in Christ reconciling the world to Himself, not counting their trespasses against them, and he has committed to us the word of reconciliation. ... He made Him who knew no sin to be sin on our behalf, so that we might become the righteousness of God in Him." (2 Corinthians 5:17-19, 21 NASB)

Whether you began this book as an atheist, an agnostic, a skeptic, or with any semblance of a confessed faith in Jesus, I want to leave you prepared as you venture out into the world and beyond your own version of Straight Street to, as Jesus said, **"Go therefore and make disciples of all nations ... teaching them to obey everything I have commanded you"** (Matthew 28:19-20 NKJV).

Rather than attempting to kill every weed as it appears and using the Bible as some sort of extra-moral anti-venom, my prayer instead is that God would give you spiritual eyes to see that our culture, our world, is desperately heart-sick. The people we speak to who are alone and without God in the world are at their core infirmed and tortured from the inside out. The real issue is festering at the root, way deep down. What we see on the surface are only outward manifestations of an entrenched darkness so all-encompassing that they may be completely unaware of it.

So be Jesus to every man or woman God places in your path, and when you go into whatever place he sends you find the pain and address it first. Approach your faith-walk from that angle and you'll find that the Holy Spirit will show you things you could not possibly know on your own, and that Jesus delights to take care of the heavy lifting for you.

I say this in love from a multi-layered and practical knowledge; addressing issues like homosexuality, abortion, sexual immorality, rebellion, spiritual deception, emotional emptiness, addiction, depression, mental illness, or suicide one by one as they sprout up is like trying to put a Band-Aid on Stage 4 Cancer. Should we continue to pray for deliverance from any or all of those things? Absolutely, without a doubt, and according to God's own Word **(1 Thessalonians 5:16-18 NASB)**. My point is to make you more aware and to admonish you to ask God in your own quiet times with him to break your heart for what breaks his.

Thank you all for reading,

Cheers!!

Mark Alan Luther

Printed in the United States
By Bookmasters